Teach® Yourself

Complete Serbian

D1616924

Teach Yourself®

Complete Serbian

Vladislava Ribnikar
and
David Norris

First published in Great Britain in 2003 by Hodder Education.
An Hachette UK company.

First published in US in 2003 by The McGraw-Hill Companies, Inc.

This edition published in 2010 by John Murray Learning

Copyright © David Norris, Vladislava Ribnikar 2003, 2010

British Library Cataloguing in Publication Data: a catalogue
record for this title is available from the British Library.

Library of Congress Catalog Card Number: on file.

ISBN 9781444102314

6

Cover image © Shutterstock.com

Typeset by Cenveo® Publisher Services.

Printed and bound in Great Britain by CPI Group (UK) Ltd.,
Croydon, CR0 4YY.

John Murray Learning policy is to use papers that are natural,
renewable and recyclable products and made from wood grown
in sustainable forests. The logging and manufacturing processes
are expected to conform to the environmental regulations of the
country of origin.

Hodder & Stoughton Ltd
338 Euston Road
London NW1 3BH
www.hodder.co.uk

Contents

Credits

Front cover: © Richard Peterson/Shutterstock

Back cover and pack: © Jakub Semeniuk/iStockphoto.com, © Royalty-Free/Corbis, © agencyby/iStockphoto.com, © Andy Cook/iStockphoto.com, © Christopher Ewing/iStockphoto.com, © zebicho – Fotolia.com, © Geoffrey Holman/iStockphoto.com, © Photodisc/Getty Images, © James C. Pruitt/iStockphoto.com, © Mohamed Saber – Fotolia.com

Pack: © Stockbyte/Getty Images

Meet the authors

The authors are both university lecturers with many years of experience teaching students the Serbian language and about the history and culture of the region. They have both lived in Serbia and travelled extensively in the region.

Vladislava Ribnikar taught at the University of Belgrade where she lectured in the Department of Comparative Literature. She lectured on Shakespeare and European literature of the eighteenth century, amongst other topics, before moving to the UK. In England she has specialised in teaching the Serbian language in the Department of Russian and Slavonic Studies at the University of Nottingham. She has published extensively on Serbian literature of the twentieth century in Serbia and abroad.

David Norris has taught at the University of Nottingham since graduating from the School of Slavonic and East European Studies in London. He has taught all levels of the Serbian language. In addition, he also lectures in the history and culture of Serbia and Southeastern Europe on degree programmes at Nottingham. He specialises in modern cultural studies, particularly the way in which Serbia has been represented in the West. He has supervised several postgraduate students who have continued to teach and research in the area.

Only got a minute?

Most Serbs live in Serbia but there are large numbers who also live in Bosnia, Croatia and Montenegro. The language which you will learn in this book concentrates on the forms used in Serbia, but by learning the language taught in *Complete Serbian* you can travel through all these countries and, although you will notice some local variations, you will be able to understand the written and spoken word.

Serbian is an unusual language in that it is written using two different alphabets, the Latin (like the one we use for English) and the Cyrillic (like the one used for Russian). But it is not a difficult language to learn, because pronunciation and spelling are phonetic. Each letter always represents the same sound. So, referring to the Latin alphabet, 'g' is always like the 'g' in 'goat' and never as in 'large'. Some letters have a different sound from the same English letter, such as 'c', which is always pronounced like the 'ts' at the end of 'cats'.

Over the years many international words have been adapted for use in Serbian, which are easily recognized, such as **taksi** (*taxi*) or **kafa** (*coffee*). You will find that other words associated with modern living like **kompjuter** (*computer*; 'j' is always pronounced like the 'y' in 'you') have been taken from English and you may even hear some people say **vikend** (*weekend*) or its slightly expanded form as **vikendica** (*a weekend-house, holiday home*).

Whatever your motive for learning to speak the language you will find a warm response from Serbs, who show a ready appreciation to foreigners who have taken the trouble to master even a few phrases of their language. Serbia is a fascinating country for the traveller. It is not too large to bewilder the visitor but offers a rich history, towns with old and new architecture and beautiful countryside. It is on its way to joining the European Union and rapidly opening up to international visitors who invariably discover the welcoming side of Serbia.

10 Only got ten minutes?

Serbian is one of the family of Slavonic languages spoken in much of Eastern Europe. They are sub-divided into three groups: the East Slavonic group (Byelorussian, Russian, Ukrainian), the West Slavonic (Czech, Polish, Slovak, Sorbian) and the South Slavonic (Bulgarian, Croatian, Macedonian, Serbian, Slovene). Some would add Bosnian and Montenegrin to this list of South Slavonic languages but these terms have not yet acquired the greater currency of the others. Until recently the language used in Bosnia, Croatia, Montenegro and Serbia was referred to as Serbo-Croat.

The first alphabet for the Serbian language was devised after the introduction of Christianity. This script, based on Greek letters and known as the Cyrillic alphabet, was adopted for use by a number of Slavonic languages. Many examples of medieval Serbian have survived in church and court documents. However, the Ottoman invasion stifled many forms of cultural development. The local population became a subjugated community, isolated in small villages, with education solely in the hands of the Church. In these circumstances, the written form of the language ossified and grew apart from the norms of the everyday spoken idiom until the nineteenth century, when the language reformer Vuk Stefanović Karadžić (1787–1864) began his work. Revising the alphabet, he promoted a new style of phonetic spelling with the maxim 'write as you speak'. With his varied activities in linguistics and cultural life he laid the foundations for the modern Serbian language as it is spoken and written today. In the twentieth century the language has also been written in the Latin alphabet. The Serbian language presented in this book is based on the standards and norms typical of the capital Belgrade and the surrounding area. There are some regional and local dialects, and with some practice you will be able to understand these variations too. By following this course you will acquire the knowledge and confidence to communicate in your new language.

The first Serbian state was founded in 1169 by Stefan Nemanja. This early kingdom was under the cultural and political influence of its much stronger neighbour, the Byzantine Empire. Traces of this influence are visible today in Serbia's medieval art and architecture. The state grew into an empire reaching its greatest extent in the mid-fourteenth century under Emperor Dušan, after which it fell into decline. Threatened by the Ottoman Empire from Asia, the Serbs fought on the plain of Kosovo on 28 June 1389. They never recovered from this battle and were eventually conquered. The Ottoman occupation of the Balkans lasted for almost 500 years and their rule forced many local communities to migrate further north and west into what is now Bosnia and Croatia.

Serbia eventually established its independence again in the nineteenth century. The First Serbian Uprising against Turkish rule was led by Kara Đorđe (Black George) Petrović in 1804. His rebellion failed but was quickly followed by another, led by Miloš Obrenović, in 1815. He became Knez (Prince) of a small Serbian principality which was still formally part of the Ottoman Empire. The last Turkish garrison and Pasha (Governor) left the country in 1867 and Serbia was recognized as an independent kingdom in 1882. By the beginning of the twentieth century Serbia was playing a central role in helping its neighbours in south-eastern Europe who were still under the domination of foreign powers. After the First World War, this unofficial regional coalition resulted in the unification of the territories inhabited by Slavs in the area. It became known as Yugoslavia, meaning 'Land of the South Slavs'. The state was made up of Serbs, Croats, Slovenes and numerous other national and religious groups. Relationships among the various communities were not always harmonious and the joint state disappeared when it was invaded during the Second World War.

The Communists of Yugoslavia, following their successful partisan war against occupying forces, reformed the country after 1945. It was constituted as a federation of six republics, including Serbia, and two autonomous provinces. Yugoslavia appeared calm in the post-war years and the country became a popular tourist destination. However, the federal structure showed signs of strain in the 1980s and amidst poor economic performance the system began to collapse. By the 1990s some republics were ready to secede from the union and sought recognition abroad as sovereign states. The former Yugoslav republics of Bosnia, Croatia, Macedonia and Slovenia became independent countries, while Serbia and Montenegro reformed themselves as the Federal Republic of Yugoslavia. Montenegrins have traditionally regarded themselves as culturally and linguistically close to the Serbs of Serbia. They both accepted the same Orthodox Church under Byzantine influence, were profoundly affected by the Ottoman occupation of the Balkans, and were founder members of the Yugoslav state after the First World War. Elsewhere, not all sections of the local populations agreed with secession and civil war broke out in Bosnia and Croatia. Peace was eventually restored with the intervention of the United Nations. Serbia did not escape internal conflict when ethnic Albanians demanded greater autonomy for the southern province of Kosovo, which has been administered by the United Nations since June 1999.

Serbia at the beginning of the twenty-first century continued to exist in a state union with Montenegro but with fairly loose political ties. However, in 2006 Montenegro decided to form an independent country and the Republic of Serbia emerged as a new state. It stretches from the border with Hungary and Romania in the north, down to Macedonia and Albania in the south. The western border with Bosnia is largely defined by the river Drina while Bulgaria lies to the east. Belgrade is the capital city situated at the confluence of the rivers Danube and Sava. North of Belgrade lie the fertile plains of Vojvodina with Serbia's second largest city of Novi Sad, and further south the towns of Kragujevac and Niš. The country faces many of the tough decisions which other Eastern European countries have had to face after the collapse of Communism. Serbia is anxious that economic restructuring attracts greater investment from abroad and integration into international markets. With the support of organizations like the European Union, Serbia is playing its role in regional conferences aimed at regenerating and strengthening stability in the Balkan peninsula.

Introduction

Welcome to Complete Serbian

Serbia is attracting an increasing number of visitors each year. Changing historical circumstances have made travel to the country much easier and greater stability is encouraging more foreign investment. Serbia is moving closer to integration with European institutions and markets. *Complete Serbian* has been designed to meet the demands of this growing interest by providing a new course which will take you through all the stages of learning Serbian. The graded units offer a structured approach, giving information in a user-friendly fashion, and presenting the language in everyday situations based around real places in Belgrade and Serbia. This book is for people who want to communicate in Serbian and to enjoy a degree of independence while in the country, whether they are leisure or business travellers, school or university students, people who have family ties in the region, or who simply enjoy the challenge of learning a new language.

The structure of *Complete Serbian*

The course contains:

- an introductory section
- 20 course units
- a reference section
- an accompanying recording. The sections which appear on the recording are marked in the book with this icon: ◆).

The introductory section features a description of the book. All the units of this course are divided into activities, often in the form of dialogues. The language is presented and explained through them under the following sections:

- 'Quick vocab' introduces new words and phrases
- 'Insight' boxes offer additional information about Serbian and everyday life in Serbia
- **How it works** – this section provides essential grammar explanations
- **Practice** and 'Test yourself' sections – these exercises will aid learning and reinforce what you have learnt.

There is also a useful reference section at the end of the course:

- **Key to the exercises** – answers are given to the exercises in each unit
- **Transcripts** – these offer a check for comprehension exercises
- **Grammar glossary** – this provides definitions of grammar terminology
- **Grammar summary** – this is a brief digest of important information
- **Vocabulary section** – this section contains alphabetical lists of words used in the course given from Serbian to English and from English to Serbian
- **Grammar index** – this provides a useful list of where specific grammar points can be found in the book

- **Taking it further** – this supplies details of useful books and internet sources on the history, language and culture of Serbia.

Since the dialogues and exercises were recorded, changes have occurred to prices and other aspects of Serbian life. Where these are significant, they are noted in the text.

Symbols and abbreviations

◀) This indicates recorded material

lit.	literally		voc.	vocative
masc.	masculine		acc.	accusative
fem.	feminine		gen.	genitive
neut.	neuter		dat.	dative
sing.	singular		ins.	instrumental
pl.	plural		loc.	locative
nom.	nominative			

How to use this course

The activities in each unit represent manageable 'chunks' of language. They allow you to reinforce what you have already learnt and to expand on that knowledge with new words, expressions and grammar points. You will be given instructions to guide you through the material. As you work your way through each activity, listen to the dialogue on the recording, repeat the phrases, read the text, and answer the accompanying questions to check that you have understood. Use the recording to improve your pronunciation and listening skills. The course offers ample scope for developing your abilities to communicate in Serbian. You can add to this scope by enlisting the help of native speakers or finding someone else who also wants to learn Serbian since studying together is a great incentive and gives you more opportunity to practise speaking.

It is more efficient to learn new words and phrases as you meet them. You will avoid the frustration of seeing a word and although you know that you have met it before you cannot quite remember what it means. It is on the tip of your tongue but needs to be activated. You will enjoy learning more if you can feel your knowledge improving without constantly checking what words mean in the reference section at the back of the book. There is no one way of learning new words. Some people prefer to write them out repeatedly, while others prefer to learn them as part of a complete phrase. Try different methods, or combinations of methods, to find the one which suits you best. The same advice, to learn as you go along, also applies to new grammar points. Grammar is simply a way to categorize parts of a language so that you see the broader picture and how it all fits together. The exercises in each unit will show what you have learnt and whether you are ready to go on. Make sure that you have mastered new words and understood the grammar patterns before proceeding to the next stage.

You do not have to work through a complete unit in one sitting. Each activity is a stage in itself with new vocabulary and questions to test your comprehension. You can work beyond the individual dialogues in order to take in the sections on grammar and the exercises if you want. It is more effective to learn a little regularly than to cram too much into one long session. Find a pace with which you feel comfortable and stick to it.

1

Beginning Serbian

In this unit you will learn:

- How to read and write Serbian
- The Latin and Cyrillic alphabets
- Pronunciation and spelling
- Some useful first phrases

Reading and writing Serbian

Walking down the streets of Belgrade or any other Serbian town, the visitor will immediately see examples of writing in both Latin and Cyrillic letters. The Latin alphabet is like the one used in English and the Serbian Cyrillic alphabet is similar to the one in Russian. Of the two alphabets Cyrillic was developed for writing first, with the Latin script introduced as Serbian culture moved closer to the West. Each alphabet contains 30 letters with a one-to-one correspondence between them – for each letter in the Latin alphabet there is an equivalent one in Cyrillic.

There is no rule to say which alphabet should be used on which occasion. Some newspapers are printed in Cyrillic and some in the Latin alphabet. Advertisements, street signs, the labelling of goods in shops, even graffiti may be found in one or the other. Of course, they are never mixed in the same word or text. However, in order to find your way around town or to be able to read the whole range of newspapers you do need to be fully conversant with both ways of writing. So, as we intend this book to be a practical course of the language in Serbia today, we have adopted an even-handed approach in presenting both scripts.

In the first three units of this book Serbian words and expressions are given in both alphabets. This approach is intended to ease the path for the learner to acquire the habit of using a new alphabet. Thereafter, they are used alternately beginning with Cyrillic in Unit 4, then Latin in Unit 5, and so on. The appendices at the end of the book are given in the Latin alphabet in order to facilitate immediate access. In Unit 1 we concentrate on introducing the sounds and printed letters of Serbian. The order of letters in the Cyrillic alphabet is given in Unit 2 and how to produce the hand-written letters in Unit 3.

Insight

Serbian uses both the Latin and the Cyrillic alphabets.
Each alphabet contains 30 letters.
There is a one-to-one correspondence between them.
Compare: HOTEL   "LONDON"
          ХОТЕЛ   "ЛОНДОН"

Latin and Cyrillic alphabets

Both the Latin and the Cyrillic alphabets contain 30 letters to represent the same 30 sounds as given below. In the first row we give the Latin alphabet and underneath each letter is the Cyrillic equivalent:

1	2	3	4	5	6	7	8	9	10
A a	B b	C c	Č č	Ć ć	D d	Dž dž	Đ đ	E e	F f
А а	Б б	Ц ц	Ч ч	Ћ ћ	Д д	Џ џ	Ђ ђ	Е е	Ф ф

11	12	13	14	15	16	17	18	19	20
G g	H h	I i	J j	K k	L l	Lj lj	M m	N n	Nj nj
Г г	Х х	И и	Ј ј	К к	Л л	Љ љ	М м	Н н	Њ њ

21	22	23	24	25	26	27	28	29	30
O o	P p	R r	S s	Š š	T t	U u	V v	Z z	Ž ž
О о	П п	Р р	С с	Ш ш	Т т	У у	В в	З з	Ж ж

Here we have used the order of letters as they appear in the Latin alphabet. The order of letters is approximately the same as in English with some additions and omissions. There are no letters for English

q, w, x or y, while some of those present are formed with the help of accents or are made out of a combination of two letters. The Cyrillic alphabet follows a different order (see Unit 2).

Spelling and pronunciation are very easy in Serbian since words are written according to phonetic principles. Each letter represents one sound, each one is pronounced separately, and each word is spelt as it is pronounced. Pronunciation is explained with the letters divided into the three following groups and practice exercises appear at the end of each stage. Latin letters are given first followed by their Cyrillic equivalents.

Activity A

◆) CD 1, TR 1, 01.52

In Group 1 we introduce the vowel sounds and those consonants which in their Latin version sound like the English letters which they resemble. The second group consists of other vowel sounds and those Latin letters which look like English letters but represent only one distinct sound. The third group is made up of those Latin letters which are formed with the help of accents (the accents are called diacritic marks). This explanation is followed by another section, which looks specifically at helpful ways to learn the Cyrillic alphabet.

Group 1

These letters are pronounced roughly as in English:

b	d	f	k	l	m	n	p	s	t	v	z
б	д	ф	к	л	м	н	п	с	т	в	з

while the vowels tend to be shorter than in English:

a	a	as in c*a*t
e	e	as in f*e*ll
i	и	as the *ea* in l*ea*n
o	o	as in kn*o*t (but try to make your lips rounder as you say the sound)
u	y	as the *oo* in m*oo*n (but with rounder lips)

Listen to the following words or names of people and places on the recording and practise your pronunciation by repeating them. The list is given first in the Latin alphabet and then it is repeated with the same words printed in the Cyrillic alphabet. Pronunciation is not at all influenced by the alphabet used to write the word. Pronounce each word carefully and confidently while looking first of all at the list of words given in Latin and then at the same list of words given in Cyrillic below:

mama (*mum*)	tata (*dad*)	brat (*brother*)

Toma
  (a man's name)
	Desa
	  (a woman's name)
		Vladislav
		  (a man's name)

Budva (a town)	Tisa (a river)	Zemun (a town)

мама	тата	брат
Тома	Деса	Владислав
Будва	Тиса	Земун

Group 2

The following vowel sounds are written as a combination of vowel + j:

aj	aj	as in n*igh*t
ej	ej	as in h*ay*
oj	oj	as in b*oy*

These letters in their Latin version resemble English letters but they represent only one distinct sound:

c	ц	pronounced like the *ts* at the end of ca*ts* (never like a *k* or *s*)
g	г	pronounced like the *g* at the beginning of *g*oat (never as in lar*g*e)
h	x	pronounced in the throat like the sound at the end of Scottish lo*ch*
j	j	pronounced like the *y* at the beginning of *y*ou
lj	љ	pronounced like the *ll* in the middle of mi*ll*ion
nj	њ	pronounced like the *ni* in the middle of o*ni*on
r	p	pronounced with a trill as commonly found in Slavonic and in other languages such as Spanish (not pronounced in the throat as in French). The letter **r/p** is sometimes treated as a vowel and placed between two consonants as in the name of the country *Serbia* **Srbija/Србија**.

Listen to the recording and practise your pronunciation by repeating the following words or names of people and places. Pronounce each word carefully and confidently while looking first of all at the list of words given in Latin and then at the same list of words given in Cyrillic below:

sestra (*sister*)	ulica (*street*)	hleb (*bread*)
konj (*horse*)	devojka (*girl*)	Srbija (*Serbia*)
Jovan	Ljiljana	Beograd (*Belgrade*)
(a man's name)	(a woman's name)	

сестра	улица	хлеб
коњ	девојка	Србија
Јован	Љиљана	Београд

Group 3

The last group of letters are formed with the help of accents above the letter but they represent sounds which are similar to ones used in English:

č	ч	pronounced like the *ch* at the beginning of *ch*ild but with the tip of the tongue raised toward the roof of the mouth and pulled back
ć	ħ	pronounced like the *t* at the beginning of *t*ube but with the tip of the tongue pushed behind the top front teeth
dž	џ	pronounced like the *j* at the beginning of *j*udge but with the tip of the tongue raised toward the roof of the mouth and pulled back
đ	ђ	pronounced like the *d* at the beginning of *d*ew but with the tip of the tongue pushed behind the top front teeth
š	ш	pronounced like the *sh* at the beginning of *sh*oe but with the tip of the tongue raised toward the roof of the mouth and pulled back
ž	ж	pronounced like the *s* in the middle of plea*s*ure but with the tip of the tongue raised toward the roof of the mouth and pulled back

The letters in the Latin alphabet Đ and đ are sometimes written as Dj and dj. All consonants which are written as a combination of two letters (dž, dj, lj, nj) are treated as single letters for dictionary purposes.

Listen to the recording and practise your pronunciation by repeating the following words or names of people and places looking first of all at the list of words given in Latin and then at the same list of words given in Cyrillic:

Čačak (a town)	Petrović (a surname)	Jovanović (a surname)
džem (*jam*)	Đorđe (a man's name)	Đerdap (place on Danube)
Šekspir (*Shakespeare*)	Živković (a surname)	Dušan (a man's name)
Чачак	Петровић	Јовановић
џем	Ђорђе	Ђердап
Шекспир	Живковић	Душан

Activity B

It is not so difficult to learn the Cyrillic alphabet as it may first appear. Look at the capital letters and you can see that some of them look and sound like their Latin equivalents:

А   Е   Ј   К   М   О   Т

ЈАК   *STRONG*
МЕК   *SOFT*

Some of them resemble letters in the Latin alphabet but they represent a different sound. They are sometimes called false friends:

Х   Н   Р   С   У   В

СУВ   *DRY*
РУС   *RUSSIAN* (man)

The remainder will take a little more effort but in time you will come to recognize them immediately:

Б   Ц   Ч   Ћ   Д   Џ   Ђ   Ф   Г   И   Л   Љ
Њ   П   Ш   З   Ж

ЦИЉ   *AIM*
ЗИД   *WALL*

Practise writing in Cyrillic by copying out the following words from the Latin alphabet (this kind of copying from one script to another is called transcribing). Use block capital letters and check your answers by looking in the lists of words given earlier in Activity A:

MAMA	TATA	BRAT
SESTRA	ULICA	HLEB
KONJ	DEVOJKA	SRBIJA
ČAČAK	DŽEM	ĐORĐE
ŠEKSPIR	ŽIVKOVIĆ	DUŠAN

Now try writing your name and the name of the place where you live in Cyrillic. Say them aloud and write down what you hear using Serbian Cyrillic letters. Do not think about English spelling rules and conventions. Foreign names of people and places are written as they are pronounced when writing in either the Latin or the Cyrillic script.

In Serbian the Latin alphabet is called **latinica/латиница** and the Cyrillic alphabet is called **ćirilica/ћирилица**.

Activity C

◆ **CD 1, TR 1, 06.16**

In order to practise reading and pronunciation while learning some useful everyday phrases listen to the following greetings on the recording and say them yourself. Repeat each phrase, taking care to pronounce it correctly, and when you are satisfied that you have mastered it move to the next. Remember to look at the phrases in both scripts:

Dobar dan	Добар дан	Good day
Dobro jutro	Добро јутро	Good morning
Dobro veče	Добро вече	Good evening

To say *goodbye*:

Do viđenja	До виђења	Goodbye
Laku noć	Лаку ноћ	Goodnight

In a more colloquial fashion you can use the word:

Zdravo	Здраво

which means both *hello* and *goodbye*, rather like *hi* and *cheerio*.

Now listen to Mr Lukić (**gospodin Lukić/господин Лукић**) greeting Mrs Petrović (**gospođa Petrović/госпођа Петровић**) in the afternoon and repeat the phrases. Do the exercise twice by firstly looking at the phrases in the Latin alphabet, then cover up that side of the page and look at the same phrases given in the Cyrillic alphabet.

Dobar dan, gospođo Petrović.	Добар дан, госпођо Петровић.
Dobar dan, gospodine Lukiću.	Добар дан, господине Лукићу.
Do viđenja, gospođo.	До виђења, госпођо.
Do viđenja, gospodine.	До виђења, господине.

The words **gospodin/господин** and **gospođa/госпођа** are common titles equivalent to *Mr* and *Mrs* in English, along with **gospođica/госпођица** *Miss*. These forms are respectively shortened to **g./г.**, **gđa/гђа** and **gđica/гђица**. In the dialogue Mr Lukić and Mrs Petrović make some small changes to the ends of words when addressing one another directly. Mr Lukić addresses Mrs Petrović as **gospođo/госпођо** instead of using the form **gospođa/госпођа**. Mrs Petrović calls Mr Lukić **gospodine Lukiću/господине Лукићу**. The ends of nouns and adjectives in Serbian change according to a system of rules. These slightly varying forms of the same word are called cases and you will learn them as part of this course.

Now listen to Mr Lukić greeting Mr Jovanović in the evening and repeat the phrases given here in Cyrillic:

Добро вече, господине Јовановићу.
Добро вече, господине Лукићу.
Лаку ноћ.
Лаку ноћ.

As in English, when you have a word of more than one syllable one part of the word is pronounced more heavily than the rest. We call this one the stressed syllable, so in English we say *lighting* and *concern* with the underlined part pronounced more forcefully than the rest. However, it is important when speaking Serbian not to reduce the vowel sound in the unstressed part of the word as we often do in English, like at the end of the word *remember* when the *er* is only a half vowel. There are no rules to say in advance which part of the word will be stressed, except that it is never the last syllable. So, Mr Lukić says **Добро вече, господине Јовановићу.**

Check your pronunciation by listening to the recording again and by carefully imitating what you hear you will soon acquire a good pronunciation.

◄● **CD 1, TR 1, 07.45**

Here are some signs in Cyrillic to practise reading, which visitors to Serbia may find useful. Try reading them for yourself first and then check your pronunciation with the recording:

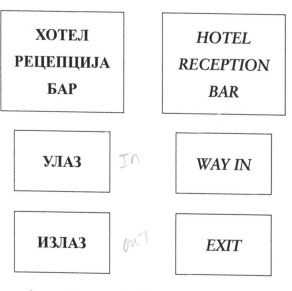

ХОТЕЛ РЕЦЕПЦИЈА БАР	HOTEL RECEPTION BAR
УЛАЗ	WAY IN
ИЗЛАЗ	EXIT

The names of some shops and buildings:

ПОШТА	POST OFFICE
АПОТЕКА	PHARMACY
БАНКА	BANK
МЕЊАЧНИЦА	EXCHANGE OFFICE
ПЕКАРА	BAKERY
РОБНА КУЋА	DEPARTMENT STORE

You may find signs inside these places such as the following (Cyrillic and Latin script):

OTVORENO	ОТВОРЕНО	OPEN
ZATVORENO	ЗАТВОРЕНО	CLOSED

> **Insight**
> Dobro jutro is usually said until about 10.00 a.m.
> Dobar dan is said until about 6.00 p.m.
> Dobro veče is used after 6.00 p.m.

Practice

1 Match these lower-case letters in Cyrillic with their Latin equivalents:

љ	у	ш	с	ф	ћ	и	в
s	š	ć	lj	u	i	f	v

2 Match these upper-case letters in Cyrillic with their Latin equivalents:

Њ	К	Р	Б	Ђ	Л	Ц	Н
N	R	K	C	L	Nj	B	Đ

3 Write out the names of the shops and buildings on the previous page in the Cyrillic alphabet and in the Latin alphabet.

4 Here is a map of Serbia with the names of some cities given in the Cyrillic alphabet. Listen to the recording and you will hear them being pronounced. Tick them as you hear and recognize the name.

◀) **CD 1, TR 1, 08.44**

10

5 It is usual when writing foreign names of people or places to spell them as phonetically as they sound to a Serbian ear, following the basic rule of 'write as you speak'. This rule applies when using either the Latin or the Cyrillic alphabet. Here are the names of some cities written in English and in Serbian Cyrillic for you to match:

a	London	**i**	Берлин
b	Manchester	**ii**	Праг
c	Nottingham	**iii**	Токио
d	Dublin	**iv**	Лондон
e	Berlin	**v**	Чикаго
f	Prague	**vi**	Њујорк
g	Sydney	**vii**	Нотингем
h	New York	**viii**	Сидни
i	Chicago	**ix**	Даблин
j	Tokyo	**x**	Манчестер

6 Some places have slightly different names than the ones we see in English, either because they have been Serbianized in some way or because they are modelled on the pronunciation of a different language. Can you tell what these place names are in English?

Рим	(capital of Italy)
Париз	(capital of France)
Москва	(capital of Russia)
Темза	(river in London)

7 Many Serbian surnames end in -ić like **Lukić**, **Petrović**, **Jovanović**. Listen to the recording and number the following names in the order in which you hear them:

◀) **CD 1, TR 1, 09.06**

some names for men:

a	Милан Лукић	**c**	Урош Максимовић
b	Драган Јовановић	**d**	Зоран Марковић

and for women:

e	Вера Петровић	**g**	Бранка Шантић
f	Весна Костић	**h**	Јелена Мићић

8 Can you identify the names of the following film stars given here in Cyrillic:

a Мел Гибсон	**e** Мерил Стрип
b Шон Конери	**f** Мег Рајан
c Том Хенкс	**g** Мелани Грифит
d Клинт Иствуд	**h** Гвинет Палтроу

9 Arriving at work in the morning what do you say to your colleagues?

10 You arrive in a hotel at noon. How would you greet the receptionist?

11 It is 8.00 p.m. and you go to a restaurant for dinner. How would you greet the waiter before ordering?

12 You meet an old Serbian friend. How would you greet him/her?

13 You have just had lunch with a new colleague from work. What do you say on parting?

14 After dinner in a restaurant what do you say to the waiter as he opens the door for you to leave?

15 It is 4.00 p.m. You have just seen Mrs Petrović in the street. How would you greet her?

Test yourself

Here you can check some of the things you have learnt in this unit. Look at the questions below and choose the right answer:

1 Which letter is the Cyrillic equivalent for the Latin letter C?

    a Ш   **b** Ц   **c** Ц

2 Which letter is the Latin equivalent for the Cyrillic letter И?

    a I   **b** U   **c** N

3 You want to change money. Which is the sign you are looking for?

    a ПОШТА   **b** ПЕКАРА   **c** БАНКА

4 You are looking for a street called **Ulica kralja Milana**. The street names are given in Cyrillic. Which street is it?

   a Улица краља Петра
   b Улица кнеза Милоша
   c Улица краља Милана

5 You are looking for a person called **Dušan Vučić**. The names on people's doors are in Cyrillic. Which door is his?

   a Дејан Вујић   **b** Душан Вучић   **c** Горан Бачић

6 How do you say *Good morning* in Serbian?

   a Dobar dan./Добар дан.
   b Dobro veče./Добро вече.
   c Dobro jutro./Добро јутро.

7 Which expression would you use to greet someone at 12 a.m.?

   a Dobar dan./Добар дан.
   b Dobro jutro./Добро јутро.
   c Laku noć./Лаку ноћ.

8 What is the Serbian for *Goodbye*?

   a Laku noć.   Лаку ноћ.
   b Do viđenja.   До виђења.
   c Dobro veče.   Добро вече.

9 When do you use the greeting **Zdravo/Здраво**?

   a when meeting and parting with friends
   b to greet people formally
   c only when parting with friends

10 Which of the following titles is equivalent to *Mrs* in English?

   a gospođica   госпођица
   b gospođa   госпођа
   c **gospodin**   господин

2

Greetings and Introductions

In this unit you will learn:

- Phrases for greeting, introducing and meeting people
- How to ask people how they are and say how you are
- How to ask someone their name and to say yours
- How to say *I am, you are, this is*
- Categories of nouns: gender
- Adjectives and gender
- The order of letters in the Cyrillic alphabet

How are you?

The first steps in learning a new language are the most important. Getting the basics right at the beginning will save you a great deal of time later. Make sure you understand the phrases and the explanations given in each part of the unit before moving to the next stage.

We are going to continue giving words and phrases in both the Cyrillic and Latin alphabets in this and the following unit. You will soon become accustomed to the fact that Serbian uses two alphabets and will stop noticing which one you are reading.

Activity A

◄ CD 1, TR 2

Some of the characters you will meet in this book are teachers and students at a language school in Belgrade. The school has foreign students who have come to learn Serbian and home students studying a foreign language. Milan Lukić is one of the teachers. As he arrives at work one morning he sees his colleague Mrs Petrović. Her name is Vera.

First of all listen to the recording and follow what they say to each other in the dialogue below. Repeat this activity by reading the dialogue in the Latin alphabet and then, covering that up, reading it again in Cyrillic:

Milan	Dobro jutro, gospođo Petrović.
Vera	Dobro jutro. Kako ste, gospodine Lukiću?
Milan	Dobro sam, hvala. Kako ste vi?
Vera	I ja sam dobro, hvala.
Милан	Добро јутро, госпођо Петровић.
Вера	Добро јутро. Како сте, господине Лукићу?
Милан	Добро сам, хвала. Како сте ви?
Вера	И ја сам добро, хвала.

Kako ste?	**Како сте?**	*How are you?*
Dobro sam.	**Добро сам.**	*I am well.*
hvala	**хвала**	*thank you*
vi	**ви**	*you*
i	**и**	*and; too, also*
ja sam	**ја сам**	*I am*

Question
How does Milan address Vera?

Activity B

🔊 **CD 1, TR 2, 00.32**

Milan works at the school and later he leaves the building. At the door he meets Dragan Jovanović, another of the teachers at the school. Listen to the recording and follow what they say to each other in the following dialogue. Repeat this activity by reading the dialogue in the Latin alphabet and then, covering that up, reading it again in Cyrillic:

Milan	Dobar dan, gospodine Jovanoviću. Kako ste?
Dragan	Dobro, hvala. A vi?
Milan	Dobro sam. Hvala. Do viđenja.
Dragan	Do viđenja.
Милан	Добар дан, господине Јовановићу. Како сте?
Драган	Добро, хвала. А ви?
Милан	Добро сам. Хвала. До виђења.
Драган	До виђења.

QV **A vi?**   **А ви?**   *And you?*

Question

How do you ask someone *How are you?*

Activity C

◆ **CD 1, TR 2, 00.57**

Two students from the school meet that evening in the street. They are Robert Trent from England who is studying Serbian, and Vesna Kostić who is from Belgrade. They greet each other in a way which is not quite so formal. Listen to the recording and follow what they say to each other in the dialogue below first in the Cyrillic alphabet and then in the Latin:

Роберт	Здраво, Весна.
Весна	Здраво, Роберте. Како си?
Роберт	Добро сам, хвала. А ти?
Весна	И ја сам добро.
Robert	Zdravo, Vesna.
Vesna	Zdravo, Roberte. Kako si?
Robert	Dobro sam, hvala. A ti?
Vesna	I ja sam dobro.

Question

What is the word which means *hi* in English?

You have met two different ways of saying *you* and *you are* in Serbian. They are **vi/ви** or **ti/ти** and **vi ste/ви сте** or **ti si/ти си**. They are sometimes called the formal and informal *you*. The form

16

vi/ви is used when talking politely to a stranger, to someone whom you know slightly or in a professional capacity. It is also the plural form to be used in all circumstances when speaking to more than one person. The form ti/ти is used when talking to a friend or relative, and by adults when talking to a child. Children, teenagers and students use the ti/ти form amongst themselves regardless of the degree of familiarity or whether they have even met before.

It is a mistake, however, to assume that the informal expressions are somehow an invitation to friendship. The social conventions ruling which is the correct form are sometimes quite complex. You could cause some offence by an inappropriate choice. Adults are best advised to stick to using vi/ви unless or until invited to do otherwise.

Insight

Adult students of Serbian should be careful not to use ti to someone just because they want to be friendly. It is always best to let the Serbian person to whom you are speaking be the first to use the ti form.

How it works

Verb *to be*

Most verbs in Serbian belong to one of three groups which follow the same pattern of changes to indicate the *I* or the *you* forms. As is the case in most languages, the verb meaning *to be* biti/бити is irregular in the present tense. These are the forms for saying *I am* and *you are*:

ja sam	ja сам	*I am*
ti si	ти си	*you are* (informal)
vi ste	ви сте	*you are* (formal and plural)

Kako ste?	Како сте?	How are you?
Ja sam dobro.	Ја сам добро.	I am well.
Kako si?	Како си?	How are you?
Dobro sam.	Добро сам.	I am well.

You do not always have to use the actual word for *I* or *you* when speaking Serbian. It tends to be used when you want to add a degree of emphasis to a question or statement. So you may say either **Ja sam dobro/Ja сам добро** or **Dobro sam/Добро сам** but notice that in this instance when using the verb *to be* there is a change in word order when omitting **ja**.

Practice

🔊 **CD 1, TR 2, 01.20**

1 Listen to the three short dialogues on the recording.
   a Which greetings are used?
   b Which of the greetings is informal?

2 a You meet Mr Lukić at noon. Say hello to him and ask him how he is.
   b Mr Lukić says he is well, and asks how you are. What do you reply?

3 You meet your friend in the street. Greet him/her and ask how s/he is.

Introductions

Activity D

🔊 **CD 1, TR 2, 03.12**

The language school is having a party for staff and students. When Milan arrives he is introduced by his colleagues to their husbands/wives. He first sees Dragan Jovanović.

Read the dialogue given below first in Cyrillic and then check your pronunciation by listening to the dialogue on the recording. Repeat the exercise using the Latin alphabet:

Драган	Добро вече, господине Лукићу. Како сте?
Милан	Добро, хвала. А како сте ви?
Драган	Добро, хвала. Да вас упознам. Ово је моја жена, Јелена.

Милан	Драго ми је, госпођо. Ја сам Милан Лукић.
Јелена	Драго ми је, господине.
Dragan	Dobro veče, gospodine Lukiću. Kako ste?
Milan	Dobro, hvala. A kako ste vi?
Dragan	Dobro, hvala. Da vas upoznam. Ovo je moja žena, Jelena.
Milan	Drago mi je, gospođo. Ja sam Milan Lukić.
Jelena	Drago mi je, gospodine.

Da vas upoznam.	Да вас упознам.	*Let me introduce you.*
ovo je	ово је	*this is*
moja žena	моја жена	*my wife*
Drago mi je.	Драго ми је.	*Pleased to meet you.*

QV

Question

How do you say *Pleased to meet you*?

Activity E

◀) CD 1, TR 2, 03.53

Later in the evening Milan sees Vera Petrović. Read the dialogue given below first in Cyrillic and then check your pronunciation by listening to the dialogue on the recording. Repeat the exercise using the Latin alphabet:

Милан	Добро вече, госпођо Петровић.
Вера	Добро вече, господине. Како сте?
Милан	Добро, хвала.
Вера	Да вас упознам. Ово је мој муж, Зоран.
Милан	Драго ми је, господине. Ја сам Милан Лукић.
Зоран	Драго ми је. Ја сам Зоран Петровић.
Milan	Dobro veče, gospođo Petrović.
Vera	Dobro veče, gospodine. Kako ste?
Milan	Dobro, hvala.
Vera	Da vas upoznam. Ovo je moj muž, Zoran.
Milan	Drago mi je, gospodine. Ja sam Milan Lukić.
Zoran	Drago mi je. Ja sam Zoran Petrović.

moj muž	мој муж	*my husband*

QV

Question

How does Vera introduce her husband to Milan?

The phrases in these dialogues are frequently employed in formal introductions:

> Da vas upoznam . . ./Да вас упознам . . .
> Ovo je . . ./Ово је . . .
> Drago mi je. Ja sam . . ./Драго ми је. Ја сам . . .

It is usual to shake hands as you say your name.

Activity F

🔊 CD 1, TR 2, 04.24

Students at the party use expressions which are less formal than the ones used by their teachers. Robert and Vesna see two other guests who also look like students. They approach the new couple and Vesna speaks to the boy first. His name is Pierre. Read the dialogue in both alphabets and then check your pronunciation by listening to the recording:

Vesna	Zdravo. Kako se zoveš?
Pjer	Zovem se Pjer. A kako se vi zovete?
Vesna	Ja sam Vesna. Ovo je moj drug, Robert.
Pjer	Drago mi je. Ovo je moja drugarica, Barbara.
Robert	Kako si, Barbara?
Barbara	Dobro, hvala.
Весна	Здраво. Како се зовеш?
Пјер	Зовем се Пјер. А како се ви зовете?
Весна	Ја сам Весна. Ово је мој друг, Роберт.
Пјер	Драго ми је. Ово је моја другарица, Барбара.
Роберт	Како си, Барбара?
Барбара	Добро, хвала.

QUICK VOCAB		
Kako se zoveš?	**Како се зовеш?**	*What's your name?*
Zovem se . . .	**Зовем се . . .**	*My name is . . .*
Kako se vi zovete?	**Како се ви зовете?**	*What are your names?*
drug	**Друг**	*friend* (male)
drugarica	**Другарица**	*friend* (female)

20

Question

How would Robert introduce Vesna?

How it works

Verb *to be*

We have now met another part of the verb *to be*; the word for *is* **je** as in the phrase **ovo je . . ./ово је** *this is. . . .*

Categories of nouns: gender

In English we talk about gender only in relation to nouns which refer to people or animals such as man/woman, author/authoress, lion/lioness. Nouns are words which name things, people or qualities. In Serbian, as in many other European languages, all nouns are classified in three groups according to gender: masculine, feminine or neuter. You can usually identify the gender of a noun by its ending:

masculine	feminine	neuter
muž/муж gospodin/господин drug/друг dan/дан	žena/жена gospođa/госпођа	jutro/јутро veče/вече

- Masculine (masc.) nouns end in a consonant.
- Feminine (fem.) nouns end in -**a**.
- Neuter (neut.) nouns end in -**o** or -**e**.

There are some subgroups, or smaller groups of nouns, which do not follow this pattern of endings. They will be pointed out and explained during the course.

Adjectives and gender

Adjectives, words which describe or define nouns, also change their ending according to the gender of the noun which they are describing. We call this kind of change an agreement when the adjective agrees with the noun which it is describing:

Masculine adjectives end with a consonant:
  dobar dan / добар дан
  moj muž / мој муж

Feminine adjectives end in -a:
  moja žena / моја жена
  moja drugarica / моја другарица

Neuter adjectives end in -o (and sometimes in -e):
  dobro jutro / добро јутро
  dobro veče / добро вече

What is your name?

There are two ways to ask *What is your name?* in Serbian depending on which form of address you use, informal or formal:

- **Kako se zoveš?/Како се зовеш?**
  (the *you* ti/ти form used when speaking informally to one person; lit. *How do you call yourself?*)

- **Kako se zovete?/Како се зовете?)**
  (the *you* vi/ви form used when speaking formally to one person, or to more than one person; lit. *How do you call yourselves?*)

The answer to this question is:
  Zovem se . . ./Зовем се . . .
  (lit. *I call myself . . .*)

Order of letters in the Cyrillic alphabet

The letters of the Cyrillic alphabet follow a different order from the letters in the Latin alphabet. It is important to know this order if you want to find a word in a dictionary.

1	2	3	4	5	6	7	8	9	10
А	Б	В	Г	Д	Ђ	Е	Ж	З	И

11	12	13	14	15	16	17	18	19	20
Ј	К	Л	Љ	М	Н	Њ	О	П	Р

21	22	23	24	25	26	27	28	29	30
С	Т	Ћ	У	Ф	Х	Ц	Ч	Џ	Ш

Practice

◀) CD 1, TR 2, 05.09

4 You have just been introduced to someone. Say you are pleased to meet them and say *I am* with your name.

5 How would you say to someone that you would like to introduce your wife/husband?

6 You are a student and see someone of your age that you do not know.
   a Using informal language how would you ask his/her name?
   b How would you respond to give your name?

7 How would you say to someone *This is my friend* (male) and *This is my friend* (female)?

8 Write out two of the dialogues in this unit transcribing from the Latin alphabet into the Cyrillic alphabet using block capitals.

Test yourself

Here you can check some of the things you have learnt in this unit. Look at the questions below and choose the right answer:

1 Which word would you use when addressing someone you don't know well?

   a Vi/Ви   **b** Ti/Ти

2 How would you ask your Serbian friend how he/she is?

   a Kako ste?/ Како сте?   **b** Kako si?/ Како си?

3 If you want to say that you are well, which word would you choose to fill the gap: **Dobro . . ./Добро . . .?**

    a ste/сте   **b** si/си   **c** sam/сам

4 What does the phrase **Da vas upoznam/Да вас упознам** mean?

    a Pleased to meet you.
    b Let me introduce you.
    c Thank you very much.

5 How would you introduce a person called Robert to your Serbian friend?

    a Ovo je Robert./Ово је Роберт.
    b Vi ste Robert./Ви сте Роберт.
    c Ja sam Robert./Ја сам Роберт.

6 When asking a child what his/her name is, what would you use?

    a Kako se zoveš?/Како се зовеш?
    b Kako se zovete?/Како се зовете?

7 Which is the usual ending for feminine nouns:

    a -o   **b** -a   **c** -e

8 What is the gender of the word **jutro/јутро** (*morning*)?

    a neuter   **b** feminine   **c** masculine

9 Which word would you choose to fill the gap in the phrase . . . . žena/. . . . . жена?

    a moj/мој   **b** moja/моја   **c** moje/моје

10 Which form of the adjective would you use in front of the word **drug/друг** when you want to say *a good friend* in Serbian?

    a dobra /добра   **b** dobro/добро   **c** dobar /добар

3

Do you speak Serbian?

In this unit you will learn:

- Phrases for talking about nationality
- How to ask which languages others speak
- How to say which languages you speak
- Some basic verb forms
- How to form questions and negative statements
- Handwritten Cyrillic and Latin

Do you speak Serbian?

Activity A

◀)) CD 1, TR 3

When you first meet someone abroad, one of the frequent topics of conversation concerns language and nationality. Here Zoran Petrović is being introduced by his wife to Robert Trent, a student from England. Listen to the dialogue on the recording and try to get the gist of what is being said. Then, listen to the recording again while following the dialogue as it is printed below. Repeat this exercise using the dialogue in Cyrillic:

Vera	Dobro veče, gospodine Trente. Da vas upoznam, ovo je moj muž, Zoran.
Robert	Drago mi je. Ja sam Robert Trent.
Zoran	Drago mi je. Ja sam Zoran Petrović. Vi ste Englez?

Robert	Da, jesam.	
Zoran	Da li govorite srpski?	
Robert	Govorim malo. Učim jezik.	
Zoran	Dobro govorite srpski.	
Robert	Hvala. Da li ste vi Srbin?	
Zoran	Da, jesam.	
Robert	Da li govorite engleski?	
Zoran	Razumem engleski, ali ne govorim dobro.	
Вера	Добро вече, господине Тренте. Да вас упознам, ово је мој муж, Зоран.	
Роберт	Драго ми је. Ја сам Роберт Трент.	
Зоран	Драго ми је. Ја сам Зоран Петровић. Ви сте Енглез?	
Роберт	Да, јесам.	
Зоран	Да ли говорите српски?	
Роберт	Говорим мало. Учим језик.	
Зоран	Добро говорите српски.	
Роберт	Хвала. Да ли сте ви Србин?	
Зоран	Да, јесам.	
Роберт	Да ли говорите енглески?	
Зоран	Разумем енглески, али не говорим добро.	

Vi ste Englez?	**Ви сте Енглез?**	*You are an Englishman?*
Da, jesam.	**Да, јесам.**	*Yes, I am.*
Da li govorite srpski?	**Да ли говорите српски?**	*Do you speak Serbian?*
Govorim malo.	**Говорим мало.**	*I speak a little.*
Učim jezik.	**Учим језик.**	*I am learning the language.*
Dobro govorite srpski.	**Добро говорите српски.**	*You speak Serbian well.*
Da li ste vi Srbin?	**Да ли сте ви Србин?**	*Are you Serbian?* (i.e. *a Serb*, male person)
engleski	**енглески**	*English* (language)
razumem	**разумем**	*I understand*
ali	**али**	*but*
ne govorim	**не говорим**	*I don't speak*

Question

How does Robert ask *Do you speak English?*

Activity B

🔊 CD 1, TR 3, 01.00

The students at the party have a similar conversation. Listen to the recording without reading the dialogue and then again while following the printed version below in both the Latin and the Cyrillic scripts.

Vesna	Barbara, da li si ti Engleskinja?
Barbara	Ne, ja sam Nemica. A ti si Srpkinja?
Vesna	Da, jesam.
Barbara	Da li govoriš nemački?
Vesna	Ne govorim nemački. Govorim engleski i malo francuski. Ali ti govoriš dobro srpski.
Barbara	Razumem srpski, ali ne govorim dobro.
Vesna	Pjer, ti si Francuz?
Pjer	Jesam.
Vesna	I ti učiš srpski?
Pjer	Da, učim.
Весна	Барбара, да ли си ти Енглескиња?
Барбара	Не, ја сам Немица. А ти си Српкиња?
Весна	Да, јесам.
Барбара	Да ли говориш немачки?
Весна	Не говорим немачки. Говорим енглески и мало француски. Али ти говориш добро српски.
Барбара	Разумем српски, али не говорим добро.
Весна	Пјер, ти си Француз?
Пјер	Јесам.
Весна	И ти учиш српски?
Пјер	Да, учим.

Da li si ti Engleskinja?	Да ли си ти Енглескиња?	*Are you* (an) *English* (woman)?
Ja sam Nemica.	Ја сам Немица.	*I am* (a) *German* (woman).
A ti si Srpkinja?	А ти си Српкиња?	*And you are* (a) *Serbian* (woman)?
Da li govoriš nemački?	Да ли говориш немачки?	*Do you speak German?*
francuski	француски	*French*
Francuz	Француз	*Frenchman*
I ti učiš srpski?	И ти учиш српски?	*You are learning Serbian too?*

QUICK VOCAB

Question

How does Barbara say that she understands Serbian but does not speak it well?

> ## Insight
>
> Notice that there is a distinction in Serbian between male and female when talking about nationalities:
>
> | | |
> |---|---|
> | Srbin/Србин | *Serbian* (male) |
> | Srpkinja/Српкиња | *Serbian* (female) |
> | Englez/Енглез | *English* (male) |
> | Engleskinja/Енглескиња | *English* (female) |
>
> The names of the languages are different from the names of nationalities and are written with a small letter:
>
> | | |
> |---|---|
> | srpski/српски | *Serbian* (language) |
> | engleski/енглески | *English* (language) |

Activity C

◆) CD 1, TR 3, 01.46

Now listen to a conversation between two other students at the party but this time, when following the dialogues, look at the Cyrillic alphabet first.

Марио	Здраво. Ја сам Марио. А како се ти зовеш?
Ана	Здраво. Ја се зовем Ана. Ти си Италијан?
Марио	Јесам.
Ана	Говориш добро српски.
Марио	Учим језик. А ти?
Ана	Не учим српски. Ја сам Српкиња. Ја учим грчки.
Марио	Да ли говориш италијански?
Ана	Не говорим, али доста разумем.
Mario	Zdravo. Ja sam Mario. A kako se ti zoveš?
Ana	Zdravo. Ja se zovem Ana. Ti si Italijan?
Mario	Jesam.
Ana	Govoriš dobro srpski.
Mario	Učim jezik. A ti?
Ana	Ne učim srpski. Ja sam Srpkinja. Ja učim grčki.
Mario	Da li govoriš italijanski?
Ana	Ne govorim, ali dosta razumem.

Italijan	Италијан	*Italian* (man)
italijanski	италијански	*Italian*
grčki	грчки	*Greek*
dosta razumem	доста разумем	*I understand a lot*

Question

How do you say *I am learning a language*?

Activity D

📢 CD 1, TR 3, 02.24

Here is what Mario and some other students have to say about themselves. Read their statements given below in the Cyrillic alphabet only and answer the questions which follow. Check your pronunciation by listening to the recording:

Марио	Зовем се Марио. Ја сам Италијан. Говорим италијански и француски. Учим српски, али не говорим добро.
Натали	Зовем се Натали. Ја сам Францускиња. Говорим француски и руски. Сада учим српски.
Ричард	Зовем се Ричард. Ја сам Американац. Говорим енглески и немачки. Учим српски и доста разумем.

Francuskinja	Францускиња	*Frenchwoman*
sada	сада	*now*
Amerikanac	Американац	*American* (man)
ruski	руски	*Russian*

Questions

i Who is American?
ii Who speaks Russian?

How it works

No word for *a* or *the* in Serbian

Serbian has no separate words for *a*, *an* or *the*. So when Vesna asks Barbara **Da li si ti Engleskinja?/Да ли си ти Енглескиња?**

it could mean either *Are you <u>an</u> Englishwoman?* or *Are you <u>the</u> Englishwoman?* depending on the context. The lack of such words may sound a little odd to the English ear at first, but you soon get used to speaking without them.

Verb *to be*

In this dialogue there is a new form to mean *I am* **jesam/jecaм** which is used for one word answers to questions of the type *Are you . . .*

Vi ste Englez?	Ви сте Енглез?	*Are you English?*
Da, jesam.	Да, јесам.	*Yes, I am.*

Verb forms – present tense

The endings for indicating the different parts of the verb (verbs are words which express actions) in the present tense are largely regular and most verbs follow a similar pattern:

the ja/ja ending is	-m/-м
the ti/ти ending is	-š/-ш
the vi/ви ending is	-te/-те

The words for *I speak* and *you speak* are significantly different at the end. The ending tells you that **govorim/говорим** means *I speak*, **govoriš/говориш** means *you speak* (informal to one person) and **govorite/говорите** means *you speak* (formal to one person and plural). As each part of the verb has its own ending, you do not have to use the personal pronouns (words for *I* and *you* etc.) in Serbian. These words are put in when you are addressing someone directly, e.g. **Da li vi govorite engleski?/Да ли ви говорите енглески?** *Do you speak English?*, or for emphasis, e.g. Zoran says to Robert **Vi ste Englez?/Ви сте Енглез?** because he finds it unusual for a foreigner to speak some Serbian. His question is more along the lines of *Are you really an Englishman? Crikey, not many of you speak Serbian.*

Having already met the forms of the verb **učim/учим** and **učiš/учиш** in the previous dialogues, by following the pattern above you can form the vi/ви part of the verb: **učite/учите**. Following the same pattern of endings **razumem/разумем** becomes **razumeš/разумеш** and **razumete/разумете** as in the table:

ja	govorim	razumem	učim
ja	говорим	разумем	учим
I speak		*I understand*	*I learn*
ti	govoriš	razumeš	učiš
ти	говориш	разумеш	учиш
you speak		*you understand*	*you learn*
vi	govorite	razumete	učite
ви	говорите	разумете	учите
you speak		*you understand*	*you learn*

Serbian has only one form of the present tense and so **govorim/говорим** means *I speak*, *I am speaking* and *I do speak*; **govoriš/говориш** means *you speak*, *you are speaking* and *you do speak*; and so on.

Forming questions and negative statements

To make a question put **da li/да ли** in front of the statement as in the example:

| Razumete srpski. | Разумете српски. | *You understand Serbian.* |
| Da li razumete srpski? | Да ли разумете српски? | *Do you understand Serbian?* |

To make a verb negative put **ne/не** in front of the verb.

| Ne, ne razumem. | Не, не разумем. | *No, I do not understand.* |

Nationalities and languages

You have met the words for an *Englishman* **Englez/Енглез** and a *Serbian (man)* **Srbin/Србин**. There are other words to designate female persons **Engleskinja/Енглескиња** and **Srpkinja/Српкиња**. In addition you have met the words for *English* and *Serbian* to mean the languages **engleski/енглески** and **srpski/српски**. Here are some other nationalities and languages. Note that the words denoting persons are spelt with a capital letter in Serbian while words denoting languages are spelt with a small letter:

Male	Female	Language	
Englez	Engleskinja	engleski	*English*
Srbin	Srpkinja	srpski	*Serbian*

Francuz	Francuskinja	francuski	*French*
Nemac	Nemica	nemački	*German*
Rus	Ruskinja	ruski	*Russian*
Amerikanac	Amerikanka	engleski	*American*
Hrvat	Hrvatica	hrvatski	*Croat*
Italijan	Italijanka	italijanski	*Italian*
Makedonac	Makedonka	makedonski	*Macedonian*
Grk	Grkinja	grčki	*Greek*

Male	**Female**	**Language**	
Енглез	Енглескиња	енглески	*English*
Србин	Српкиња	српски	*Serbian*
Француз	Францускиња	француски	*French*
Немац	Немица	немачки	*German*
Рус	Рускиња	руски	*Russian*
Американац	Американка	енглески	*American*
Хрват	Хрватица	хрватски	*Croat*
Италијан	Италијанка	италијански	*Italian*
Македонац	Македонка	македонски	*Macedonian*
Грк	Гркиња	грчки	*Greek*

Handwritten Cyrillic

Handwritten, or cursive, forms of the Cyrillic alphabet differ from the printed forms.

print	capital	small	example
А	*А*	*а*	*Ана*
Б	*Б*	*б*	*Баба*
В	*В*	*в*	*Вава*
Г	*Г*	*г*	*Гага*
Д	*Д*	*д*	*Деда*
Ђ	*Ђ*	*ђ*	*Ђиђа*
Е	*Е*	*е*	*Еђе*
Ж	*Ж*	*ж*	*Жижа*

З	*З*	*з*	Заза
И	*И*	*и*	Иди
Ј	*Ј*	*ј*	Јаје
К	*К*	*к*	Кика
Л	*Л*	*л*	Лела
Љ	*Љ*	*љ*	Лиља
М	*М*	*м*	Мама
Н	*Н*	*н*	Нена
Њ	*Њ*	*њ*	Њања
О	*О*	*о*	Око
П	*П*	*п̄*	Поп
Р	*Р*	*р*	Рибар
С	*С*	*с*	Саса
Т	*Т*	*т̄*	Тата
Ћ	*Ћ*	*ћ*	Ћопић
У	*У*	*у*	Унук
Ф	*Ф*	*ф*	Фифа
Х	*Х*	*х*	Хула-хоп
Ц	*Ц*	*ц*	Цица
Ч	*Ч*	*ч*	Чича
Џ	*Џ*	*џ*	Џиџа
Ш	*Ш*	*ш*	Шаша

Handwritten Latin

Handwritten, or cursive, forms of the Latin alphabet are very similar to English with the exception of the diacritic marks above certain consonants which have to be clearly placed. Look at the examples:

gospodin Živković   *gospodin Živković*

učim srpsiki   *učim srpski*

Note that the letters z and ž are written like the printed form as in these examples:

Francuz   *Francuz*

žena   *žena*

Practice

1 Fill in the blanks in the grid below identifying people and the languages they speak. First look at the example:

Роберт	Енглез	енглески
a Марио		италијански
b Весна	Српкиња	
c Иван		руски
d Сандра	Американка	
e Барбара		немачки
f Пјер	Француз	

2 Look at the following pattern:

Ja sam Maja.   Ja sam Hrvatica.   Govorim hrvatski.

Now repeat the pattern using the names

   a Natalie (French)   **b** Mario (Italian)
   c Richard (American)   **d** Jovan (Serb).

3 Now use the same pattern to describe yourself.

4 You are at a party where there are people of many different nationalities. You are playing the role of B in the following dialogue. Replace the English phrases with their Serbian equivalents:

🔊 **CD 1, TR 3, 03.04**

A	Ја сам Зоран Петровић.
B	*Pleased to meet you. I am Richard Thompson.*
A	Ви сте Американац?
B	*No, I am English.*
A	Да ли разумете српски?
B	*I understand a little. I am learning the language.*
A	Добро говорите српски.
B	*Thank you.*

5 Choose the correct forms of the verbs given in brackets in order to complete the sentences below:

  a Ja (govorim, govorite, govoriš) engleski.
  b Vi dosta (razumeš, razumem, razumete) srpski.
  c Ti (ne učite, ne učiš, ne učim) francuski.
  d Učim srpski, ali (ne govoriš, ne govorite, ne govorim) dobro.
  e Da li ti (razumeš, razumem, razumete) engleski?
  f Da li (sam, si, ste) vi Engleskinja?
  g Da li (si, ste, sam) ti Amerikanac?
  h Ja (si, sam, ste) dobro.

6 Listen to Milan, Ana and Laura introducing themselves and fill in the table below with the nationality (**nacionalnost**) and languages corresponding to each person:

🔊 **CD 1, TR 3, 03.57**

ime	nacionalnost	jezik
a Milan		
b Ana		
c Laura		

7 Here is a short letter written by a girl called Branka to her cousin in Belgrade. Branka lives in England, but her parents are from

Serbia. Read the letter and then answer the questions which follow:

Здраво, Весна!

Како си? Ја сам добро. Сада
учим српски. Разумем доста,
али мало говорим.

a What greeting does Branka use in her letter?
b Which question does she ask her cousin?
c Does Branka speak Serbian?

8 Here are the names of some of the people you've met during your stay in Serbia. Write out their names using the handwritten forms of Cyrillic:

a Бојан Поповић   **b** Милена Рајић
c Владан Гордић   **d** Љиљана Жикић

Test yourself

Here you can check some of the things you have learnt in this unit. Look at the questions below and choose the right answer:

1 Which of these Serbian words is used to refer to the English language?

  a Englez/Енглез
  b engleski/енглески
  c Engleskinja/Енглескиња

2 If you want to say that you are an Englishman, which word do you have to insert into the following sentence: Ja ...... Englez/ Ja ...... Енглез?

  a ste/сте   **b** si/си   **c** sam/сам

3 Which word would you use to refer to a Frenchman?

  a Francuskinja/Францускиња
  b Francuz/Француз
  c francuski/француски

4 Which of the following would you use if you want to say that you are learning Serbian?

   a Učim srpski./Учим српски.
   b Učiš srpski./Учиш српски.
   c Učite srpski./Учите српски.

5 Which of these statements is the most appropriate response to the question **Da li govorite srpski/Да ли говорите српски?**

   a Da, jesam./Да, јесам.
   b Ne, hvala./Не, хвала.
   c Govorim malo./Говорим мало.

6 If someone asks you **Da li razumete srpski?/Да ли разумете српски?** he/she wants to know:

   a if you are learning Serbian
   b if you understand Serbian

7 The meaning of the word **malo/мало** is:

   a a little   **b** a lot   **c** enough

8 If someone asks you if you are English and you want to respond with *Yes, I am*, how would you fill the gap in the phrase **Da/Да, ...?**

   a sam/сам   **b** jesam/јесам

9 How would you ask the waiter in a restaurant politely if he speaks English?

   a Da li govorite engleski?/Да ли говорите енглески?
   b Da li govoriš engleski?/Да ли говориш енглески?

10 How would you ask the little daughter of your Serbian friend if she understands what you are telling her?

   a Da li razumeš?/Да ли разумеш?
   b Da li razumete?/Да ли разумете?

4

....

Ordering a drink

In this unit you will learn:

- How to order a drink
- Some polite expressions
- How to ask what someone wants
- Cases: genitive and accusative singular
- Numbers 1–4
- How to express *of*

Ordering a drink

The Cyrillic and the Latin alphabets are from now on used alternately, beginning with Cyrillic.

Activity A

◀) CD 1, TR 4

Milan and Dragan are going for a drink after work. Listen to the following dialogue on the recording, follow what they say to the waitress by reading the printed text below, and answer the questions at the end:

Конобарица	Добро вече. Изволите?
Милан	Једно пиво, молим вас.
Конобарица	А за вас?
Драган	И ја бих пиво.

The waitress brings the beer.

Конобарица	Два пива. Изволите.
Драган	Хвала.
Конобарица	Молим.

Milan turns to Dragan and, raising his glass, says **Живели!**

конобарица	*waitress*
Изволите	*Can I help you?/Here you are.*
једно пиво	*one beer*
молим вас	*please* (lit. *I beg you*)
А за вас?	*And for you?*
И ја бих пиво.	*I would like a beer too.*
два пива	*two beers*
молим	*you are welcome; please*
Живели!	*Cheers! To your health!*

QUICK VOCAB

Questions

i How do you say *please* in Serbian?

ii Which phrase does Milan use to order a beer?

iii How would he order *two beers*?

Activity B

◀)) **CD 1, TR 4, 00.45**

Vesna and Robert are going for a drink. Listen to the following dialogue on the recording, follow what they say to the waiter by reading the printed text below, and answer the questions at the end:

Весна	Добар дан.
Конобар	Добар дан. Изволите?
Весна	Ја бих једну кафу и један сок, молим вас.
Конобар	Сок од боровнице или сок од поморанџе?
Весна	Сок од боровнице, молим вас.
Конобар	А за вас?
Роберт	Дајте ми кафу и киселу воду, молим вас.
Конобар	У реду. Две кафе, кисела вода и сок. Одмах.

конобар	*waiter*
ја бих једну кафу	*I would like a (one) coffee*

QV

један сок	*one juice*
сок од боровнице	*blueberry juice*
или	*or*
сок од поморанце	*orange juice*
дајте ми кафу	*give me a coffee*
. . . и киселу воду	*and a mineral water*
у реду	*OK, all right*
две кафе	*two coffees*
одмах	*immediately, at once*

Questions

i How does Vesna order a coffee?

ii How do you say *Give me . . .* in Serbian?

iii How would Vesna order *two coffees*?

It is not difficult to find somewhere to eat and drink in Belgrade or other Serbian towns. The **кафана** *café* is a traditional institution which can range from a simple affair offering drinks and basic snacks to a larger place with a full menu. There is sometimes little to distinguish a **кафана** from a **ресторан** *restaurant*, but bear in mind that some tables may be reserved for diners only. In all these places the general rule is to find a table, sit down and wait for the waiter or waitress. They will take and serve your order, and when you are ready to leave bring your bill. If you have a sweet tooth choose a **посластичарница**, where you can get soft drinks, coffee and choose from a large variety of cakes. A **кафић** is generally a small bar catering for the younger generation where drinks are often ordered and paid for at a counter. Those wishing to go on into the small hours can look for a **ноћни клуб** *night club*.

Cafés in Belgrade offer a wide selection of non-alcoholic and alcoholic drinks; for example **кисела вода** *mineral water*, **сок** *juice*, **кока-кола** *Coca-Cola*, **пиво** beer, **бело вино** *white wine*, **црно вино** *red wine* (**црн** actually means *black*), **ракија** *brandy*. Beer is usually sold in bottles of $^1/_3$ or $^1/_2$ litre, and increasingly you can find draught beer (**точено пиво**). In summer months most cafés put tables and chairs outside for customers.

Кафа *coffee* is drunk at all times of the day and is traditionally taken in a black, strong brew called **турска кафа** *Turkish coffee* in which sugar and water are boiled together before adding very finely ground coffee. You will be asked whether you take it **слатка** *sweet*, **средња** *medium* or **горка** *without sugar*.

How it works

Polite expressions

The waiter uses **изволите** with two different meanings depending on the context. When you walk in he may ask **Изволите?** meaning *Can I help you?*. When bringing your order he will say with a different intonation **изволите** meaning *here you are*. The word indicates that the waiter is offering his help or giving you something.

Similarly, the word **молим** has more than one meaning depending on the context and intonation. It is a polite response when someone says **хвала** to you, meaning *you're welcome* or *don't mention it*. It is the word meaning *please*, often used in the phrase **молим вас** (lit. *I beg you*). The same phrase may be used to attract someone's attention (*excuse me*).

Insight

When someone says **хвала** to you, it is the custom to respond with **молим**. Not to do so might appear impolite.

Ordering

The waiter indicates that he is ready to take an order in two ways:

Изволите?	*Can I help you?*
А за вас?	*And for you?*

The customers respond in one of three ways:

Једно пиво, молим вас.	*A beer, please.*
Ја бих пиво/кафу/сок, молим вас.	*I would like a beer/coffee/ juice, please.*
Дајте ми кафу, молим вас.	*Give me a coffee, please.*

All three are perfectly acceptable responses: simply stating what you want, saying first *I would like . . .* or *Give me . . .* The last example may sound a little abrupt but is polite when, as usual, you add **молим вас**.

Cases

You are already aware that the endings of nouns vary slightly. We have met some changes already when **господин** becomes **господине** and **госпођа** becomes **госпођо**. The first forms given here are called the nominative (nom.) case. They are regarded as the first or basic case, used to state the subject of a sentence. It is the form of the word used for dictionary headings and you identify the gender of the noun according to its ending. The second forms given here are in the vocative (voc.) case used when addressing someone directly. Serbian has seven cases and they fulfil certain functions in the language.

Accusative case

You have examples here of words for drinks in all three genders:

сок	*juice* – ends in a consonant, masc.
кафа	*coffee* – ends in -a, fem.
пиво	*beer* – ends in -o, neut.

When ordering drinks, the words for juice, coffee or beer are put in the accusative (acc.) case. For example, Vesna says **Ја бих једну кафу** *I would like a (one) coffee*.

When you say *I would like X*: *I* is the subject of the verb, the one performing the action (Serbian nom. case **ja**), *X* is the direct object of the verb, the thing on which the action is performed (Serbian acc. case **кафу**). This is because it is the thing which is wanted, it is the object of wanting. In English the object usually comes after the verb.

You can see this distinction between subject and object more clearly in English in the difference between *he/him* and *she/her* as in the following examples:

He likes her.
She likes him.

The words *he/she* come before the verb as the subject, the ones doing the liking. The words *her/him* come after the verb as the direct object, the ones towards whom the action of the verb is directed.

The object of the verb in a Serbian sentence is put in the acc. case. Each gender has its own rules for these case endings with some overlaps and similarities. The acc. case endings generally follow this pattern:

case	masc.	fem.	neut.
nom. acc.	сок сок (no change)	кафа кафу (-a to -u)	пиво пиво (no change)

Numbers *one* and *two* and the genitive case

The word for *one* is **један** and for *two* is **два**.

Један is an adjective in Serbian and as such has to agree with the gender of the noun which it qualifies whether it be masc., fem. or neut. To specify one of something say:

један сок   masculine

једна кафа   feminine   (**једну кафу** in the accusative case when ordering)

једно пиво   neuter

The correct form of the words for *two* also depends on the gender of the noun:

два   with masc. and neut. nouns

две   with fem. nouns

The noun which follows this number goes into the genitive (gen.) singular case:

два сока

два пива

две кафе

We can build on our table of case endings from above to show the pattern of cases with the gen.:

case	masc.	fem.	neut.
nom. acc. gen.	сок сок (no change) сока (add -a)	кафа кафу (-a to -u) кафе (-a to -e)	пиво пиво (no change) пива (-o to -a)

We shall gradually develop the patterns of the language as you go through the dialogues and exercises so that you can learn the correct forms in order to make your own sentences. These patterns are rather like building blocks which will enable you to understand and respond in a great variety of situations and contexts.

What kind of juice?

If you ask for a *juice* сок to drink, the waiter will have to ask what kind of juice you want. A common way of expressing flavours or ingredients in drinks and dishes is shown in Activity B when Vesna asks for **сок од боровнице** meaning *a juice made from blueberry*. The word **од** *from* is followed by the name of the fruit in the gen. case. The names of many fruits are fem.:

поморанџа	*orange*
боровница	*blueberry*
јабука	*apple*
малина	*raspberry*
јагода	*strawberry*
сок од јабуке	*apple juice*

You may be asked if you would like a **џус**, which will always be *orange juice*.

Practice

1 Look at the following drinks (**пиће**) from a list in a café and answer the questions below:

ПИЋЕ
пиво
бело вино
црно вино
ракија
виски
џин
турска кафа
чај

кисела вода
лимунада
кока-кола
тоник
сок од малине

a What kind of wine is on the list?
b What is the Serbian word for *tea*?
c What does the word **лимунада** mean?
d Can you get a gin and tonic in this cafe?
e What kind of juice is on the menu?

2 Listen to what Vesna, Barbara and Robert order in turn from the waiter in a **кафана** and fill in the table below with their orders:

◄) **CD 1, TR 4, 01.17**

a Весна	
b Барбара	
c Роберт	

3 You have invited a friend for a drink. Using the list of drinks given above, try to order:

◄) **CD 1, TR 4, 01.46**

a two teas
b a brandy and a coffee
c two lemonades.

What would you like?

Activity C

◄) **CD 1, TR 4, 02.22**

Vera is taking Barbara, Pierre and Robert for a drink. Listen to the following dialogue, follow what they say by reading the printed text below, and answer the questions at the end:

Вера	Шта желите, Барбара?
Барбара	Ја бих кафу.
Вера	Хоћете ли и киселу воду?
Барбара	Да, хвала. Жедна сам.
Вера	У реду. А за вас, Роберте?
Роберт	Не пијем кафу. Ја бих пиво.
Вера	Хоћете ли и ви пиво, Пјер?
Пјер	Хоћу, хвала.
Вера	Дајте нам, молим вас, три пива, једну кафу и чашу киселе воде.

Шта желите?	*What do you want/wish?*
Хоћете ли . . . ?	*Do you want . . . ?*
Жедна сам.	*I am thirsty.*
не пијем	*I don't drink*
и ви	*you too*
хоћу	*I want* (irregular verb)
Дајте нам . . .	*Give us . . .*
три пива	*three beers*
. . . и чашу киселе воде	*. . . and a glass of mineral water*

Questions

i How does Vera ask Barbara what she wants to drink?

ii What is the Serbian equivalent for *three beers*?

How it works

Asking what someone wants

There are two phrases in the dialogue above (Activity C) which are used to ask someone else what they want:

Шта желите?	*What do you want?*
Хоћете ли и ви пиво?	*Do you want a beer too?*

The first phrase using **желите** is a formal way of asking someone what they would like, whereas the word **хоћете** is equally polite, means exactly the same, but is less formal. You are quite likely to hear both words being used.

In order to ask a question you have already used:

Да ли говорите српски?   *Do you speak Serbian?*

The phrase **Хоћете ли пиво?** represents an alternative formula for making questions. Instead of using **да ли** followed by the verb as in **Да ли хоћете пиво?** you simply put the particle **ли** after the verb followed by the subject if one is used, as in **Хоћете ли и ви пиво?**

Irregular verb *хоћу*

The verb **хоћу** *I want* follows an irregular pattern. The **ja, ти** and **ви** forms of this verb are:

ja	хоћу
ти	хоћеш
ви	хоћете

Responding to questions

In English, when answering a direct question we tend to say *yes* or *no* with a *please* or *thank you* to be polite. In Serbian, people typically answer questions by repeating the verb, or by adding the word **да** *yes* in front of the verb:

Хоћете ли пиво?
Хоћу./Да, хоћу.

I am thirsty

When adjectives are used to describe people, they have to agree with the gender of the person, ending in a consonant for a male and in -a for a female:

Жедна сам.   *I am thirsty.* (Barbara says of herself.)
Жедан сам.   *I am thirsty.* (Robert would say of himself.)

It is quite common when adding endings to nouns and adjectives that a penultimate **a** disappears as in **жедан** (masc.) but **жедна** (fem.). This feature is known as the moveable **a**.

Numbers *three* **and** *four*

три	*three*
четири	*four*

These numbers, like **два/две**, are followed by the gen. singular:

три сока	*three juices*
три кафе	*three coffees*
три пива	*three beers*

To say *of*

The genitive case in Serbian is also used when in English we would say *of*, as in the following phrase:

Дајте нам чашу кисел<u>е</u> вод<u>е</u>, молим вас.	*Give* (or *Bring*) *us a glass of mineral water, please.*

Compare these phrases:

чаша сока	*a glass of juice*
чаша воде	*a glass of water*
чаша пива	*a glass of beer*

You will find that cases are often used when, in English, we use *of* or some other similar word like *by*, *to* etc. These words are called prepositions and they relate two or more items together as in the phrase *a glass of water*.

Practice

4 In Practice 1 there is a list of drinks. Write out the drinks given using the Latin alphabet.

5 You go to a **кафана** with a colleague. Fill in your part of the conversation:

🔊 **CD 1, TR 4, 03.05**

> *What do you want?*
> Ја бих кафу.
> *I would like a coffee too. Do you want a glass of mineral water?*
> Хоћу, хвала.
>
> Добро вече, изволите?
> *Good evening. Two coffees and two mineral waters, please.*

6 Complete the sentences by putting the nouns in brackets into the correct forms using the acc. or gen. case:

a Желите ли (вино) или (пиво)?

b Не пијем (ракија).

c Дајте ми, молим вас, чашу (сок).

d Хоћу сок од (боровница).

e Дајте нам једну (кафа) и две (лимунада).

f Да ли хоћете (чај)?

g Дајте нам четири (пиво).

h Ја бих чашу (кока-кола).

7 Imagine that you are at a conference or a business meeting in Belgrade. There is a break and you want to buy a round of drinks for the people sitting at your table.

    a How would you ask them what they would like?

    b How would you order four coffees, one orange juice, one mineral water and two beers?

8 You order a drink for yourself and immediately you are joined by two friends. Change the following orders from one to three drinks:

    a Једно пиво, молим вас.

    b Једну чашу лимунаде, молим вас.

    c Једну ракију, молим вас.

    d Један сок од јабуке, молим вас.

    e Један џус, молим вас.

    f Једну кока-колу, молим вас.

Test yourself

Here you can check some of the things you have learnt in this unit. Look at the questions below and choose the right answer:

1 The traditional place where you can have a drink in Serbia is called:

    a кафана   **b** бифе   **c** бар

2 What would you say in response to **хвала**?

    a Изволите.   **b** Живели.   **c** Молим.

3 Which word should be used to complete the sentence **Дајте ми .... пиво?**

   a једна   **b** једно   **c** један

4 Which phrase should be used to complete the sentence **Дајте ми .... when asking for one coffee?**

   a једну кафу   **b** једна кафа   **c** једне кафе

5 Which form of the word **лимунада** would you use to complete the sentence **Не пијем ....?**

   a лимунада   **b** лимунаду   **c** лимунаде

6 What is the genitive case of the noun **чај**?

   a чају   **b** чаја   **c** чај

7 Which of these forms is used after the number **три**?

   a кисела вода   **b** киселу воду   **c** киселе воде

8 What kind of juice is **сок од јабуке**?

   a apple juice   **b** orange juice   **c** strawberry juice

9 What is the meaning of the word **жедан**?

   a hungry   **b** thirsty   **c** tired

10 Which form of the word **чаша** would you use when asking **Дајте ми .... воде?**

   a чаша   **b** чаше   **c** чашу

5

Ordering food

In this unit you will learn:

- How to buy a snack
- How to read a menu
- Cases: nominative and genitive plurals
- Numbers 5–100
- Types of regular verbs
- Cases: instrumental singular and soft endings

As the Cyrillic alphabet was used in Unit 4, the Latin alphabet is used here for writing Serbian. Opportunity to practise Cyrillic continues to be given.

New nouns in the vocabulary boxes are given in the nom. case and adjectives in the masc. nom. form where the meaning of the phrase in which they occur is clear.

Fast food

If you are a visitor or a tourist in a Serbian town, you may want to buy a snack as you wander the streets or grab a quick bite between appointments. Look out for a **pekara** *bakery*, a **kiosk** *kiosk* where they sell different kinds of fast food, or a **picerija** (also spelt as in Italian **pizzeria**).

Activity A

🔊 **CD 1, TR 5, 00.05**

Words for food and ways of cooking often betray cultural influences. In Serbia you find many different types of cuisine from Central

Europe, the Mediterranean area and Turkey. In the bakery, alongside bread, you may find **burek** on sale. It is a word from Turkish which denotes a kind of pie made of thin leaves of filo pastry which are layered with cheese or meat.

Below is a price list of a bakery on one of Belgrade's central streets. This bakery is open 24 hours (**otvoreno 0–24**). Its prices are given in dinars, shortened to **din.**, and **burek** is sold in units of 100 grams. Listen to the information about items and prices on the recording while following the list below and answer the questions at the end:

PEKARA	
otvoreno 0–24	
HLEB	20 din.
KIFLE	10 din.
BUREK sa sirom	20 din. (100 g.)
BUREK sa mesom	25 din. (100 g.)
JOGURT	8 din.

QUICK VOCAB

hleb	loaf, bread
kifle	crescent-shaped bread rolls
burek	pie (made with filo pastry)
sa sirom	with cheese
sa mesom	with meat
jogurt	yoghurt

Questions

i Robert goes into the bakery to buy a loaf of bread and two **kifle**. How much does he pay?

ii Vesna goes to the bakery for 100 grams of **burek sa mesom** and a yoghurt. How much does she pay?

Activity B

◀» CD 1, TR 5, 01.33

Robert and Vesna are buying a sandwich and something to drink at a kiosk. Listen to their conversation on the recording, read the printed text and answer the question at the end:

Robert	Gladan sam, Vesna. Hoću sendvič. Ah, ovde je kiosk.
Vesna	I ja sam gladna. Hoću sendvič sa sirom i sok.
Robert	Ja hoću sendvič sa šunkom. Molim vas, dajte nam jedan sendvič sa sirom, jedan sa šunkom i dva soka. Da li imate sok od jabuke?
Prodavačica	Da, imamo. Izvolite. Jedan sendvič je osamnaest dinara, sok je petnaest. Molim vas, šezdeset šest dinara.

gladan	*hungry*
sendvič	*sandwich*
ovde	*here*
sa šunkom	*with ham*
da li imate ...	*do you have ...*
prodavačica	*saleswoman*
imamo	*we have*
osamnaest	*eighteen*
petnaest	*fifteen*
šezdeset šest	*sixty-six*

Question

What kind of sandwiches do Robert and Vesna buy?

Bakeries sell a range of different things and sometimes provide space for you to eat them inside. In addition to the items mentioned earlier, you can buy **pašteta** which is a pasty made with flaky pastry and baked with a filling such as cheese. There is also **pogačica** which is a small pie and **đevrek** which is a bread roll shaped in a hoop and topped with sesame seeds. There are kiosks where you can buy sandwiches, cold drinks, and other snacks, including a type of hamburger called **pljeskavica** served in a special type of bread bun called **lepinja**.

How it works

Forming the nominative plural of nouns

The word **kifle** is plural. It is a fem. word and the singular form is **kifla**. If you go into a shop and want just one of them you ask **Dajte mi, molim vas, jednu kiflu**. Masc., fem. and neut. nouns form their plurals according to the following pattern:

	masculine	feminine	neuter
singular nom. plural nom.	sendvič sendviči (add -i)	kafa kafe (-a to -e)	pivo piva (-o to -a)

One of the variations on this pattern occurs with many masc. nouns which have only one syllable, like **sok** *juice*. These short roots are lengthened in the plural **sok + ov + i**. The nominative plural of **sok** is **sokovi**.

Not all monosyllabic masc. nouns form their plural with this extended stem. The plural of **dan** *day* is **dani** *days*.

Numbers 5–100

In the previous unit you learnt how to use the numbers 1–4. Here are the numbers 5–100:

5	pet	21	dvadeset jedan
6	šest	22	dvadeset dva
7	sedam	23	dvadeset tri
8	osam	24	dvadeset četiri
9	devet	25	dvadeset pet
10	deset	26	dvadeset šest
11	jedanaest	27	dvadeset sedam
12	dvanaest	28	dvadeset osam
13	trinaest	29	dvadeset devet
14	četrnaest	30	trideset
15	petnaest	40	četrdeset
16	šesnaest	50	pedeset
17	sedamnaest	60	šezdeset
18	osamnaest	70	sedamdeset
19	devetnaest	80	osamdeset
20	dvadeset	90	devedeset
		100	sto

To express the numbers 20 and above, simply put the number of units after the tens as in the example with 21, 22, etc.

31	trideset jedan
42	četrdeset dva

56 pedeset šest
78 sedamdeset osam
99 devedeset devet

The same principle applies after 100 (**sto**):

125 sto dvadeset pet
163 sto šezdeset tri
187 sto osamdeset sedam

Genitive plural after numbers

Jedan is an adjective, while **dva/dve**, **tri**, **četiri** are followed by the gen. singular of the noun as in **dva soka**, **tri kafe**.

The numbers **pet** to **dvadeset** are followed by the gen. plural, which is formed in the following way:

	masculine	feminine	neuter
nom. plural gen. plural	sendviči sendviča (-**i** to **a**)	kafe kafa (-**e** to -**a**)	piva piva (no change)

pet sendviča	*five sandwiches*
osam kafa	*eight coffees*
deset piva	*ten beers*

Masculine nouns with one syllable, such as **sok**, will of course continue to add the extra **-ov** in all cases in the plural:

dvanaest sokova *12 juices*

Which case you use with numbers above 20 depends on the last word of the compound number. Numbers which finish with **jedan** continue to be followed by nouns in the singular and **jedan** behaves like an adjective. Numbers which finish with **dva/dve**, **tri**, **četiri** are followed by the genitive singular, and all others are followed by the genitive plural:

dvadeset jedan sendvič (singular after **jedan** which agrees with the noun)
dvadeset dve kafe (gen. singular after **dve**)
sto osamnaest sokova (gen. plural after **osamnaest**)

Types of regular verbs

Regular verbs in Serbian fall into one of three groups depending on which vowel is used to form the endings of the present tense. You have seen examples of all of them and we can classify them as follows:

the a group	such as **imam**	*I have*
the e group	such as **pijem**	*I drink*
the i group	such as **govorim**	*I speak*

Each verb has six endings in the present tense (called persons). There are three in the singular (corresponding to the forms for *I*, *you* and *he* or *she*) and three in the plural (corresponding to the forms for *we*, *you* and *they*). In Activity B you met the first person plural form of the verb **imamo** *we have* (the word for *we* is **mi**). The ending for the first person plural of the present tense is **-mo**:

ja imam	*I have*	mi imamo	*we have*
ja pijem	*I drink*	mi pijemo	*we drink*
ja govorim	*I speak*	mi govorimo	*we speak*

Sa with instrumental and soft endings

The word **sa** *with* is a preposition followed by the instrumental (ins.) case. You have three such expressions in this unit **sa sirom**, **sa mesom** and **sa šunkom**. The endings for masc., fem. and neut. nouns are as follows:

case	masc.	fem.	neut.
nom. singular ins. singular	sir sirom (add **-om**)	šunka šunkom (**-a** to **-om**)	meso mesom (**-o** to **-om**)

Following this pattern, if Robert wanted to say that he was buying a sandwich *with Vesna* he would say **sa Vesnom**, and Vesna would say **sa Robertom**.

Some neut. nouns, such as **pozorište** *theatre*, end in -e. For these nouns change -e to -em: **pozorište** to **pozorištem**.

Some masc. nouns end in a soft consonant. The soft consonants are c, č, ć, dž, đ, j, lj, nj, š and ž. To form the instrumental singular after one of these consonants add -em instead of -om: **sendvičem**, **čajem**.

This is a spelling rule which requires that -e instead of -o be written after a soft consonant and it applies to all masc. and neut. noun and adjective endings. This rule does not apply to fem. noun and adjective endings: for example the instrumental form of the word čaša is čašom.

Insight

To say that you drink coffee with milk (**mleko**), use the preposition **sa** followed by the instrumental case:

Pijem kafu sa mlekom.

To say that you drink it without milk, use the preposition **bez** (*without*) followed by the genitive case:

Pijem kafu bez mleka.

Practice

1 Write out the list of bakery items from Activity A in Cyrillic.

2 Listen to Barbara buying items in the bakery. What has she bought and how much does she have to pay?

◀) CD 1, TR 5, 02.18

3 Write out the following numbers in words using first the Latin and then the Cyrillic alphabet:

   15, 16, 28, 37, 44, 59, 62, 76, 123, 165, 189, 191

4 The teachers in the language school are having a meeting which has gone on longer than expected. Milan, with Dragan to help him, has been sent to get some drinks and food to keep everyone going. He has made a list of items. Listen to him reading it and work out what he is going to buy, then check with the list printed below:

◀) CD 1, TR 5, 03.09

   pet sokova; tri od borovnice i dva od pomorandže
   jedna koka-kola
   dva tonika
   četiri sendviča; jedan sa šunkom, tri sa sirom
   dve paštete sa sirom

dva đevreka
šest jogurta

5 Fill in the table below by putting the nouns given in their singular nom. form into the nom. plural:

kifla	
sendvič	
jabuka	
vino	
pomorandža	
sok	

6 Write down the correct form of the noun in brackets after the number indicated:

3	(kafa)
5	(sendvič)
7	(koka-kola)
10	(jogurt)
17	(pašteta)
20	(sok)
24	(hleb)

Reading a menu

Activity C

Read the following explanations and the menu that follows:

> ## Insight
>
> **Predjela**
> A classic first course in a Serbian restaurant is a plate of cheese and smoked ham **sir i pršut**. The **pršut** is a delicacy, served in very thin slices, like Italian prosciutto.
>
> **Supe i čorbe**
> **Supa** is a clear soup with noodles while **čorba** is a much thicker affair with vegetables.

Jela po porudžbini

These are main meals and may well include fried potatoes in the order too. They tend to be quite meaty and vegetarians may have to enquire for something **bez mesa** *without meat*.

JELOVNIK

Predjela

Sir
Šunka
Pršut
Omlet
Pečurke na žaru

Supe i čorbe

Goveđa supa
Pileća čorba

Jela po porudžbini
Biftek
Bečka šnicla
Medaljoni sa pečurkama

Roštilj

Ćevapčići
Ražnjići
Pljeskavica
Piletina na žaru

Salate
Salata od paradajza
Srpska salata
Šopska salata
Zelena salata

Slatkiši
Baklava
Sladoled

MENU

First courses
Cheese
Ham
Smoked ham
Omelette
Grilled mushrooms

Soups and broths
Beef soup
Chicken broth

BBQ
Ćevapčići
Ražnjići
Pljeskavica
Grilled chicken

Salads
Tomato salad
Serbian salad
Šopska salad
Green salad

Dishes to order	Sweets
Steak	Baklava
Wiener schnitzel	Ice cream
Medallions with mushrooms	

Roštilj

This is the mainstay of most restaurants and kafanas and is the more traditional way of cooking and serving meat. **Ćevapčići** are sausage-shaped lengths of minced meat, often a combination of beef and pork but there are many variations and recipes. They are usually served with chopped raw onion. **Ražnjići** are chunks of meat threaded on a skewer. **Pljeskavica** is round and flat, made of minced meat, and usually has onions and hot peppers added.

Salate

Salads are ordered as accompaniments to main courses rather than cooked vegetables. Look out for words like **paradajz** *tomato*, **krastavac** *cucumber*, **cvekla** *beetroot*, **kupus** *cabbage*. Popular types of mixed salad are **srpska salata** (tomato, cucumber, pepper, onion) and **šopska salata** (same but with feta cheese too).

Slatkiši

Sweets are either of the **baklava** type made with honey, or the Central European kind of **torta** *cake*.

Bread

When you order a meal the waiter will bring bread (**hleb**) to accompany your food as a matter of course.

Question
How would you order an omelette and a tomato salad?

Activity D

◀ CD 1, TR 5, 03.50

Vera and Zoran are taking Barbara and Robert to a restaurant for dinner. Listen to the recording and make a list of drinks and dishes that they order. Check your list with the printed text that follows:

Konobar	Dobro veče. Izvolite, šta želite?
Zoran	Dobro veče. Da li imate jelovnik?
Konobar	Imamo. Izvolite.
Zoran	Hvala.
Konobar	Da li želite aperitiv?
Zoran	Želimo. Hoćete li jednu rakiju, Barbara?
Barbara	Da, molim vas.
Zoran	A vi, Roberte?
Robert	I ja bih rakiju, molim vas.
Zoran	A ti, Vera?
Vera	Ja bih kiselu vodu.
Zoran	Dobro. Konobaru, dajte nam tri rakije i flašu kisele vode.
Konobar	Odmah. A za jelo?
Zoran	Dajte nam, molim vas, četiri supe.
Konobar	U redu. Šta još želite?
Zoran	Tri bifteka, molim vas, i jednu bečku šniclu.
Konobar	Želite li salatu?
Zoran	Hoćemo dve srpske salate i dve salate od paradajza.
Konobar	A za piće?
Zoran	Dajte nam flašu vina.
Konobar	Želite li crno ili belo vino?
Zoran	Crno, molim vas.

At the end of the meal Zoran calls the waiter and asks for the bill: **Račun, molim vas.**

QUICK VOCAB

jelovnik	*menu*
flaša	*a bottle*
za jelo	*for food* (meaning *what do you want to eat?*)
šta još	*what else*
za piće	*for drink* (meaning *what do you want to drink?*)
račun	*the bill*

Practice

7 You are ordering a meal in a **restoran**. Fill in the missing part of the following dialogue:

> Dobro veče. Izvolite?
> *Good evening. Do you have a menu?*
> Imamo. Da li želite supu?
> *Yes. Give me a beef soup, please.*
> Šta još želite?
> *I would like one steak and a šopska salad, please.*
> A za piće?
> *A glass of wine, please.*
> Crno ili belo vino?
> *Red, please.*
> U redu. Odmah.
> *The bill, please.*

8 Dragan and his wife Jelena are having dinner in a restaurant. Listen to the recording in order to find out what they are going to have and answer the questions below:

◀) CD 1, TR 5, 06.35

  a Why is Jelena not having a starter?
  b What main dish is Jelena going to have?
  c Is Dragan having a Wiener schnitzel?
  d Is Jelena having a tomato salad or a green salad?
  e Which salad is Dragan having?

9 You want to order a vegetarian pizza without mushrooms and a pizza with ham:

  a When is the pizzeria open?
  b Which pizzas will you order?
  c How much will they cost?
  (Note: **masline** *olives*)

PICERIJA VLADIMIR	OTVORENO 18.00–24.00	
Margarita	paradajz, sir, masline, origano	150 din.
Fungi	paradajz, sir, pečurke, masline, origano	170 din.
Vladimir	paradajz, sir, pečurke, šunka, masline, origano	190 din.

Test yourself

Here you can check some of the things you have learnt in this unit. Look at the questions below and choose the right answer:

1 A savoury pie made of filo pastry often sold in Serbian bakeries is called:

   a kifla   **b** burek   **c** đevrek

2 A ham sandwich in Serbian is **sendvič sa . . . .**

   a šunkom   **b** šunka   **c** šunke

3 The meaning of the word **hoćemo** is:

   a I want   **b** You want   **c** We want

4 Which number comes after **sedamnaest**?

   a devetnaest   **b** osamnaest   **c** osamdeset

5 Which number is **sto četrdeset četiri**?

   a 114   **b** 104   **c** 144

6 Which form of the word **sendvič** would you use after the number **šest**?

   a sendviči   **b** sendviča   **c** sendvič

7 How would the waiter say *We have good barbequed meat*?

   a Imamo dobar roštilj.
   b Imate dobar roštilj.
   c Imaš dobar roštilj.

8 What is **pljeskavica**?

   a roast pork
   b Serbian version of a hamburger
   c chunks of meat on a skewer

9 How would you ask for a menu?

   a Imate li jelovnik?   **b** Imate li predjelo?   **c** Imate li jelo?

10 In which situation is the phrase **Račun, molim vas** used?

   a when ordering food
   b when ordering a taxi
   c when asking for the bill

6

Going shopping

In this unit you will learn:

- How to ask for things in shops
- How to ask the price of something
- How to say how much of something
  you want
- Cases: accusative plural nouns, nominative and
  accusative adjectives
- Numbers above 100
- Verbs: all persons and infinitives
- Irregular verbs хоћу, могу

How much does it cost?

When out shopping, you will be asked certain standard questions for
which there are standard responses. It will help to be aware of these
in advance. The activities in this unit will teach you most of them.
This unit is in the Cyrillic script.

Activity A

◀) CD 1, TR 6

Robert goes shopping (**у куповину**) to the centre of town. First he
goes to a bookshop (**књижара**) to buy a dictionary (**речник**). Listen
to the dialogue and see if you can find out what else he wants to buy,
then read the text to check you have understood:

Роберт	Добар дан. Да ли имате енглеско-српски речник?
Продавачица	Имамо, господине. Изволите, овај речник је добар.
Роберт	Колико кошта?
Продавачица	Кошта петсто двадесет динара.
Роберт	У реду. А да ли имате мапу Србије?
Продавачица	Немамо, господине. Не продајемо мапе.
Роберт	Добро. Дајте ми, онда, тај енглеско-српски речник.
Продавачица	Још нешто?
Роберт	Не, то је све. Изволите шестсто динара.
Продавачица	Изволите ваш кусур, осамдесет динара. Хвала вам и пријатно.
Роберт	До виђења, пријатно.

енглеско–српски речник	*English–Serbian dictionary*
овај	*this*
колико	*how much, how many*
кошта	*it costs*
петсто	*500*
мапа Србије	*map of Serbia*
немамо	*we do not have*
не продајемо	*we do not sell*
тај	*that*
још нешто	*something else*
то је све	*that is all*
шестсто	*600*
ваш кусур	*your change*
хвала вам	*thank you* (lit. *thanks to you*)
пријатно	*cheerio, bye*

QUICK VOCAB

Activity B

🔊 **CD 1, TR 6, 01.09**

The kiosks which you can see on the streets of a Serbian town sell a wide variety of goods. Robert buys a map of Serbia and some other things at one of them. Listen to the dialogue to find out the price of the map, then read the printed text to check your understanding:

Роберт	Добар дан. Да ли имате мапу Србије?
Продавац	Имамо, господине. Кошта сто двадесет динара.

Роберт	А да ли продајете разгледнице?
Продавац	Имамо само ове велике разгледнице.
Роберт	Колико коштају?
Продавац	Оне коштају десет динара.
Роберт	Дајте ми три. И дајте ми један план Београда.
Продавац	Изволите. Овај план града је нов. Он кошта осамдесет пет динара. Још нешто?
Роберт	Не, хвала. Ништа више.

продавац	*salesman*
велике разгледнице	*large postcards*
само	*only*
ове	*these*
коштају	*they cost*
оне	*they* (feminine)
план Београда	*plan of Belgrade*
план града	*city plan*
нов	*new*
ништа више	*nothing more*

At certain points in the last 100 years Serbia has experienced huge political and social changes. There was the creation of a unified Yugoslavia after the First World War, the beginning of Communist rule in 1945, and most recently the end of Communism in the early 1990s. At each stage streets have been given new names in recognition of the new historical era. In recent cases the changes have involved a return to a name previously used before the Second World War. For example, the longest street in Belgrade was known as **Булевар револуције** *Boulevard of the Revolution* until recently when its name was changed back to **Булевар краља Александра** *Boulevard of King Aleksandar*, after Alexander Karađorđević, King of Yugoslavia 1921–34.

How it works

Asking for things in a shop

There are some expressions in these dialogues which are commonly used in shops. When you have finished your shopping and taken it to the checkout or till (**каса**) the cashier may ask **Још нешто?** *Anything else?* You may want to add another purchase or say **То је све** *That is everything* or **Не, хвала. Ништа више** *No, thank you. Nothing more.*

There is an expression used in the first of the dialogues above which you will often hear in Serbia. The expression **пријатно** literally means *pleasantly* but is often used to say *goodbye*, even in conjunction with **до виђења** as Robert uses it here.

Insight

To ask for the price of one thing, use the singular form of the verb:

Колико кошта сендвич? *How much is the sandwich?*

To ask for the price of two or more things, use the plural:

Колико коштају сендвичи? *How much are the sandwiches?*

Verb endings in the present tense

In this unit you have learnt the final parts of the verb in the present tense. They are the third person singular for expressing *he*, *she* or *it* does something, and the third person plural for expressing *they* do something. The verbs used are **кошта** *it costs* and **коштају** *they cost*. The singular form simply ends with the identifying vowel of that group: **-а**, **-е** or **-и**. The ending for the third person plural is different for each group as can be seen from the complete list of regular verb endings for the present tense given in the table below:

	a verbs	**e** verbs	**и** verbs
ја	имам	пијем	учим
ти	имаш	пијеш	учиш
он	има	пије	учи
ми	имамо	пијемо	учимо
ви	имате	пијете	учите
они	имају	пију	уче

Most verbs in Serbian fall into one of these groups. The vowel at the end immediately reveals to which group a verb belongs. You can construct any person of a verb in the present tense by knowing just one of its parts.

Third person singular and plural pronouns

A pronoun is a word which stands in for another word. When you say *John is my brother. He is tall*, the word *he* is a pronoun which is replacing *John*.

Serbian has three third person pronouns in the singular and three in the plural depending on the gender of the noun or nouns to which they refer:

gender	singular	
masc.	он	*he* (or *it*), to replace a masc. noun
fem.	она	*she* (or *it*), to replace a fem. noun
neut.	оно	*it*, to replace a neut. noun

gender	plural	
masc.	они	*they*, to replace masc. plural nouns
fem.	оне	*they*, to replace fem. plural nouns
neut.	она	*they*, to replace neut. plural nouns

Compare the following examples:

masc. singular

Ово је Пјер. Он је Француз.   *This is Pierre. He is French.*

Ово је хлеб. Он кошта 20 динара.   *This is a loaf of bread. It costs 20 dinars.*

fem. singular

Ово је Барбара. Она је Немица.   *This is Barbara. She is German.*

Ово је мапа. Она кошта 120 динара.   *This is a map. It costs 120 dinars.*

neut. singular

Ово је пиво. Оно кошта 30 динара.   *This is a beer. It costs 30 dinars.*

masc. plural

Роберт је Енглез. Пјер је Француз. Они уче српски.   *Robert is English. Pierre is French. They are learning Serbian.*

fem. plural

| Барбара је Немица. Натали је Францускиња. Оне уче српски. | Barbara is German. Natalie is French. They are learning Serbian. |

When talking about a mixed group of men and women, or nouns of different genders, the masc. plural form **они** is used:

| Роберт и Весна имају кафу. Они пију кафу. | Robert and Vesna have coffee. They are drinking coffee. |

In the explanations and summaries in this course we use the masc. pronouns **он** and **они** in order to refer to the third person parts of the verb for the sake of brevity.

Saying *this* and *that*

The words **овај** *this* and **тај** *that* are the masc. singular forms of these demonstrative adjectives. They have fem. and neut. forms too:

masc.	fem.	neut.
овај	ова	ово
тај	та	то

| овај план | *this plan* | ова разгледница | *this postcard* |
| тај план | *that plan* | та разгледница | *that postcard* |

Accusative plural

In this unit we have the acc. plural forms:

| Не продајемо мапе. | *We do not sell maps.* |
| Да ли продајете разгледнице? | *Do you sell postcards?* |

The words for *map* **мапа** and *postcard* **разгледница** in Serbian are fem. We can add the endings to the models we have studied before to see them in all genders:

	masc.	fem.	neut.
nom. plural	сендвичи	кафе	пива
acc. plural	сендвиче (**-и** to **-е**)	кафе (no change)	пива (no change)

Nominative and accusative forms of adjectives

In this unit we have plural forms of adjectives:

> **Имамо само ове велике разгледнице.**
>
> *We have only these large postcards.*

The nom. and acc. forms of adjectives in the singular and plural follow similar patterns to the noun endings as shown by the example of **добар** in the following table:

	Singular			Plural		
	masc.	fem.	neut.	masc.	fem.	neut.
nom.	добар	добра	добро	добри	добре	добра
acc.	добар	добру	добро	добре	добре	добра

Numbers above 100

100	сто	199	сто деведесет девет
200	двеста	206	двеста шест
300	триста	315	триста петнаест
400	четиристо	422	четиристо двадесет два
500	петсто	537	петсто тридесет седам
600	шестсто	644	шестсто четрдесет четири
700	седамсто	751	седамсто педесет један
800	осамсто	868	осамсто шездесет осам
900	деветсто	973	деветсто седамдесет три
1,000	хиљада	1,111	хиљаду сто једанаест
		2,000	две хиљаде
		5,000	пет хиљада
		1 million	милион

When speaking of *1,000* the word is often used in its accusative form of **хиљаду**. With more than 1,000 **хиљада** takes gen. singular or gen. plural endings depending on the preceding number, as does **милион** *million*.

Practice

1 You are buying things at a kiosk. Fill in your part of the following dialogue:

70

> Изволите?
> *Do you sell postcards, please?*
> Продајемо.
> *How much do they cost?*
> Једна разгледница кошта дванаест динара. Колико желите?
> *Give me five, please. And do you have a city plan?*
> Немамо. Желите ли још нешто?
> *No, thank you. That is all.*

2 Replace the nouns in the sentences below with the appropriate pronoun as in the example:

e.g. **Роберт** говори енглески.
Он говори енглески.

a **Роберт и Пјер** уче српски.
b **Јелена** не разуме руски.
c **Зоран и Вера** не говоре француски.
d **Ова мапа** кошта сто двадесет пет динара.
e **Разгледнице** коштају десет динара.
f **Продавачица** продаје сендвиче и сокове.
g **Пиво** кошта тридесет динара.
h **Сендвичи са сиром** коштају двадесет динара.
i **Весна и Барбара** не желе вино.
j **Драган и Вера** пију кафу са Миланом.

3 Robert paid **петсто двадесет динара** for his English–Serbian dictionary. Before buying it he visited a few other bookshops where he was offered other dictionaries at different prices. Listen to the recording and find their prices. Write them down in the box below and compare them with what Robert finally paid. Has he bought the cheapest dictionary?

🔊 **CD 1, TR 6, 03.13**

a	
b	
c	
d	

4 Write out the following numbers in words using the Cyrillic alphabet:

286, 418, 659, 947, 361, 1600, 2580.

I want to buy

Activity C

◀) CD 1, TR 6, 04.24

Quite often you need to buy food or other items in kilos or by the bottle and so need to know how to express quantities. Vera uses some words for quantities in her shopping list below. Listen to her reading the list on the recording and try to find out the answer to the questions below before reading the printed text:

i How many bottles of beer does Vera want to buy?
ii How much wine?
iii How much bread?
iv How many apples?
v How much coffee?

> флаша сока
> три пива
> две лименке кока-коле
> литар вина
> литар киселе воде
> пола литра млека
> кило хлеба
> кило јабука
> пола кила лимуна
> пола кила парадајза
> један бутер
> сто грама кафе
> двеста грама сира
> сапун
> шампон
> зубна паста

лименка	can
литар	litre
пола литра	half a litre
млеко	milk
кило	kilo
пола кила	half a kilo
лимун	lemon
бутер	butter
сто грама	100 grams
сапун	soap
шампон	shampoo
зубна паста	toothpaste

Activity D

🔊 CD 1, TR 6, 05.47

Listen to Barbara and Pierre going home after their classes talking about what they want to buy:

Пјер	Хоћу да купим бурек. Гладан сам. Барбара, хоћеш ли и ти бурек?
Барбара	Не, нећу. Нисам гладна. Али морам да купим нешто за доручак.
Пјер	У реду. Овде продају бурек. Молим вас, двеста грама бурека са сиром.
Продавац	Изволите. Двадесет динара.
Пјер	Хвала.
Продавац	Молим.
Барбара	Тамо је бакалница. Могу тамо да купим ствари за доручак... Дајте ми, молим вас, кило хлеба, сто грама шунке, један јогурт и један џем од јагода.
Продавачица	Хлеб имам, и џем, и шунку, али немам јогурт.
Барбара	Да ли имате млеко?
Продавачица	Имам.
Барбара	Дајте ми једно млеко.
Продавачица	Изволите, госпођице. Још нешто?
Барбара	Не, хвала. Ништа више.

| хоћу да купим | I want to buy |
| нисам | I am not |

нећу	I do not want
морам	I must, have to
нешто	something
за доручак	for breakfast
тамо	there
бакалница	grocery shop
могу да купим	I can/may buy
ствари	things
џем од јагода	strawberry jam
немам	I do not have
госпођица	Miss

Questions

i What does Barbara want to buy?

ii What does she buy instead of yoghurt?

There are many words for different kinds of shops. **Бакалница** is a traditional term for a shop selling different kinds of foodstuffs and household items. You will often hear it but rarely see it written. A small shop selling food usually has the sign **мини-маркет**, while a bigger self-service shop is called **самопослуга** or **супермаркет**. Common words meaning *shop* without being specific are **радња** and **продавница**. The till or checkout in a shop is called a **каса**. When writing a half in figures note that a comma is used instead of a full stop: **пола** *half* 0,5.

How it works

Infinitive

In English the infinitive of a verb is made up of two words: *to do, to buy*. It is usually used after another verb with a person: *I want to buy*. In Serbian the infinitive of a verb is one word usually ending in -**ти** and sometimes in -**ћи**: **имати** *to have*, **пити** *to drink*, **учити** *to learn*. It is the form of the verb which is used as a dictionary entry. The present tense of the verb is sometimes based directly on the infinitive, like **имати - имам**, and sometimes it is not, like **пити**

- **пијем**. In this course new verbs will be listed under the infinitive with the first person singular also given where the present tense forms are not based directly on the infinitive. Given the regularity of the verbal system in Serbian, when you know both the infinitive and the first person singular of the present tense you can form all parts of that verb in any tense.

Alternative infinitive construction

Serbian generally avoids using the infinitive and prefers instead an alternative construction formed by using the word **да** with the present tense:

Хоћу да купим . . .	*I want to buy . . .*
Морам да купим . . .	*I have to buy . . .*
Могу да купим . . .	*I can buy . . .*

In these examples the word **да** means *that* and you are really saying *I want that I buy . . .*

You simply use the same person in the second verb as in the first:

Роберт мора да купи хлеб.	*Robert has to buy bread.*
Ми хоћемо да учимо српски.	*We want to learn Serbian.*

It is possible to use the infinitive and say:

Роберт мора купити хлеб.
Ми хоћемо учити српски.

But, the alternative expression is generally preferred.

This is the same construction used for saying *I want you to do something . . .*

Ја хоћу да ти учиш српски.	*I want you to learn Serbian. (lit. I want that you learn Serbian.)*

Irregular verbs: *хоћу, могу*

The vast majority of verbs in Serbian follow one of the regular patterns outlined above. A few verbs, however, are irregular. In this unit there are two: they are **хоћу** *I want* and **могу** *I can, I am able*:

ja	хоћу	могу
ти	хоћеш	можеш
он	хоће	може
ми	хоћемо	можемо
ви	хоћете	можете
они	хоће	могу

The infinitives of these verbs are **хтети** and **моћи**.

Irregular negative forms

To form the negative of most verbs you simply put **не** in front of the verb:

| **Не могу.** | *I cannot.* |
| **Не говорим руски.** | *I do not speak Russian.* |

You have now seen examples of the three verbs which form their negative as one word:

ja сам *I am* **нисам** *I am not*

The other persons of this verb follow the same pattern (see Unit 7).

хоћу *I want* **нећу** *I do not want*

All persons of this verb follow the same pattern to form the negative:

нећу нећеш неће нећемо нећете неће

имам *I have* **немам** *I do not have*

All persons of the verb follow the same pattern to form the negative:

немам немаш нема немамо немате немају

Noun subgroups: *ствар* thing

There is a subgroup of fem. nouns which end in a consonant with a separate set of endings, mostly in **-и**:

singular	nom.	ствар
	acc.	ствар
	gen.	ствари
	ins.	ствари (and an alternative form стварју)

plural	nom.	ствари
	acc.	ствари
	gen.	ствари

Practice

5 Vera went to a shop with her shopping list but then decided to change the quantity of some of the items from the list. How did she ask for the following items:

a two bottles of juice
b five bottles of beer
c a litre of milk
d two kilos of bread
e half a kilo of apples
f a kilo of tomatoes
g 200 grams of coffee
h 300 grams of cheese

6 Make your own shopping list using words and phrases from this unit.

7 You are buying food in a **бакалница**. Fill in the missing part of the dialogue:

◀) **CD 1, TR 6, 07.20**

> *Hello. I want to buy bread and milk.*
> Колико хоћете?
> *Give me half a kilo of bread, please, and a litre of milk.*
> Још нешто?
> *Give me a bottle of mineral water too.*
> Да ли је то све?
> *Do you have apples?*
> Немамо. Желите ли поморанце?
> *All right. Give me a kilo.*
> Још нешто?
> *No, thank you. Nothing more.*

8 Change the person of the verbs in the present tense as indicated by the pronoun given in brackets. First look at the example:

e.g. Ја морам да купим хлеб. (**ти**)
     Ти мораш да купиш хлеб.

a Ми морамо да учимо француски. (**они**)
b Да ли ти хоћеш да говориш немачки? (**она**)

c Ви нећете да купите сендвиче. **(ја)**

d Да ли она може да разуме српски? **(ти)**

e Они неће да пију чај. **(он)**

f Ја не морам да купим кафу. **(ви)**

g Он хоће да има добар речник. **(ми)**

Test yourself

Here you can check some of the things you have learnt in this unit. Look at the questions below and choose the right answer:

1 You are in a shop and have asked for all the items you need. How would you respond if the salesman asked you if you wanted anything else?

   a Изволите.   **b** Пријатно.   **c** Ништа више.

2 How would you say that you and your companion do not speak Serbian well?

   a Не говорим добро српски.

   b Не говори добро српски.

   c Не говоримо добро српски.

3 Which pronoun would you use to replace the noun **мапа** in the sentence **Мапа кошта сто динара?**

   a он   **b** она   **c** оно

4 Which pronoun would you use to replace the noun **хлеб** in the sentence **Хлеб кошта осамдесет динара?**

   a он   **b** она   **c** оно

5 Which form of the word would you use to fill the gap in the question **Да ли продајете . . . . . ?**

   a разгледница   **b** разгледници   **c** разгледнице

6 Which number is 60,550?

   a шеснаест хиљада петсто петнаест

   b шездесет хиљада петсто педесет

   c шездесет хиљада петсто петнаест

7 How do you say *a bottle* in Serbian?

   a флаша   **b** чаша   **c** лименка

8 What is the meaning of the sentence **Хоће да купе речник**?

   a I want to buy a dictionary.
   b They want to buy a dictionary.
   c You want to buy a dictionary.

9 What form of the word **грам** would you add to say *two hundred grams of cheese*: **двеста** . . . . **сира**?

   a грам   **b** граму   **c** грама

10 What form of the word **шунка** would you add to say *half a kilo of ham*: **пола кила** . . . .?

   a шунка   **b** шунке   **c** шунку

7

In town

In this unit you will learn:

- How to describe where things are
- How to ask and say where people live and work
- How to give telephone numbers and addresses
- Cases: locative, spelling rules and uses of cases
- Irregular verb ja sam
- Possessive adjectives

In town

Activity A

◀ CD 1, TR 7

There are numerous places of interest to see in the centre of Belgrade. Listen to Vesna talking to Robert. She is holding a map and points out some of the main attractions to him. Listen to the recording and see if you can find the places which she mentions on the map before reading the text:

Vesna	Mi smo ovde. Tamo je Kalemegdan. To je veliki park. U parku je tvrđava. Ona je iznad reke.
	Ulica Kneza Mihaila se nalazi blizu parka. Ta ulica je duga. U ulici su prodavnice, galerije, kafane i restorani.
	Trg Republike je u centru grada. Na trgu su Narodni muzej i Narodno pozorište. U pozorištu možemo da gledamo operu i balet.

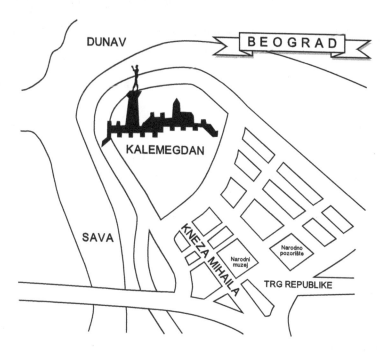

mi smo	*we are*
to je	*that is*
veliki	*large*
u parku	*in the park*
tvrđava	*fortress*
iznad	*above* (preposition with gen.)
reka	*river*
ulica	*street*
nalaziti se	*to be situated*
blizu	*near* (preposition with gen.)
dug	*long*
u ulici	*in the street*
su	*are* (third person plural)
galerija	*gallery*
Trg Republike	*Republic Square*
u centru grada	*in the centre of town*
na trgu	*on the square*
Narodno pozorište	*National theatre*

QUICK VOCAB

Narodni muzej	*National museum*
gledati	*to watch*
opera	*opera*
balet	*ballet*

QV

Activity B

🔊 **CD 1, TR 7, 01.02**

Vesna then tells Robert about Richard who has recently arrived from America. She tells him where he lives and his telephone number. Listen to the recording and try to find out this information before reading the text below:

Vesna Ričard stanuje ovde u Beogradu, blizu Trga Republike. Njegova adresa je Gospodar Jevremova 18. Njegov telefonski broj je 637–208.

Škola stranih jezika je ispod ulice gde stanuje Ričard. Njegov stan nije daleko od škole.

QUICK VOCAB

stanovati, stanujem	*to live, to reside*
u Beogradu	*in Belgrade*
njegov	*his*
adresa	*address*
telefonski broj	*telephone number*
škola stranih jezika	*school of foreign languages*
ispod	*below* (preposition with gen.)
gde	*where*
stan	*flat*
daleko	*far*
od	*from* (preposition with gen.)

Question
Is Richard's flat far from Republic Square?

Activity C

🔊 **CD 1, TR 7, 01.48**

As Vesna and Robert walk down the street looking in the shop windows, Robert thinks he sees someone they both know.

Robert	Vesna, ko je to?
Vesna	Ko, gde?
Robert	Ona žena tamo u apoteci. Je li to gospođa Petrović?
Vesna	Da, jeste. Je li gospođa Petrović tvoja nastavnica srpskog jezika?
Robert	Da, jeste. Jesmo li blizu škole?
Vesna	Pa, nismo daleko.
Robert	Dobro, imam sada čas.

ko je to?	*who is that?*
ona žena	*that woman*
u apoteci	*in the pharmacy*
je li to . . .	*is that . . .*
jeste	*he/she/it is*
tvoj	*your*
nastavnica	*teacher* (female)
Jesmo li . . .	*Are we . . .*
pa	*well*
sada	*now*
čas	*class*

Question

What does Mrs Petrović teach Robert?

Belgrade is called **Beograd** in Serbian which literally means *white city*. The name is derived from the light colour of the walls of the old Turkish fortress in what is now the central park **Kalemegdan**. Belgrade, with its commanding position over the confluence of the rivers Sava (**Sava**) and Danube (**Dunav**), was an important strategic outpost of the Ottoman Empire for almost 400 years. Walking from the park towards the centre of town, you cross into **ulica Kneza Mihaila** *Knez Mihailo Street*. This street is named after Knez, or Prince, Mihailo who was the ruler of Serbia when the Ottoman Empire finally relinquished its fortress and left the city in 1867. Now pedestrianized, this is one of the main commercial and shopping areas. It is very busy in the early evening when many people take a stroll along its length. At the far end of Knez Mihailo Street is Belgrade's main square **Trg Republike** *Republic Square*, surrounded by many smart cafés and a favourite place to sit and sip coffee.

Most people in Belgrade and other Serbian towns live in flats or apartments. Some of the older buildings from the late nineteenth and early twentieth centuries are elegant constructions, although many areas are dominated by large blocks of flats, typical of the newer suburbs across the River Sava from the centre of town in New Belgrade (**Novi Beograd**). There are three bridges (**most**) across the River Sava linking the two parts of town.

Richard's address is **ul.** (short for **ulica** *street*) **Gospodar Jevremova 18/III**. The numbers tell you that his flat is in house number 18 on the 3rd floor.

How it works

Saying *in* and *on*

To say *in* somewhere or *on* somewhere you use the words **u** or **na** with the locative (loc.) case. Here we have examples of phrases with all three genders:

u parku	(**park** masc.)
u ulici	(**ulica** fem.)
na trgu	(**trg** masc.)
u pozorištu	(**pozorište** neut.)
u Beogradu	(**Beograd** masc.)

case	masc.	fem.		neut.
nom.	park	ulica	stvar	pozorište
loc.	parku	ulici	stvari	pozorištu
	(add -**u**)	(**-a** to **-i**)	(add -**i**)	(-**o** or -**e** to -**u**)

Spelling rules

There is a spelling rule in Serbian that when a noun adds a case ending you cannot write i after the consonants **k**, **g** and **h**. These three consonants change to **c**, **z** and **s** respectively. When Robert sees Mrs Petrović in the pharmacy (**apoteka**) and he wants to say that she is in the pharmacy, the change of -**a** to -**i** at the end of the noun also requires that the consonant **k** change to **c**. Robert says **u apoteci** *in the pharmacy*.

Other examples of this spelling rule:

1 fem. loc. singular -a to -i

banka	u banci
Amerika	u Americi
samoposluga	u samoposluzi

Exceptions are made for people's proper names: **Branka** (a girl's name) becomes **Branki**.

2 masc. nom. plural add -i

jezik	jezici
kiosk	kiosci
Grk	Grci

Note that most monosyllabic masc. nouns add an extra syllable in the plural:

| park | parkovi |
| trg | trgovi |

Insight

When describing location, the prepositions **u** (*in, at*) and **na** (*on*) are followed by the locative case.

| **Restoran je u parku.** | *The restaurant is in the park.* |
| **Muzej je u tvrđavi.** | *The museum is in the fortress.* |

Remember that the letters **k**, **g** and **h** change into **c**, **z** and **s** respectively before the letter **i** in the locative case of the feminine nouns:

| banka | u banci |
| samoposluga | u samoposluzi |

Above, below, near, far from

Many prepositions in Serbian are followed by the genitive case including:

| **iznad/ispod** | *above/below* |
| **iznad reke** | *above the river* |

ispod ulice	*below the street*
blizu/daleko od	*near/far from*
blizu parka	*near the park*
daleko od stana	*far from the flat*

Uses of cases

Cases in Serbian have three different uses:

1 They are used to show a grammatical function, such as the acc. case to show which noun is the direct object of the verb.

2 They are used to show a certain meaning where in English we would use a preposition, such as the gen. case to mean *of*.

3 They are used after prepositions (the nominative case is never used following a preposition), such as the loc. case after **u** and **na** to show location.

Sometimes a phrase in Serbian may contain more than one case as in **u centru grada** *in the centre of town* where we have the loc. used after the preposition **u** (**centar** masc. noun) and the gen. case of the word for *town* (**grad** masc. noun) to mean *of*.

Irregular verb *ja sam*

The words for *is* and *are* are used in the text for Activity C, so we can now see the pattern of this verb in the present tense:

infinitive: biti		
short form	**long form**	**negative**
ja sam	jesam	nisam
ti si	jesi	nisi
on je	jeste	nije
mi smo	jesmo	nismo
vi ste	jeste	niste
oni su	jesu	nisu

We have mostly used the short form of the verb *to be* which may not come as the first word of a sentence. The long form is more emphatic and has two other uses:

1 for giving one-word answers to questions. When asked if that is Mrs Petrović Vesna replies: **Da, jeste.** *Yes, it is.*

2 for asking questions

> **Jesmo li blizu škole?**   *Are we close to the school?*

except for the third person singular when the short form is used

> **Je li to gospođa Petrović?**   *Is that Mrs Petrović?*

There is the other way of making a question by putting **da li** in front of the verb as in **Da li smo blizu škole?** or **Da li je to gospođa Petrović?**

Possessive adjectives

You have now met most of the possessive adjectives (*my, your, his* etc.). As adjectives they have to agree with the gender of the noun which they describe:

	masc.	fem.	neut.
my	moj	moja	moje
your (sing.)	tvoj	tvoja	tvoje
his	njegov	njegova	njegovo
her	njen	njena	njeno
our	naš	naša	naše
your (pl.)	vaš	vaša	vaše
their	njihov	njihova	njihovo

The ending of the adjective depends on the gender of the noun it describes. When Vesna tells Robert about Richard, she tells him *his address* **njegova adresa** (**adresa** fem. noun) and about *his flat* **njegov stan** (**stan** masc. noun).

The neut. ending of the possessive adjectives is **-o**, or **-e** following a soft consonant. Just to remind you, the soft consonants are **c, č, ć, dž, đ, j, lj, nj, š** and **ž**.

That *onaj*

There is another adjective to mean *that* in Serbian:

masc.	fem.	neut.
onaj	ona	ono

It always refers to something or someone who is far away from you as the speaker and from the person to whom you are speaking.

In Activity C Robert and Vesna are standing together and he points to someone in the distance:

Ona žena tamo u apoteci.   *That woman over there in the pharmacy.*

Reflexive verbs with *se*

In Activity A Vesna describes where things are to Robert. She says:

Ulica Kneza Mihaila se   *Knez Mihailo Street is situated*
nalazi blizu parka.   *near the park.*

Some verbs in Serbian are used with an additional particle **se** meaning literally *oneself*. Depending on the person of the verb it may mean *myself, yourself* etc. as in the phrases **Kako se zoveš?** *What is your name?* (lit. *How do you call yourself?*) and the reply **Zovem se . . .** *My name is . . .* (lit. *I call myself . . .*).

Practice

1 Put the nouns in brackets below into the correct case for the preposition as in the example:

e.g.   Kalemegdan je park u (Beograd).
        Kalemegdan je park u Beogradu.

a Restoran se nalazi u (park).
b Vera je nastavnica u (škola).
c Njihov stan je u (grad).
d Robert je u (apoteka).
e Muzej je na (trg).
f Pjer i Barbara su u (knjižara).
g Gledamo balet u (pozorište).
h Dragan i njegova žena nisu u (hotel).
i Imamo sada čas u (škola).
j Ričard i njegova drugarica piju kafu u (kafana).

2 Fill in the missing possessive adjectives in the following sentences. First look at the example:

e.g.   Ja stanujem u centru grada. Ovo je _____ adresa.
       Ja stanujem u centru grada. Ovo je moja adresa.

a Vesna stanuje blizu parka. Ovo je _____ adresa.
b Jelena i Dragan stanuju u Beogradu. Ovo je _____ stan.
c Robert uči srpski. Ovo je _____ škola.
d Ja imam nov telefonski broj. Ovo je _____ telefonski broj.
e Ričard pije pivo. Ovo je _____ pivo.
f Vesna i ja pijemo kafu. Ovo je _____ kafa.
g Ti hoćeš da piješ vino. Ovo je _____ vino.
h Vi želite sendvič sa sirom. Ovo je _____ sendvič.

3 Listen to the recording and you will hear two conversations in which people request telephone numbers. Listen and write each number as you hear it:

◀) CD 1, TR 7, 02.43

> *Milan Janković*
>
> *adresa: Molerova 46*
> *telefon:*

> *Restoran Kolarac*
>
> *adresa: Kneza Mihaila 46*
> *telefon:*

Where do you live and work?

Activity D

◀) CD 1, TR 7, 03.42

Vesna is inviting Barbara to come to her place for lunch. Listen to the recording, repeating the phrases, and read the text before answering the questions that follow:

Vesna	Barbara, dođi sutra kod mene na ručak.
Barbara	Hvala na pozivu. Gde stanuješ?
Vesna	Stanujem u ulici Svetozara Markovića broj 6.
Barbara	Gde je ulica Svetozara Markovića?
Vesna	Da li znaš gde se nalazi crkva Svetog Marka?
Barbara	Znam, pored parka Tašmajdan.
Vesna	Moja ulica je odmah preko puta parka. Posle ručka možemo da šetamo u parku.
Barbara	Odlično. Zdravo, do sutra.
Vesna	Zdravo.

QUICK VOCAB

dođi	*come* (an imperative form of the verb, informal)
sutra	*tomorrow*
kod mene	*to/at my place* (house, flat)
na ručak	*for lunch*
Hvala na pozivu	*Thank you for the invitation*
broj	*number*
crkva Svetog Marka	*church of St Marko's*
pored	*next to, by, beside* (preposition with gen.)
znati	*to know*
park Tašmajdan	*park Tašmajdan*
preko puta	*opposite* (preposition with gen.)
posle	*after* (preposition with gen.)
šetati	*to walk*
odlično	*excellent*
do sutra	*until tomorrow*

Questions

i How does Barbara ask Vesna for her address?
ii Which phrase does Vesna use to give Barbara her address?
iii Where is Vesna's street?

Activity E

◆) CD 1, TR 7, 04.38

Zoran and Vera Petrović are at a party. Zoran introduces himself to a new aquaintance. Listen to the dialogue, read the text and answer the questions that follow:

Zoran	Ja sam Zoran Petrović.
Dušan	Drago mi je. Ja sam Dušan Milanović.
Zoran	Vi ste iz Beograda?
Dušan	Nisam. Ja sam iz Niša. Ali sada živim u Beogradu. Imam stan ovde blizu, ispod hotela *Slavija*. Odakle ste vi? Gde vi stanujete?
Zoran	Ja sam iz Beograda. Naš stan nije u centru grada. Moja žena i ja živimo daleko od centra. Ali to je lep kraj.
Dušan	Gde radite?
Zoran	Da li znate gde je *Kosmaj*?
Dušan	Šta je to?
Zoran	Bioskop u centru grada.
Dušan	Ah, da, znam, na Terazijama, preko puta hotela *Balkan*.
Zoran	Moja kancelarija je tačno između bioskopa i Trga Republike. A gde vi radite?
Dušan	Ja sam lekar. Radim u bolnici blizu železničke stanice.

iz	*out of, from* (preposition with gen.)
Niš	*Niš* (a town in southern Serbia)
Odakle ste vi?	*Where are you from?*
živeti, živim	*to live*
lep	*nice, beautiful*
kraj	*area*
raditi	*to work, to do*
Šta je to?	*What is that?*
bioskop	*cinema*
kancelarija	*office*
tačno	*exactly*
između	*between* (preposition with gen.)
lekar	*doctor*
bolnica	*hospital*
železnička stanica	*railway station*

QUICK VOCAB

Questions

i Where does Dušan live?

ii Where is Zoran's office?

Activity F

🔊 CD 1, TR 7, 05.46

Listen to Zoran as he asks Dušan for his address and telephone number. Try to find out Dušan's address and telephone number at home (**kućni broj**) and at work (**broj na poslu**). Listen and write each number as you hear it. Does Dušan have a mobile phone? Can you work out his e-mail address? Check your answers by reading the text below:

Dušan Milanović

adresa:

kućni broj:

broj na poslu:

e-mail:

Zoran	Koja je vaša adresa?
Dušan	Moja adresa je Resavska 34.
Zoran	A koji je vaš telefonski broj?
Dušan	Moj kućni broj je 3233–741.
Zoran	Koji broj imate na poslu?
Dušan	Moj broj na poslu je 684–997.
Zoran	Imate li mobilni telefon?
Dušan	Nemam.
Zoran	Da li imate mejl?
Dušan	Imam. Adresa je dusanmil@eunet.yu.

Koja je vaša adresa?	*What is your address?*
Koji je vaš telefonski broj?	*What is your telephone number?*
Imate li mobilni telefon?	*Do you have a mobile phone?*
Da li imate mejl?	*Do you have e-mail?*

There are a number of pleasant places to go for a stroll in or close to the centre of town in Belgrade as Vesna invites Barbara. One favourite spot is at Kalemegdan, and another is the park Tašmajdan with the church of Sveti Marko.

The typical working day is from 7 a.m. to 3 p.m. *Breakfast* **doručak** usually consists of a snack and coffee taken during a mid-morning break at work. After work, *lunch* **ručak** is the main meal of the day, followed by a rest before evening. *Dinner* **večera** may be something small and simple or quite elaborate and taken late.

Work and communication practices are changing in Serbia, not least with the arrival of e-mail and the *internet* **internet**. E-mail is officially called **elektronska pošta** lit. *electronic post* by which you send an **elektronska poruka** *electronic message*. More colloquially people refer to **imejl** or just **mejl**. On business cards and the like it is written as in English 'E-mail'. When reading addresses, say **at** for the sign @ (sometimes also called **majmun** lit. *monkey*) and **tačka** for *dot*. E-mail addresses do not have diacritic marks.

How it works

To live

There are two verbs *to live* **stanovati, stanujem** and **živeti, živim** in this unit. The first verb means specifically *to reside* and it has linked words like a *flat* **stan** and an *inhabitant* **stanovnik**. **Živeti** is a more general word which can mean both *to reside* or *to be alive*.

Question words

A number of words used for formulating questions are used in this unit:

gde	*where*
odakle	*where from*
ko	*who*
šta	*what*
koji	*what, which one*

Of these words note that **koji** is an adjective and so must agree with the noun as in the phrase **Koja je vaša adresa?**

Telephone numbers

There are different ways of reading telephone numbers. Each number may be pronounced separately, or they may be put together in combinations. Dušan's telephone number at work could be said as 6-8-4-9-9-7 or as two larger numbers 684–997 (*six hundred and eighty four-nine hundred and ninety seven*). The word for *zero* is **nula**.

Noun subgroups: *posao* work, job

There are some masc. nouns which end in -o. Historically speaking, these nouns had an ending in -l but over time it has either disappeared or mutated into -o. In these words the -l reappears when the noun adds case endings. For example, here are the endings which you know so far for **posao**:

singular	nom.	posao
	acc.	posao
	gen.	posla
	ins.	poslom
	loc.	poslu (**na poslu** *at work*)
plural	nom.	poslovi
	acc.	poslove
	gen.	poslova

In forms other than the nom. and acc. singular the moveable **a** drops out and the **-o** mutates back to **-l** before you add case endings. In the plural forms this change leaves a monosyllabic stem **posl-** which is then extended according to the same principle as other masc. monosyllabic nouns to **poslovi**.

Practice

4 You are working at a Serbian town and have been asked to help a group of colleagues who have recently arrived and do not know the area well. Look at the map that follows and try to tell which of the following statements are true and which are not:

a Restoran je u parku.
b Hotel je pored pošte.
c Banka je preko puta pozorišta.

d Bioskop je na trgu.

e Apoteka je između hotela i kafane.

f Železnička stanica je daleko od parka.

5 Looking at the map again, try to give your own answers to the questions using one or more of the following expressions:

u	na	pored	između	preko puta	blizu	daleko od

First, look at the example:

Gde je pozorište?
Pozorište je na trgu, preko puta muzeja.

a Gde je železnička stanica?
b Gde je banka?
c Gde je crkva?
d Gde je muzej?
e Gde je pošta?

6 Now use the map again to make up more questions and to answer them as fully as possible using the models from Practice 5.

7 You are talking to a new acquaintance in a Belgrade café. Fill in your part of the dialogue:

◄))) **CD 1, TR 7, 06.46**

Vi ste iz Londona?
Yes, I am. But I live in Belgrade now. Where are you from?
Ja sam iz Niša.
Do you live there?
Ne, ne živim. Stanujem ovde, u Beogradu. Imam ovde posao.
Where do you work?
Radim u knjižari. A gde vi radite?
I work in a school.
Gde stanujete?
I have a nice flat near the centre of town.

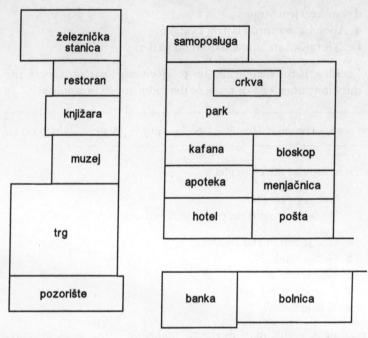

8 You have been given business cards by various people. Your Serbian boss needs some information about them. Study the cards in order to answer his questions:

Слободан Јовановић
Булевар краља Александра 237
11000 Београд

Тел: 011/422-678
Факс: 011/422-679

MILICA PAVLOVIĆ

Kneza Miloša 65
11000 Beograd
tel. 648-391
mobilni tel. 062/237-918
E-mail: milicapav@eunet.rs

АНА ПРОТИЋ

адреса: Влајковићева 13

кућа: 3231-677
посао: 1284-012
моб. тел. 063/8051-655

a Koja je adresa gospodina Slobodana Jovanovića?
b Da li on ima faks? Koji broj?
c Koji je kućni broj gospođe Ane Protić?
d Koji je njen broj na poslu?
e Gde stanuje Milica Pavlović?
f Koja je njena e-mail adresa?

Test yourself

Here you can check some of the things you have learnt in this unit. Look at the questions below and choose the right answer:

1 How do you say *here* in Serbian?

   a tamo   **b** daleko   **c** ovde

2 You want to inform your Serbian friend that you and your group of English tourists are waiting for him/her at the square. Which word would you add to the sentence **Mi . . . . na trgu?**

   a smo   **b** ste   **c** su

3 What is **pozorište?**

   a a fortress   **b** a cinema   **c** a theatre

4 You are renting a flat in **ulica Kneza Miloša**. Which form of the word would you use to give your Belgrade colleague your address: **Stanujem u . . . . Kneza Miloša?**

   a ulicu   **b** ulice   **c** ulici

5 How do you say *our telephone number*?

   a njegov telefonski froj
   b naš telefonski broj
   c vaš telefonski broj

6 You are told **Vaš hotel je blizu parka**. Where is your hotel?

   a near the park   **b** opposite the park   **c** by the park

7 What is the meaning of the word **pored:**

   a above   **b** between   **c** next to

8 How would you ask your Serbian acquaintance where he/she works?

a Gde živite?   **b** Gde radite?   **c** Gde šetate?

9 Which form of the word **koji** would you use to ask for somebody's address: .... **je vaša adresa?**

a koja   **b** koji   **c** koje

10 What is the Serbian word for *a job*?

a kancelarija   **b** posao   **c** bioskop

8

....

Directions

In this unit you will learn:

- How to follow and give directions
- Phrases for using public transport
- Expressions for use in the post office
- How to form the imperative
- How to form ordinal numbers
- How to use modal verbs
- Cases: vocative, masculine animate nouns, more about genitive plurals

---

Getting to the restaurant

Activity A

🔊 **CD 1, TR 8**

Robert and Richard are in the language school and ask Dragan where to go for dinner. Listen to their conversation on the recording and read the printed text. While reading the text try to follow the directions on the map and find the restaurant yourself. You can then check your accuracy by looking at the map:

Роберт	Ричард и ја идемо данас у ресторан на вечеру. Који ресторан је добар? Куда можемо да идемо?
Драган	Можете да идете у ресторан *Вук*. Храна је тамо врло добра.
Роберт	Да ли је то далеко?

Драган	Није далеко. Можете да идете пешке. Идите горе на Трг Републике, а онда скрените десно у улицу Кнеза Михаила. Идите право и скрените у трећу улицу лево. Ресторан *Вук* се налази са десне стране, на ћошку.
Роберт	Хвала.
Драган	Нема на чему.

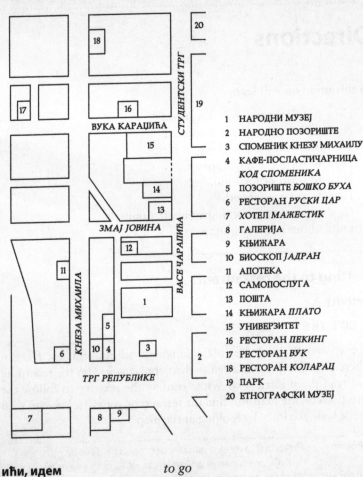

1 НАРОДНИ МУЗЕЈ
2 НАРОДНО ПОЗОРИШТЕ
3 СПОМЕНИК КНЕЗУ МИХАИЛУ
4 КАФЕ-ПОСЛАСТИЧАРНИЦА *КОД СПОМЕНИКА*
5 ПОЗОРИШТЕ *БОШКО БУХА*
6 РЕСТОРАН *РУСКИ ЦАР*
7 ХОТЕЛ *МАЖЕСТИК*
8 ГАЛЕРИЈА
9 КЊИЖАРА
10 БИОСКОП *ЈАДРАН*
11 АПОТЕКА
12 САМОПОСЛУГА
13 ПОШТА
14 КЊИЖАРА *ПЛАТО*
15 УНИВЕРЗИТЕТ
16 РЕСТОРАН *ПЕКИНГ*
17 РЕСТОРАН *ВУК*
18 РЕСТОРАН *КОЛАРАЦ*
19 ПАРК
20 ЕТНОГРАФСКИ МУЗЕЈ

ићи, идем	*to go*	
данас	*today*	
на вечеру	*for dinner*	
куда	*where, where to*	

храна	food
врло	very
пешке	on foot
идите горе	go up
онда	then
скренути, скренем	to turn
скрените десно	turn right
право	straight on
. . . у трећу улицу	into the third street
лево	left
са десне стране	on the right side
на ћошку	on the corner
нема на чему	don't mention it

QUICK VOCAB

Activity B

🔊 CD 1, TR 8, 00.59

Robert and Richard go to Republic Square and turn right into Knez Mihailo Street. They walk along the street but are not sure where to go next, so they ask a lady who is passing by. Listen to the instructions she gives them and read the dialogue below. Find the restaurant *Vuk* on the map again and see if you can say where Robert and Richard are at the moment when they lose their way:

Ричард	Извините, госпођо. Ми смо странци. Да ли знате где је ресторан *Вук*?
Госпођа	Наравно, господине. То је одмах овде, иза ћошка. Скрените у прву улицу лево, идите мало даље и опет скрените лево.
Ричард	Хвала лепо.
Госпођа	Молим лепо.

извините	excuse (me)
странац	foreigner
наравно	of course
иза ћошка	round the corner
. . . у прву улицу	into the first street
мало даље	a little further

QUICK VOCAB

опет	*again*
хвала лепо	*thank you very much*
молим лепо	*you're welcome* (response to **хвала лепо**)

Activity C

🔊 **CD 1, TR 8, 01.38**

Following her instructions Robert and Richard find themselves in a small side street and still unable to locate the restaurant. They ask another passer-by for directions. Find out what he tells them and see if you can say what mistake they have made:

Роберт	Извините, господине. Где се налази ресторан *Вук*?
Господин	Ресторан *Вук*? Погледајте десно. Ресторан је одмах ту, на крају улице.
Роберт	Хвала.

погледајте	*look, have a look*
ту	*here*
на крају улице	*at the end of the street*

How it works

To go to somewhere

You already know from the previous unit to use **у** or **на** with the loc. to say that you are *in* or *on* somewhere. To say that you are going *to* a place you use **у** or **на** with the acc. case.

Compare

Ја сам у ресторану.	*I am in the restaurant.*
Ја сам на тргу.	*I am on the square.*

with

Идем у ресторан.	*I am going to the restaurant.*
Идем на Трг Републике.	*I am going to Republic Square.*

The loc. case expresses where you are located. When you use the same prepositions with the acc. case they then indicate *going to* those places.

The word **куда** is only used to ask or talk about *where you are going* and invites a reply using **у** or **на** with the acc. case. The word **где** can be used to mean both *where are you* and *where are you going*.

Uses of *на*

You have used the preposition **на** to mean *on* somewhere or to say *going onto*. It is sometimes used in Serbian when you might expect to find the preposition **у**. For example, when talking about the post office, points of the compass, the bus or railway station, the university or faculty building we use **на**:

Ја сам на пошти.	*I am in the post office.*
Идем на пошту.	*I am going to the post office.*

The preposition **на** is also used when talking about meals or going for a drink:

Ми смо на вечери/на ручку/на доручку.	*We are at dinner/lunch/ breakfast.*
Идемо на вечеру/на ручак/ на доручак.	*We are going for dinner/lunch/ breakfast.*
Идемо на пиће/на кафу.	*We are going for a drink/for a cup of coffee.*

Directions

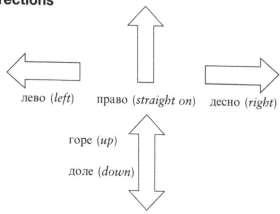

лево (*left*) право (*straight on*) десно (*right*)

горе (*up*)

доле (*down*)

Imperatives

The forms **идите, скрените, погледајте** are called imperatives. They are command words, i.e. *Go!* or *Turn!* There are two forms of the word. There is an informal one for someone to whom you would normally say **ти** and a formal one for someone to whom you would normally say **ви**.

The imperative is formed by taking the third person plural of the present tense of the verb (i.e. **они** *they*) and removing the last letter:

verb	infinitive	3rd person plural	stem
go	ићи	иду	ид-
turn	скренути	скрену	скрен-
look	погледати	погледају	погледај-

The **ти** form is made from the stem in one of two ways:

1 if the stem ends in -ј, it makes the informal form

     погледај

2 if the stem ends in a consonant, add -**и** to make the informal form

     иди
     скрени

The formal **ви** form is made by adding -**те** to the informal form

     погледајте
     идите
     скрените

Ordinal numbers

When giving directions, you often need to say *turn into the third street on the left* **скрените у трећу улицу лево** or similar. You need to know the words for *first, second, third,* etc. These are called ordinal numbers. They are adjectives and agree with the gender of the noun which they accompany:

	masc.	fem.	neut.
first	први	прва	прво
second	други	друга	друго

third	трећи	трећа	треће*
fourth	четврти	четврта	четврто
fifth	пети	пета	пето
sixth	шести	шеста	шесто
seventh	седми	седма	седмо
eighth	осми	осма	осмо

*Трећи is an adjective with a soft ending and so takes -e in the neuter.

The higher numbers are made by simply adding adjective endings to the cardinal number (so *ninth* девети). The masc. nom. singular ending for these adjectives is -и.

Adjective endings also change to indicate case and in the expression **скрените у прву улицу лево** the adjective ending for fem. acc. singular is the same as for the noun.

Vocative case

When addressing someone directly, you need the vocative (voc.) case. You have seen examples already: **господине, госпођо, госпођице, Роберте**. In theory, any noun may form this case, but it is practically limited to personal names and nouns denoting people.

- Masc. nouns add -e: **господине, Роберте**
- Masc. nouns in a soft consonant add -y: **Господине Јовановићу**
- In the vocative case **p** is considered to be a soft consonant so when you want the waiter call: **конобару,**
- Fem. nouns change -a to -o: **госпођо**
- Fem. nouns ending in -ица change -a to -e: **госпођице**
- However, many female names stay the same as the nom.: voc. of **Весна** is **Весна**.
- Neut. nouns do not change in the voc., they remain the same as the nom.: **дете** *child*.
- The voc. plural endings are the same as the nom. plural for all genders.

The majority of Serbian surnames end in -ић and when addressing men as *Mr so-and-so* both words change to the voc.: **Господине**

Петровићу. However, when addressing a woman as *Miss* or *Mrs so-and-so* the surname does not change: **Госпођо Петровић.**

There is a spelling rule for masc. names and nouns in the voc. singular; -г changes to -ж, -к changes to -ч, -х changes to -ш:

Предраг	Предраже
Вук	Вуче

More prepositions of place

In addition to **у** or **на** with the loc. and acc. cases, you have met other expressions used with the gen. case to say where things are:

поред
преко пута
између
испод
изнад
близу
далеко од

We can now add two more prepositions with the gen. case:

иза	*behind*
испред	*in front of*

and the expressions:

са десне стране	*on the right*
са леве стране	*on the left*
на крају улице	*at the end of the street*
на ћошку	*on the corner*
иза ћошка	*round the corner*

Practice

1 A tourist who has recently arrived in a town in Serbia has stopped a passer-by and is asking for directions. Listen to the recording and answer these questions:

🔊 **CD 1, TR 8, 02.16**

  a What is the first place he is asking for?
  b Does he have to turn left or right to get there?
  c Is the post office on the left or on the right?
  d Where is the hotel *London*?

2 Look at the map of Belgrade for Activity A. You are standing in front of the post office in **улица Васе Чарапића** facing **Трг Републике**. In order to answer the questions from a group of tourists, follow the directions on the map and choose the correct reply:

  a Где је Народни музеј?

  i Скрените десно. Музеј је одмах овде, иза ћошка.
  ii Идите право на трг. Музеј је на тргу, са десне стране.
  iii Скрените у прву улицу лево. Музеј је мало даље са десне стране.

  b Где се налази апотека?

  i Апотека је лево, на ћошку.
  ii Идите право на Трг Републике, а онда скрените лево.
  iii Идите десно и скрените у другу улицу лево. Апотека је тамо, са десне стране.

  c Где је ресторан *Коларац*?

  i Идите десно и опет скрените десно. Ресторан је са десне стране.
  ii Идите лево и скрените у прву улицу десно. Ресторан је на ћошку.
  iii Идите право. Ресторан је на крају улице.

  d Где се налази хотел *Мажестик*?

  i Идите лево. Хотел је на ћошку са десне стране.
  ii Идите право на трг и на тргу скрените лево. Хотел је мало даље лево, близу музеја.
  iii Идите десно и скрените у другу улицу лево, а онда опет скрените десно.

3 This time you are standing in front of the hotel *Мажестик* facing **Трг Републике**. Study the map again and answer the questions of passers-by as fully as possible. First look at the example:

e.g. Да ли знате где је књижара?
Идите право на трг. Књижара је на тргу десно, поред галерије.

a Да ли знате где је пошта?
b Молим вас, где је позориште *Бошко Буха*?
c Где се налази самопослуга?
d Извините, где је ресторан *Пекинг*?

4 Now use the map to make up similar dialogues. Choose the spot where you are standing and use the dialogues above as a model.

5 Put the nouns in brackets below into the correct case:

a Позориште се налази на (трг).
b Не можемо сада да идемо у (кафана).
c Они не живе у (град).
d Идемо сутра у (биоскоп).
e Драган и Јелена иду у (ресторан) на (вечера).
f Морамо да идемо у (апотека).
g Да ли можеш данас да идеш у (град)?
h Идите на (трг) и скрените лево.
i Хоћемо да идемо на (пиво).
j Ова госпођа ради у (апотека).

Public transport

Activity D

◀) CD 1, TR 8, 02.55

Barbara is on Knez Mihailo Street. She has to go to the National Library of Serbia (**Народна библиотека Србије**) for some books which she needs. She stops a passer-by to ask for directions. Listen to their dialogue, read the text and answer the questions:

Барбара	Извините, господине. Да ли знате како могу да дођем до Народне библиотеке?

Господин	Народна библиотека није близу. Немојте ићи пешке. Можете тамо да идете аутобусом.
Барбара	Који аутобус треба да узмем?
Господин	Узмите аутобус број тридесет један.
Барбара	А где је аутобуска станица?
Господин	Да ли знате где је Народни музеј?
Барбара	Наравно, господине.
Господин	Аутобус број тридесет један стаје испред музеја. Сиђите на четвртој станици. Библиотека је у парку, са леве стране улице.
Барбара	Молим? Извините, не разумем. Ја сам странкиња. Поновите, молим вас. Где треба да сиђем?
Господин	На четвртој станици.
Барбара	Добро, хвала.
Господин	Молим.

како	*how?*
доћи, дођем	*to come*
до	*to, up to* (preposition with gen.)
немојте ићи	*don't go*
аутобусом	*by bus*
Који аутобус треба да узмем?	*Which bus should I take?*
треба	*should, ought*
узети, узмем	*to take*
аутобуска станица	*bus stop* (also *bus station*)
аутобус стаје	*the bus stops*
испред	*in front of* (preposition with gen.)
сићи, сиђем	*to get off, get down*
на четвртој станици	*at the fourth stop*
Молим?	*Pardon? What did you say?*
странкиња	*foreigner* (woman)
поновити	*to repeat*

QUICK VOCAB

Questions

i Which phrase did the gentleman use in order to explain that the bus stop was in front of the museum?

ii What did Barbara say when she could not understand the instructions?

In the post office

Activity E

🔊 CD 1, TR 8, 04.22

Robert has some items to post. He asks Vesna where to go. Listen to the dialogue, read the text and answer the questions:

Роберт	Где могу да купим марке? Продају ли марке у киоску?
Весна	У киоску немају марке за иностранство. Треба да идеш на пошту.
Роберт	Где је пошта?
Весна	Пошта није далеко, само пет минута пешке. Одавде иди право до семафора. Пређи улицу и скрени лево. Тамо је пошта. Уђи и иди на шалтер. Тражи на шалтеру марке за Енглеску.

Роберт иде на пошту. Тамо види човека на шалтеру. Он продаје марке.

Службеник	Изволите? Шта желите?
Роберт	Дајте ми, молим вас, пет марака за Енглеску.
Службеник	Желите ли марке за разгледнице или за писма?
Роберт	За разгледнице.
Службеник	Још нешто?
Роберт	Имам овде и два писма, за Енглеску и за Аустралију.
Службеник	Шаљете ли писма авионом?
Роберт	Да, наравно, авионом.
Службеник	У реду. Дајте ми писма. Изволите пет марака за разгледнице. Поштанско сандуче је на улазу, са леве стране.

QUICK VOCAB		
	марка	*stamp*
	иностранство	*abroad*
	само	*only*
	минут	*minute*
	одавде	*from here*
	семафор	*traffic lights*
	прећи, пређем	*to cross*
	ући, уђем	*enter*
	шалтер	*window, desk* (in post office, bank, etc)

110

тражити	ask for, look for
Енглеска	England
видети, видим	to see
човек	person, man
службеник	clerk
пет марака	five stamps
писмо	letter
Аустралија	Australia
слати, шаљем	to send
авионом	by air mail (ins. of **авион**, aeroplane)
поштанско сандуче	postbox, mailbox
улаз	entrance

Questions

i How far does Vesna say the post office is?

ii How would you correct her and say that it takes 15 minutes to get there on foot?

iii What would you ask in order to find out where the postbox is?

How it works

Instrumental case with transport

A frequent meaning of the ins. case in Serbian is *by* in the sense of *by means of*: **ићи аутобусом** *to go by bus*

tram	трамвај	by tram	трамвајем (soft ending)
trolleybus	тролејбус	by trolleybus	тролејбусом
car	ауто	by car	аутом
train	воз	by train	возом
taxi	такси	by taxi	таксијем

Такси is an adopted foreign word which does not conform to the normal pattern of endings. It is a masc. noun and adds j before case endings for ease of pronunciation.

nom.	такси
acc.	такси
gen.	таксија

ins.	таксијем
loc.	таксију

Negative commands

The passer-by advises Barbara not to walk to the library as it is too far but to take a bus. He tells her **Немојте ићи пешке.** The way to say not to do something is to use **немој** or **немојте** (informal and formal forms) with the infinitive or more often with the alternative (**да** and present tense) infinitive expression:

немој ићи	немој да идеш
немојте ићи	немојте да идете

Modal verbs

Verbs which come in front of other verbs and govern them are called modal verbs. The second verb is usually in the alternative (**да** with the present tense) infinitive form:

Хоћу да . . .	*I want to . . .*
Могу да . . .	*I may, am able to*
Морам да . . .	*I must, have to*
Треба да . . .	*I should, ought to*

The verb in this last example does not change like other verbs do. It has only one form but is followed by the appropriate form after **да**:

Који аутобус треба да узмем?	*Which bus should I take?*
Који аутобус треба да узмемо?	*Which bus should we take?*

When you do not understand

There are a few expressions to be used when you do not understand or catch what someone says:

Молим?	*Pardon? Sorry?*

(same as the word for *please* but with a questioning intonation)

Извините, не разумем.	*Excuse me, I don't understand.*
Поновите, молим вас.	*Repeat it, please.*

Animate masc. nouns

You have learnt that the acc. singular ending for masc. nouns is the same as the nom. case. However, when a masc. noun refers to a human being or animal (all animate nouns are included: people, animals, fish, insects, etc.), the acc. case takes the same ending as the gen. case. This rule applies to nouns in the singular only. Nouns in the plural take the usual acc. plural ending. In the previous dialogue in Activity E Robert arrives at the post office where *he sees a man* **види човека**. Compare:

Весна види парк.	(inanimate masc. noun *park*)
Весна види Роберта.	(animate noun *Robert*)
Роберт види другарицу.	(fem. noun **другарица**)
Роберт види друга.	(masc. animate noun **друг**)

Insight

When a masculine noun denotes something inanimate, the accusative singular is the same as the nominative. When it denotes a living being, the accusative singular is the same as the genitive.

Добро знам Београд.	*I know Belgrade well.*
Добро знам господина Поповића.	*I know Mr Popović well.*

More about genitive plurals

In the post office Robert asks for *five stamps* **пет марака**. The word *stamp* **марка** is fem. Following the pattern for forming the gen. plural of fem. nouns, we normally take the nom. plural and change the **-е** to **-а: кафе – кафа** (see Unit 5).

However, when forming the gen. plural in Serbian, if there are two consonants at the end of the stem (i.e. the word minus its case ending), then an extra **а** is inserted between those consonants in all genders:

	masc.	fem.	neut.
nom. singular	Американац	банка	писмо
nom. plural	Американци	банке	писма
gen. plural	Американаца	банака	писама

Fem. nouns like **ствар** *thing* have a gen. plural ending in **-и: ствари.**
Some fem. nouns with -a and with two consonants at the end of the
stem also form their gen. plural with the same **-и** ending:

nom. singular	радња
nom. plural	радње
gen. plural	радњи

Practice

6 Look at the map below. You are at the spot marked with a star.
Answer Barbara's questions by giving her the directions to the
places she wants to go:

e.g.   Где могу да купим план Београда?
План Београда можете да купите у књижари.
Где је књижара?
Скрените у прву улицу лево. Књижара је одмах иза ћошка.

a Где могу да купим хлеб?
b Где могу да купим шампон?
c Где могу да купим марке?
d Где могу да купим аспирин?

7 You are in a town which you do not know well and you stop a
passer-by to ask for directions. Fill in your part of the dialogue:

◆ CD 1, TR 8, 06.00

> *Excuse me, how can I get to the museum?*
> Музеј је далеко. Не треба да идете пешке. Идите аутобусом.
> *Which bus goes there?*
> Можете да узмете аутобус број 42. Сиђите на трећој станици.
> *Where is the bus stop, please? Is it near?*
> Није далеко. Идите право до семафора, скрените лево и онда
> скрените у прву улицу десно.
> *Excuse me, I don't understand. Repeat that, please.*
> Идите до семафора, скрените лево и онда десно.
> *Now I understand. Thank you.*
> Нема на чему. До виђења.

8 Put the nouns in brackets into the correct case after the preposition
   or according to their function in the sentence (nouns are given in
   the nom. case: apply sing. or pl. endings as indicated):

   a Аутобуска станица се налази испред (парк).
   b Узмите (трамвај) број осам.
   c Можемо да идемо у центар града (аутобус).
   d Треба да видимо (Вера и Зоран).
   e Морају да иду на (пошта) да купе (марке).
   f Биоскоп је на (трг), поред (кафана).
   g Наш хотел је у (центар) (град), преко пута (музеј).

Test yourself

Here you can check some of the things you have learnt in this unit.
Look at the questions below and choose the right answer:

1 Which word would you use to attract someone's attention?

   a Изволите   **b** Погледајте   **c** Извините

2 You ask a passer-by for directions and are told **Идите лево, а
   онда право**. That means that you have to go:

   a straight on and then left
   b left and then straight on
   c left and then right

3 What does **иза ћошка** mean?

    a near the corner   **b** at the corner   **c** around the corner

4 Which of the following would you use when you want to hear something again:

    a Поновите   **b** Узмите   **c** Дајте

5 You have been told **Скрените у другу улицу лево, а онда у трећу улицу десно**. This means that you have to turn:

    a into the second street on the right and then into the third on the left

    b into the second street on the left and then into the third on the right

    c into the second street on the left and then into the first on the right

6 You want to ask could you go somewhere by bus. Which form of the word would you use to fill the gap in the question **Могу ли тамо да идем . . . .** ?

    a аутобусом   **b** аутобусу   **c** аутобус

7 How would you ask a passer-by where the bus stop is?

    a Где је аутобус?   **b** Где стаје аутобус?   **c** Где иде аутобус?

8 You are in a bus and are not sure where you should get off. Which question should you ask?

    a Где треба да идем?
    b Где треба да уђем?
    c Где треба да сиђем?

9 You want to buy five stamps for England. Which form of the word would you use to fill the gap in the sentence **Дајте ми пет . . . . за Енглеску?**

    a марка   **b** марке   **c** марака

10 You want to say that you know Mr Petrović. How would you fill the gap in the sentence **Знам . . . .** ?

    a господин Петровић   **b** господина Петровића
    c господину Петровићу

9

Arriving in Belgrade

In this unit you will learn:

- Phrases for the airport
- Expressions for arriving at a hotel
- How to change money
- How to form the past tense
- About verbal aspect
- How to tell the time

Arrival at the airport

Activity A

◆ **CD 1, TR 9**

Marko Pavlović was born in England. His father is Serbian and his mother is English. He works for a British company with business in Serbia and he is visiting Belgrade. Here he arrives at Surčin, Belgrade airport, where he is met by his business partner Stevan Marić. Listen to the description of Marko's journey on the recording and read the text below.

> Marko Pavlović je putovao iz Londona u Beograd avionom. Dobio je vizu u ambasadi u Londonu i onda je kupio kartu. Let je bio udoban. Stigao je u Beograd i prošao kroz pasošku kontrolu. Dobio je svoj kofer i odmah išao na carinu. Na izlazu je čekao Stevan Marić.

putovao	*travelled*
avion	*aeroplane*
dobio	*received, got*
viza	*visa*
ambasada	*embassy*
kupio	*bought*
karta	*ticket*
let	*flight*
bio	*was*
udoban	*comfortable*
stigao	*arrived*
prošao	*went, passed*
kroz	*through* (preposition with acc.)
pasoška kontrola	*passport control*
svoj	*his*
kofer	*suitcase*
išao	*went*
carina	*customs*
izlaz	*exit*
čekao	*was waiting*

Question

When did Marko go to customs?

How it works

Forming the past tense: infinitives ending in *-ti*

The past tense in Serbian is formed by a verbal adjective taken from the infinitive and using the verb *to be* as an auxiliary verb. For an infinitive ending in **-ti** remove the final two letters, which gives you the stem from which to make the verbal adjective:

infinitive	stem	verbal adjective
putovati	putova-	putovao

In this example the infinitive is **putovati** meaning *to travel*. Remove the last two letters which leaves you with **putova-** to which are added the endings which agree with the subject of the verb. In this example the subject is Marko, a male person, and the masc. ending is **-o** to give **putovao** (this is another example of **-o** which used to be a consonant **-l** like the ending on **posao** *job*).

There are separate endings for fem. and neut., singular and plural, as given in the table below:

	Singular			Plural		
masc.	fem.	neut.		masc.	fem.	neut.
putovao	putovala	putovalo		putovali	putovale	putovala

If the sentence concerned Vesna and not Marko, then the form of the verbal adjective would be fem.: **putovala**.

When talking about groups of men and women, the endings used are masc.:

Robert i Vesna su čekali.   *Robert and Vesna waited.*

All verbs which end in a **vowel + ti** in the infinitive follow this pattern:

dobiti	dobio	dobila	dobilo
	dobili	dobile	dobila
kupiti	kupio	kupila	kupilo
	kupili	kupile	kupila
biti	bio	bila	bilo
	bili	bile	bila
čekati	čekao	čekala	čekalo
	čekali	čekale	čekala

Forming the past tense: infinitives in *-ći*

Verbs of this type have a stem which is not immediately recognizable from the infinitive. There are far fewer verbs in this category and they have to be learnt separately, e.g. **ići** *to go*

	Singular			Plural		
masc.	fem.	neut.		masc.	fem.	neut.
išao	išla	išlo		išli	išle	išla

The endings are basically the same except that the penultimate **a** disappears:

stići	stigao	stigla	stiglo
	stigli	stigle	stigla
proći	prošao	prošla	prošlo
	prošli	prošle	prošla

> ## Insight
> Remember that the verbal adjective used to form the past tense has to agree with the subject in gender:
>
> | **Moj drug je kupio kartu.** | *My male friend bought a ticket.* |
> | **Moja drugarica je kupila kartu.** | *My female friend bought a ticket.* |

Forming the past tense: auxiliary verb

Alongside the verbal adjective, *to be* is used as an auxiliary or helping verb.

The form of *to be* required depends on the subject of the sentence:

Marko Pavlović je putovao.	*Marko Pavlović travelled.*	(masc. third person singular)
Mi smo putovali.	*We travelled.*	(masc. first person plural)
Barbara i Vesna su čekale.	*Barbara and Vesna waited.*	(fem. third person plural)

If you have two or more verbs in a sentence and the subject of them is the same, the auxiliary verb may be omitted from the second verb:

Stigao je u Beograd i prošao kroz pasošku kontrolu.

When using the short forms of *to be*, remember that these forms cannot come at the beginning of a sentence or clause, i.e. part of a sentence. This explains why the first sentence begins **Marko Pavlović je putovao . . .** while the next one begins **Dobio je . . .** The auxiliary verb has to follow the verbal adjective in the second example.

The short form will usually come after the introductory word or phrase at the beginning of a sentence as in **Na izlazu je čekao Stevan**

Marić. *Stevan Marić was waiting at the exit.* It is important to note here that in Serbian the subject of a verb does not have to come before the verb as in English. You must follow the case endings to see the function of a noun in a sentence. Compare these two sentences in which Stevan is first in nom. as the subject of the sentence and then in acc. as the object:

Na izlazu je čekao Stevan.	*Stevan was waiting at the exit.*
Na izlazu je Marko čekao Stevana.	*Marko was waiting for Stevan at the exit.*

Use of *svoj*

In the passage above it says that Marko collected his suitcase **Dobio je svoj kofer.**

In English the word *his* may refer to *his own* or to *somebody else's*. In Serbian you distinguish between these two meanings:

Marko ima svoju kartu.	*Marko has his* (his own) *ticket.*
Marko ima njegovu kartu.	*Marko has his* (not his own, perhaps Robert's) *ticket.*

When using possessive adjectives in Serbian, you can avoid ambiguities by using **svoj** when you want to say that the owner of the object is the same person as the subject of the sentence (i.e. **svoj** refers back to the subject of the verb):

Dobio sam svoj kofer.   *I collected my own suitcase.*
but
Dobio sam njen kofer.   *I collected her suitcase.*
                                        (i.e. someone else's)

The word **svoj** is an adjective:

masc.	fem.	neut.
svoj	svoja	svoje

Activity B

◀» **CD 1, TR 9, 00.49**

Listen to the dialogue and try to understand the verbs used in the past tense. Then read the passage.

Marko i Stevan su išli na piće. Na aerodromu su pili kafu i razgovarali.

Stevan	Da li ste dobro putovali?
Marko	Da, jesam, hvala.
Stevan	Jeste li dobili moje pismo?
Marko	Nisam. Kada ste poslali pismo? Je li bilo važno?
Stevan	Nije. Poslao sam neke informacije o Beogradu.
Marko	Već sam bio u Beogradu. Dobro znam grad.
Stevan	Zaista? Nisam znao. Hajde, treba da krenemo.

Marko i Stevan su popili kafu i krenuli. Nisu čekali autobus. Uzeli su taksi i brzo stigli u hotel *Park*. Marko je tamo imao rezervaciju.

<table>
<tr><td rowspan="14" style="writing-mode:vertical-rl">QUICK VOCAB</td></tr>
<tr><td>aerodrom</td><td>airport</td></tr>
<tr><td>razgovarati</td><td>to discuss, have a conversation</td></tr>
<tr><td>kada</td><td>when</td></tr>
<tr><td>poslati, pošaljem</td><td>to send</td></tr>
<tr><td>važno</td><td>important</td></tr>
<tr><td>neke informacije</td><td>some information</td></tr>
<tr><td>o</td><td>about (preposition with loc.)</td></tr>
<tr><td>već</td><td>already</td></tr>
<tr><td>zaista</td><td>really</td></tr>
<tr><td>hajde</td><td>come on</td></tr>
<tr><td>krenuti, krenem</td><td>to set off</td></tr>
<tr><td>popiti, popijem</td><td>to drink</td></tr>
<tr><td>brzo</td><td>quickly</td></tr>
<tr><td>rezervacija</td><td>reservation</td></tr>
</table>

Question
Did Marko receive Stevan's letter?

How it works

Past tense: making a question

When asking a question in the past tense, follow the usual rules and either put **Da li . . .** in front with a short form of *to be* or put **li** after the long form:

| Da li ste dobro putovali? | *Did you travel well?* |
| Jeste li dobili moje pismo? | *Did you receive my letter?* |

When answering a question with a simple *yes*, use the long form of the auxiliary verb on its own **Da, jesam.**

Agreement with *vi*

When using the **vi** form, i.e. addressing one person formally as in Activity B, the agreement is always with the masc. plural even when speaking to a female:

| Kada ste poslali pismo? | *When did you send the letter?* |

Marko addresses this question to Stevan, but he would have used the same plural ending if speaking to a female colleague.

The same principle applies to adjective agreements. To ask either Robert or Vesna if he or she is hungry you would say in both cases **Da li ste vi gladni?**

Past tense: making a negative statement

The negative form of the past tense is made simply from the appropriate part of the verb *to be*: **Nisam dobio vaše pismo.** *I did not receive your letter.*

The negative forms of *to be* in Serbian are not short forms and so they usually come before the verbal adjective:

Dobio sam vaše pismo.
Nisam dobio vaše pismo.

Verbal aspect

In English and many other languages there is more than one form of a verb in the past tense to differentiate between saying *they were drinking coffee* and *they drank their coffee* (i.e. finished it). This difference in Serbian, and other Slavonic languages, is made through verbal aspects.

Most verbs in Serbian come in pairs representing the imperfective aspect and the perfective aspect. In the passage above there are two verbs *to drink* **piti** and **popiti**. The first verb **piti** is the imperfective aspect of the pair and **popiti** is the perfective. Imperfective verbs indicate that the action is or was in the process of being done. Additionally, they may indicate that the action is or was done frequently. Perfective verbs indicate that the action was (or will be) completed.

Pili su kafu i razgovarali.	*They were drinking coffee and chatting.* (in the process of drinking and talking at the same time)
Popili su kafu i krenuli.	*They drank their coffee and set off.* (they finished their coffee, drank up, and then left)

In both these examples the past tense is formed in the same way (verbal adjective from infinitive with *to be* as the auxiliary verb). The difference in the quality of the action is indicated by choosing the correct aspect from the pair of verbs meaning *to drink*. Also, you can make the English pluperfect by adding the word **već** lit. *already* to the perfective verb: **već su popili** . . . *they had drunk* . . .

Using the correct aspect is important in the past tense, future tense, imperatives and other forms in order to differentiate between incomplete or frequent actions and a single completed action.

Pij mleko.	*Drink milk.* (Drink it regularly because it is good for you.)
Popij mleko.	*Drink your milk up.* (Come on now, finish your milk.)

When talking about ongoing actions in the present tense, you logically use the imperfective.

We shall list verbs in their aspectual pairs, giving the imperfective aspect first, noting present and past tense forms when they are not based directly on the infinitive.

Come on! *Hajde!*

This word is frequently heard in conversations. It means *come on* when you want to urge or chivvy someone on. There is also the expression **hajdemo** which is similarly used as a first person plural to mean *come on* or *let's go*.

Practice

1 Answer the following questions about the dialogues in Activity A and Activity B:

  a Kako je Marko Pavlović putovao u Beograd?
  b Gde je dobio vizu?
  c Da li je let bio udoban?
  d Ko je čekao Marka na izlazu?
  e Gde su Marko i Stevan pili kafu?
  f Da li je Marko već bio u Beogradu?
  g Da li su Marko i Stevan čekali autobus?
  h Kako su stigli do hotela?

2 Complete the sentences below putting the verbs given in brackets into the appropriate form of the past tense. First look at the example:

  e.g. Marko (biti) u Beogradu.
       Marko je bio u Beogradu.

  a Vera (piti) kafu.
  b Barbara i Vesna (ići) u školu peške.
  c Marko (putovati) avionom.
  d Mi (živeti) blizu parka.
  e Ja (kupiti) kartu.
  f Dragan i Jelena (čekati) taksi.
  g Vi (biti) u centru grada?
  h Robert (stići) na aerodrom.

3 Make the following sentences negative, taking care with word order:

  a Znala sam dobro Beograd.
  b Vesna je išla u Narodnu biblioteku Srbije.
  c Dobili smo vaše pismo.
  d Gledao si taj film.
  e Milan i Dragan su bili na poslu.
  f Imao sam stan u Beogradu.
  g Dobro je govorio srpski.
  h Videli ste njegovu ženu.

Hotel reception

Activity C

🔊 CD 1, TR 9, 01.47

Marko Pavlović arrives at his hotel where he approaches the reception to register. Listen to the recording and try to find out Marko's room number before reading the dialogue below:

Marko	Dobar dan. Imam ovde rezervaciju.
Recepcioner	Dobar dan, gospodine. Vaše prezime, molim vas?
Marko	Pavlović.
Recepcioner	Hm . . . ne mogu da nađem vašu rezervaciju. Vaše ime?
Marko	Marko, Marko Pavlović iz Londona.
Recepcioner	Ah, da, našao sam vašu rezervaciju. Potpišite ovde i dajte mi, molim vas, pasoš. Vi ste u sobi broj 273. To je na drugom spratu. Ovo je vaš ključ. Lift je ovde, pored recepcije. Izvolite, ovo su neke informacije o hotelu.

QUICK VOCAB

recepcioner	*receptionist*
prezime	*surname*
nalaziti; naći, nađem, našao	*to find*
ime	*name*
potpisivati, potpisujem; potpisati, potpišem	*to sign*
potpišite	*sign (imperative)*
pasoš	*passport*
soba	*room*
na drugom spratu	*on the second floor*
ključ	*key*
lift	*lift, elevator*
recepcija	*reception*
informacija	*information*

Activity D

Read the information about the hotel and answer the questions that follow:

PARK
hotel

***

Njegoševa 4, 11000 Beograd
Telefon: 3234-723
Telefaks: 3233-029

Hotel se nalazi u centru grada u mirnoj ulici i ima 130 soba i apartmana.
Sve sobe imaju kupatilo i telefon.
U hotelu su restoran, aperitiv bar, salon i sala za bankete.
Hotel ima parking i garažu.
Cena uključuje noćenje i kontinentalni doručak.
Doručak se služi od sedam do devet sati.

u mirnoj ulici	*in a quiet street*	
apartman	*apartment*	
kupatilo	*bathroom*	
telefon	*telephone*	
salon	*lounge*	
sala za bankete	*banqueting hall*	
parking	*car park*	
garaža	*garage*	QUICK VOCAB
cena uključuje	*price includes*	
noćenje	*overnight stay*	
kontinentalni doručak	*continental breakfast*	
doručak se služi	*breakfast is served*	
od sedam do devet sati	*from seven to nine o'clock*	

Questions

i What is the address of the hotel *Park*?
ii How big is the hotel?

How it works

Hotel floors

The word for *floor* or *storey* is **sprat**.

prizemlje	*ground floor*	u prizemlju	*on the ground floor*
prvi sprat	*first floor*	na prvom spratu	*on the first floor*
drugi sprat	*second floor*	na drugom spratu	*on the second floor*
treći sprat	*third floor*	na trećem spratu	*on the third floor*
četvrti sprat	*fourth floor*	na četvrtom spratu	*on the fourth floor*

Telling the time

Breakfast is served in the hotel *Park* from seven to nine o' clock (**Doručak se služi od sedam do devet sati**).

The word for *hour* or *o'clock* is **sat** (gen. singular **sata**; gen. plural **sati**) as follows:

jedan sat	*1.00*	sedam sati	*7.00*
dva sata	*2.00*	osam sati	*8.00*
tri sata	*3.00*	devet sati	*9.00*
četiri sata	*4.00*	deset sati	*10.00*
pet sati	*5.00*	jedanaest sati	*11.00*
šest sati	*6.00*	dvanaest sati	*12.00*

To give times between the hours:

Jedan (sat) i pet (minuta)   *1.05 (five minutes past one)*

(The word **minut** *minute*, like **sat**, is usually omitted.)

Dva i deset	*2.10*
Tri i petnaest	*3.15*
Četiri i dvadeset	*4.20*
Pet i dvadeset pet	*5.25*
Pola sedam	*6.30*
Dvadeset pet do sedam	*6.35 (twenty-five to seven)*
Dvadeset do osam	*7.40*
Petnaest do devet	*8.45*
Deset do deset	*9.50*
Pet do jedanaest	*10.55 (five minutes to eleven)*

The pattern for telling the time is simply to add on minutes past the hour to half past, and then count the number of minutes up to the next hour. Half past the hour is expressed as if saying *halfway to seven* **pola sedam** for 6.30.

Expressions for telling the time

Koliko je sati?	*What time is it?*
Sada je pet i petnaest.	*It is now 5.15.*
Sada je oko pola šest.	*It is now about 5.30.*

U koliko sati . . . ?	*At what time . . . ?*
U petnaest do šest.	*At 5.45.*
Oko petnaest do šest.	*At about 5.45.* (without **u**)
Od šest do pola sedam.	*From 6.00 to 6.30.*

24-hour clock

The 24-hour clock is used for timetables and in official programmes. The word for *hour* or *o'clock* in these circumstances is sometimes čas, gen. singular časa, gen. plural časova:

| Let je u četrnaest časova i trideset minuta. | *The flight is at 14.30.* |
| Voz polazi u sedamnaest časova i stiže u devetnaest časova i četrdeset minuta. | *The train leaves at 17.00 and arrives at 19.40.* |

Changing money

Activity E

◀) CD 1, TR 9, 02.48

Marko wants to change money and goes to the hotel reception:

Marko	Izvinite, gde je u blizini banka? Treba da promenim novac.
Recepcioner	Novac možete da promenite ovde, u hotelu. Koju valutu želite da promenite?
Marko	Engleske funte.
Recepcioner	Koliko funti želite da promenite?
Marko	Kakav je danas kurs za funtu?
Recepcioner	Funta je danas devedeset devet dinara.
Marko	Želim da promenim pedeset funti.
Recepcioner	Dobro. Da vidim . . . To je četiri hiljade devetsto pedeset dinara. Izvolite.
Marko	Hvala.
Recepcioner	Molim. Prijatno.

u blizini	*in the vicinity*
menjati; promeniti	*to change*
novac	*money*
valuta	*currency*
funta	*pound* (gen. plural **funti**)
Kakav je kurs?	*What is the exchange rate?*
kurs	*exchange rate*
Da vidim . . .	*Let me see . . .*

Question

How much money does Marko change and for how many dinars?

Serbia's currency is the dinar, divided into 100 para, although you are unlikely to see any of these as their value is so small. Large hotels offer money-changing facilities and currency can also be changed in a bank (**banka**) or in one of the bureau de change offices (**menjačnica**) licensed by the National Bank.

Practice

4 During his stay in Belgrade Marko has to book a room for his boss who is unexpectedly coming from England. His main requirement is that the hotel is situated in the very centre of town. There are three hotels with free rooms available. Read the information below and find out which hotel best suits his requirement:

HOTEL TURIST
Sarajevska 37

Hotel se nalazi u blizini železničke i autobuske stanice. Poseduje bar, aperitiv bar, restoran, menjačnicu, letnju baštu i parking. Sve sobe su sa kupatilom.

Aerodrom: 14 km; železnička stanica 800 metara.

HOTEL PUTNIK
Palmira Toljatija 9, Novi Beograd

Hotel je lociran u Novom Beogradu, 12 kilometara od aerodroma i pet minuta autom od centra grada. Sve sobe imaju kupatilo i TV i moderno su opremljene. Hotel ima dva restorana i svoj parking.

HOTEL SPLENDID
Dragoslava Jovanovića 5

Hotel se nalazi u centru grada, u mirnoj ulici pored parka. U blizini hotela nalaze se mnoge kulturne i istorijske znamenitosti (muzeji, galerije, pozorišta), radnje i restorani. Lokacija hotela pogodna je i za turiste i za poslovne ljude. Hotel ima 42 sobe i salon gde se služi doručak i piće. Sve sobe imaju tuš, WC i telefon.

5 Marko's Belgrade colleague Stevan Marić phones him in the morning to give him a list of times for meetings that day (*meeting* **sastanak**). Listen to the recording and write down the times Marko is given with the details of his appointments:

◀)) **CD 1, TR 9, 03.42**

	time	details
a		
b		
c		
d		
e		
f		

6 You are walking along a street in Belgrade and a passer-by asks you the time. How would you say the following:

◀)) **CD 1, TR 9, 04.26**

a nine o'clock   **b** quarter past ten
c twenty-five past two   **d** twenty to five
e five to eight   **f** half past eight

7 Here is the foreign currency exchange rate **devizni kurs** (**devize** *foreign currency*) which you are given in a bank when you go there to change money. (**Zemlja** means *country*, **Danska** *Denmark*, **Norveška** *Norway*, **Švedska** *Sweden*, **Švajcarska** *Switzerland* and **SAD, Sjedinjene Američke Države** *USA, United States of America*.) Remember that in Serbia 60,36 = 60.36. Study the list and answer the questions that follow:

DEVIZNI KURS		
ZEMLJA		KURS
Evropska monetarna unija	1 evro	60,36
Australija	1 dolar	36,44
Kanada	1 dolar	43,16
Danska	1 kruna	8,11
Japan	100 jena	52,11
Kuvajt	1 dinar	222,42
Norveška	1 kruna	7,90
Švedska	1 kruna	6,58
Švajcarska	1 franak	41,08
Velika Britanija	1 funta	98,44
SAD	1 dolar	68,28

a What is the Serbian word for a *euro*?
b How would you ask what is the exchange rate for the pound?
c How would you say that you want to change 50 pounds?
d How would you say that you want to change 100 euros?
e How would you say that you want to change 200 dollars?

Test yourself

Here you can check some of the things you have learnt in this unit.
Look at the questions below and choose the right answer:

1 Which form would you use to fill the gap in the sentence **Moj
   drug je . . . . avionom?**

   a putovao   b putovala   c putovali

2 Which form would a female person use if she wanted to say that
   she has changed her money in the hotel: **Ja sam . . . .
   novac u hotelu?**

a promenio   **b** promenila   **c** promenilo

3 You and your friend have come by taxi to a meeting with your Serbian collegue. How would you respond if asked **Kako ste došli?**

  a Došli su taksijem.   **b** Došli smo taksijem.   **c** Došli ste taksijem.

4 Which word would you choose to fill the gap when asking your Serbian collegue if he/she has ever been to London **Da li ste već . . . . u Londonu?**

  a bili   **b** bila   **c** bio

5 If a male person wanted to say that he has finished his coffee, what would he say?

  a Pio sam kafu.   **b** Popio sam kafu.

6 How would you fill the gap to say that Marko has his own ticket **Marko ima . . . . kartu?**

  a njegovu   **b** njenu   **c** svoju

7 You are tired from your journey and looking for a hotel where you can get a good night's sleep. Where should your hotel be?

  a u blizini restorana i barova
  b blizu železničke stanice
  c u mirnoj ulici

8 What is the meaning of the word **prizemlje?**

  a basement   **b** ground floor   **c** first floor

9 What is the meaning of the phrase **cena ne uključuje doručak?**

  a no breakfast is served
  b breakfast is included in the price
  c breakfast has to be paid for separately

10 Which form of the word would you use if you wanted to change £100: **Želim da promenim sto . . . .?**

  a funti   **b** funta   **c** funte

10

At home with the family

In this unit you will learn:

- Phrases for discussing family matters
- How to say your age and to ask others
- How to say your occupation and to ask others
- How to describe where you live
- Cases: dative, locative and instrumental plurals
- Adjectives formed from personal names

Marko's Belgrade family

Marko Pavlović has finished his business meetings and has a little time left in Belgrade. He decides to visit his aunt and uncle, Biljana and Miloš, and their daughter, Maja.

Activity A

◄) CD 1, TR 10

Listen to the recording without looking at the printed text and try to answer these questions:

i What does Marko's Aunt Biljana do?
ii What is his cousin Maja studying?

Now read the text below:

> Биљана и Милош су муж и жена. Имају ћерку Мају и сина Дејана. Живе у Београду. Биљана ради у школи као наставница историје, а њен муж је инжењер. Маја већ две године студира енглески језик на универзитету.

> Она је студенткиња и није удата. Мајин брат Дејан више не живи са родитељима. Он има свој стан. Ожењен је и има два детета. Дејанова жена ради као секретарица.

QUICK VOCAB

ћерка	*daughter*
син	*son*
као	*as, like*
историја	*history*
инжењер	*engineer*
већ	*already*
година	*year*
студирати	*to study*
универзитет	*university*
студенткиња	*student* (female)
удата	*married* (of a woman)
брат	*brother*
више не	*no longer, no more*
са родитељима	*with parents*
ожењен	*married* (of a man)
два детета	*two children*
Дејанов	*Dejan's*
секретарица	*secretary* (female)

Activity B

◆ CD 1, TR 10, 01.08

Marko, Maja and Biljana are chatting. Listen to the recording and read the dialogue below, then answer the questions:

Марко	Мајо, колико имаш година?
Maja	Имам двадесет година.
Марко	Шта радиш? Имаш ли посао?
Maja	Не, ја сам још увек студенткиња. Студирам енглески.
Марко	Да ли учиш само енглески или још неки страни језик?
Maja	Учила сам француски у школи, а на факултету учим и италијански.
Марко	Шта хоћеш да радиш после факултета?
Maja	Још не знам. Али волим да путујем. Желим да нађем неки посао где могу да путујем.

Биљана	Марко, шта раде твоји мама и тата?
Марко	Тата има нов посао у великој фирми. Мама више не ради.
	Она је сада домаћица.
Биљана	А ти? Јеси ли ожењен?
Марко	Нисам. Али имам девојку.
Биљана	И Маја већ има младића. Зове се Влада.

Колико имаш година?	How old are you?
још увек	still
још неки	one more, another
страни	foreign
факултет	faculty
још не	not yet
волети, волим	to like, to love
мама	mother, mum
тата	father, dad
нов	new
у великој фирми	in a large company
домаћица	housewife
девојка	girl, young lady, girlfriend
младић	youth, young man, boyfriend

Questions

i Which phrase did Marko use to ask Maja about her age?

ii How would she respond to that question if she were 22?

Here are everyday terms to denote family relationships:

муж	husband	жена	wife
тата	dad	мама	mum
отац	father	мајка	mother
син	son	ћерка	daughter
брат	brother	сестра	sister
деда	grandfather	бака (or баба)	grandmother
унук	grandson	унука	granddaughter

You can also use the words **супруг** and **супруга** to mean *husband* and *wife* but these are formal terms which you may find on official documents rather than in everyday speech, rather like the English word *spouse*.

The words **тата** and **мама** are commonly used by people of all ages while **отац** and **мајка** are somewhat more formal.

To say *aunt* and *uncle* you have to decide which side of the family you are talking about. The brother of your father is your **стриц**, and his wife is your **стрина**. The brother of your mother is your **ујак**, and his wife is your **ујна**. The sister of either your mother or father is your **тетка**, and her husband is your **теча**. Biljana is Marko's **тетка**, Miloš is his **теча** (Biljana is his father's sister). The words for cousin are the same as the words for brother and sister, i.e. the son of your **стриц** is your **брат од стрица**.

How it works

Expressing age

To ask how old someone is, use the word **колико** *how much, how many* with the gen. plural of the word **година** *year* and note the word order:

Колико имате година?	*How old are you?* (lit. *How many do you have years?*)
Колико има Маја година?	*How old is Maja?*

To answer the question, use the verb **имати** with the appropriate form of **година**:

Имам дванаест година.	*I am 12* (years old).
Влада има двадесет једну годину.	*Vlada is 21.*
Марко има двадесет четири године.	*Marko is 24.*

Talking about occupations

To say *I work as* . . . use **Радим као** . . .

Most jobs or occupations have separate forms for men and women. The forms for men usually end in a consonant and for women end in -a:

occupation	feminine	masculine
teacher	наставница	наставник
teacher (primary)	учитељица	учитељ
student	студенткиња	студент
journalist	новинарка	новинар
pupil	ученица	ученик
doctor	лекарка	лекар
dentist	зубарка	зубар
secretary	секретарица	секретар
actor	глумица	глумац
singer	певачица	певач

However, the word **инжењер** is used for both men and women. The same is the case with some other names of occupations:

translator	преводилац
lawyer	адвокат

Saying someone is married

To say that someone is married depends on whether we speak of a man or a woman:

Он је ожењен.	*He is married.*
Она је удата.	*She is married.*

There is another expression when you want to say that two people are married:

Они су у браку.	*They are married.* (lit. *They are in marriage.*)

Noun subgroups: *тата* and *дете*

Тата

From the beginning of the book you have been recognizing the gender of nouns by their final letter (masc. nouns end with a consonant; fem. nouns with -a; neut. nouns with -o or -e). However, there are some exceptions which form small subgroups. Some masc. nouns end in -a like **тата** and **Влада**.

Those which end in -a denote a person; **тата** means *dad* and **Влада** is a man's name (short for **Владимир** or **Владислав**). Although they look and change cases like a fem. noun, all adjective and other agreements behave as if they were masc.

Он је мој тата.

Дете

This is a word belonging to a small group of neut. nouns which add an extra syllable **-ет-** before adding the case ending:

nom.	**дете**
acc.	**дете**
gen.	**детета**
ins.	**дететом**
loc.	**детету**

Also in this group is the word **дрво** (gen. singular **дрвета**) *tree*.

More about adjectives

Mixed noun agreements

When you have one adjective used to describe two nouns of different genders, the adjective takes masc. endings as in the phrase: **твоји мама и тата**.

Omitting possessive adjectives

Serbian does not use possessive adjectives as often as English does. If the meaning of the sentence is clear from the context, then they tend to be omitted as in:

Дејан више не живи са родитељима.	*Dejan no longer lives with <u>his</u> parents.*

Adverbs in time phrases

The words **више не, још, још не, већ** are used in the following way:

више не	*no longer*	**Мама више не ради.**
		Мама више није радила. (past tense)
још увек	*still*	**Маја је још увек студенткиња.**
још не	*not yet*	**Још не знам.**
		Још нисам знао. (past tense)
већ	*already*	**Маја већ две године студира енглески.**

The word **већ** is used more often than *already* is heard in English. Note that when in English we would say *Maja has been studying English for two years*, in Serbian you use the present tense as in the sentence above.

Adjectives formed from personal names

You can form adjectives from personal names to show that something belongs to someone:

- for a man's name ending in a consonant or **-o** add **-ов** or **-ев** after a soft consonant:

Дејан	**Дејанов**	*Dejan's*
Марко	**Марков**	*Marko's*
Милош	**Милошев**	*Miloš's*
Дејанова жена		*Dejan's wife*
Маркови родитељи		*Marko's parents*

- for names (masc. or fem.) which end in -a add **-ин**:

Маја	**Мајин**	*Maja's*
Весна	**Веснин**	*Vesna's*
Влада	**Владин**	*Vlada's*
Мајин младић		*Maja's boyfriend*
Владини мама и тата		*Vlada's mum and dad*

- similar adjectives can be formed from words denoting family relationships:

мама	**мамин**	*mum's*
тата	**татин**	*dad's*

Practice

1 You have been asked to take part in a formal interview with a candidate applying for a job in your company in Belgrade. First study the words and phrases used in the form and make sure that you understand them. Then listen to the candidate introducing herself and fill in the form with the information she gives you:

a	име и презиме	
b	боравиште	
c	занимање	
d	године старости	
e	брачно стање	
f	име мужа	
g	занимање мужа	
h	године старости мужа	
i	син/ћерка	
j	име и године старости детета	

боравиште	*place of residence*
занимање	*profession*
године старости	*age*
брачно стање	*marital status*

QUICK VOCAB

2 Robert is talking to Ana at a party organized at their language school in Belgrade. Fill in his part of the dialogue:

◄) CD 1, TR 10, 02.53

Ана	Јеси ли ти студент, Роберте?
Роберт	*Yes, I am.*
Ана	Шта студираш?
Роберт	*I am studying history and Serbian language.*
Ана	Где живе твоји родитељи?
Роберт	*They live in London.*
Ана	Шта они раде?
Роберт	*My mum doesn't work, and my dad is a doctor.*
Ана	Имаш ли брата или сестру?
Роберт	*I have a sister and a brother.*
Ана	Колико имају година?
Роберт	*My sister is 27.*
Ана	Да ли она живи са родитељима?
Роберт	*No, she doesn't. She is already married. She works as a teacher in Birmingham.*

Ана	А твој брат?
Роберт	*My brother is 17.*
Ана	Шта он ради?
Роберт	*He still goes to school.*

3 Gordana is the daughter in the family group below. What would she say to introduce herself and the other members of her family?

Гордана	Милица	Бранко	Бојан
21	50	54	28
студенткиња	учитељица	адвокат	новинар

4 Change the name in brackets into an adjective and supply the correct ending. First look at the example:

e.g. (Биљана) муж се зове Милош.
Биљанин муж се зове Милош.

a (Зоран) жена је наставница српског језика.
b (Јелена) другарица ради у банци.
c (Роберт) родитељи живе у Лондону.
d (Маја) младић воли да путује.
e (Јован и Мира) дете има већ две године.
f (Милан) сестра је глумица и ради у позоришту.

Flats and houses

Activity C

🔊 **CD 1, TR 10, 04.50**

The conversation between Marko and his Serbian relatives turns to flats and ways of life in England and in Serbia. Listen to the dialogue, read the text and then answer the questions:

142

Марко	Имате леп стан.
Маја	Стан је удобан, али је мали, трособан. Ово је наша дневна соба. Имамо и две спаваће собе, купатило и велику кухињу. Немамо трпезарију, једемо у кухињи. Тамо држимо сто и столице.
Биљана	Хтели смо да тражимо стан са трпезаријом, али су станови овде скупи.
Маја	Твоји тата и мама имају кућу близу Лондона, зар не?
Марко	Да, имају велику кућу са баштом. Тамо станују и моје сестре, Јелена и Ана. Мој брат Филип је купио кућу у Шефилду, где сада живи са породицом.
Биљана	А ти?
Марко	Ја сам изнајмио мали стан у Лондону, због посла.
Биљана	Људи у великом граду овде ретко имају своје куће. Обично живе у становима.

мали	*small, little*
трособан (стан)	*three-roomed (flat)*
дневна соба	*sitting room*
спаваћа соба	*bedroom*
кухиња	*kitchen*
трпезарија	*dining room*
јести, једем, past tense **јео**	*to eat*
држати, држим	*to keep*
сто	*table*
столица	*chair*
скуп	*expensive*
кућа	*house*
зар не?	*is that not so?*
башта	*garden*
породица	*family*
изнајмљивати, изнајмљујем, изнајмити	*to rent, to hire*
због	*because of* (preposition with gen.)
људи	*people* (plural of **човек**)
ретко	*rarely*
обично	*usually*

QUICK VOCAB

Questions

i How big is Biljana's and Miloš's flat?

ii Where does Marko's brother live?

Buying presents

Activity D

🔊 **CD 1, TR 10, 06.00**

Marko, Biljana and Maja are continuing their conversation. Listen to the recording, read the text below and then answer the questions:

Maja	Наша бака Љубица има кућу у селу близу Београда. Треба да видиш како је лепо њено село. Хоћеш ли да идемо тамо сутра?
Марко	На жалост, не могу. Сутра морам да купим поклоне сестрама и брату.
Биљана	А мами и тати?
Марко	Треба да купим нешто и мами и тати, али не знам колико ствари могу да носим. Тати сам већ купио флашу шљивовице, а мама је тражила неке биљне чајеве.
Биљана	Иди сутра у куповину са Мајом.

QUICK VOCAB

село	*village*
на жалост	*unfortunately*
поклон	*present*
сестрама и брату	*for my sisters and brother*
нешто	*something*
колико ствари	*how many things*
носити	*to carry*
шљивовица	*brandy made from plums*
неки	*some, a certain*
биљни чајеви	*herbal teas*
ићи, идем у куповину	*to go shopping*

Questions

i Where does Maja's grandmother live?

ii What has Marko bought for his father?

144

Activity E

🔊 CD 1, TR 10, 06.39

Listen to the recording, read the text below and then answer the questions:

> Марко је са Мајом ишао у град у куповину. Купио је брату два постера са фотографијама Београда. Сестри Јелени је купио књигу и ЦД, а Ани два филма на видео-касетама. Онда су ишли на кафу и колаче у једну посластичарницу близу Мајиног факултета. Увече је Марко ишао у интернет-кафе и послао поруку оцу и мајци. Ево шта је написао:
>
> Драги мама и тата,
> Био сам код тетке Биљане и тече Милоша. Били су врло љубазни. Ишао сам са Мајом у град. Упознао сам њено друштво. Ишли смо у шетњу на Калемегдан. Било је лепо и хоћу ускоро опет да дођем у Београд.
> Ваш
> Марко

постер	*poster*
фотографија	*photograph*
књига	*book*
ЦД	*CD* (pronounced 'tse-de')
филм	*film*
видео-касета	*video cassette*
колач	*cake*
посластичарница	*cake shop*
близу Мајиног факултета	*near Maja's faculty*
увече	*in the evening*
интернет-кафе	*internet café*
слати, шаљем, послати, пошаљем	*to send*
порука	*message*
оцу и мајци	*to his father and mother* (dat. case)
ево	*here is*
писати, пишем, написати, напишем	*to write*
драги	*dear*

QUICK VOCAB

код	at, at the house of (preposition with gen.)
љубазан	kind
упознавати, упознајем, упознати	to get to know, to become aquainted with
друштво	company, group of friends
ићи, идем у шетњу	to go for a walk
било је лепо	it was nice
ускоро	soon

Questions

i What did Marko buy for Jelena?

ii What did he say about Biljana and Miloš to his mother and father?

Most people in Serbian cities live in flats or apartments. The size of a flat is usually given according to the number of rooms overall, excluding bathroom and kitchen. You can talk about a *one-roomed flat*, *two-roomed flat*, *four-roomed flat* **једнособан, двособан, четворособан стан**.

Marko has bought his father a bottle of **шљивовица** *plum brandy*. You can find many different sorts of fruit-based brandies in Serbia: **кајсијевача** *apricot brandy*, **крушковача** *pear brandy*, **јабуковача** *apple brandy*. The one made from plums is regarded by many as the national drink.

After his day spent with Maja, Marko went to an internet café in the evening to send an e-mail home. There are numerous internet cafés in the centre of Belgrade. One of the well-known ones is in the *Plato* bookshop and café by the University's Faculty of Philosophy (**Филозофски факултет**).

How it works

Dative case

The dative (dat.) is the last of the seven cases in Serbian. It is used after some prepositions and when in English we would normally say *to* or *for* after a verb. Such a construction is called the indirect object:

| *I want to buy a present for my brother.* | **Хоћу да купим поклон брату.** |

You already know the endings for the dat. case as they are exactly the same as for the loc.:

Singular	masc.	fem.		neut.
nom.	брат	сестра	ствар	дете
dat.	брату add **-у**	сестри **-а** to **-и**	ствари add **-и**	детету **-о**, **-е** to **-у**

Because of the usual spelling rules **к**, **г** or **х** will change to **ц**, **з** or **с** before the ending **-и**, so **мајка** becomes **мајци**.

Dative, instrumental and locative plurals

The plural forms for the dat., ins. and loc. cases are the same for each noun. There are some examples in this unit:

поклон сестрама	*a present for his sisters* (dat.)
са родитељима	*with his parents* (ins.)
у становима	*in flats* (loc.)
на видео-касетама	*on video cassettes* (loc.)

The endings of these cases in the plural for all genders are:

Plural	masc.	fem.		neut.
nom.	родитељи	сестре	ствари	позоришта
dat., ins., loc.	родитељима **-и** to **-има**	сестрама **-е** to **-ама**	стварима **-и** to **-има**	позориштима **-а** to **-има**

Is that not so?

It is possible to make a question by adding the phrase **зар не?** after a statement.

| **Ти мораш да купиш поклоне сестрама, зар не?** | *You have to buy presents for your sisters, is that not so?* |

Nouns: *човек, отац, сто*

The word **човек** means a *person* or it can also refer to a *man* depending on the context. The plural form of that word is **људи** *people, men* which takes the regular masc. plural endings except that the gen. plural form is **људи**.

> ## Insight
> Remember that the word **човек** has an unusual plural **људи** and that the same form **људи** is used in the genitive plural:
>
> | | |
> |---|---|
> | Људи обично живе у становима. | *People usually live in flats.* |
> | Видела сам испред куће пет људи. | *I saw five people in front of the house.* |

When case endings are added to **отац** the stem of the word also changes:

nom.	**отац**
voc.	**оче**
acc.	**оца**
gen.	**оца**
dat.	**оцу**
ins.	**оцем**
loc.	**оцу**

The moveable **-а** disappears which leaves the consonants **т** and **ц** together. Since the sound of the letter **ц** incorporates the sound of **т**, this consonant is also dropped to leave a stem of **оц-**.

The plural of **отац** behaves like a monosyllabic noun with the nom. form **очеви**.

Сто *table* is one of those masc. nouns which used to end in **-л**. The sound returns when the word adds case endings, like **посао** (gen. **посла**):

nom.	**сто**
acc.	**сто**
gen.	**стола**
dat.	**столу**
ins.	**столом**
loc.	**столу**

148

The plural of **сто** behaves like a monosyllabic noun with the nom. form **столови.**

Some, a certain

The adjective **неки** is used to mean *some* or *a certain*:

Она учи неки страни језик.	*She is studying some (a certain) language.*
Мама је тражила неке чајеве.	*Mum asked for some (certain kinds of) teas.*

Practice

5 Look at Biljana's, Marko's and Maja's family tree and answer the questions below. First look at the example:

e.g. Шта је Љубица Биљани и Стевану?
Љубица је њихова мајка.

a Шта је Стеван Биљани?
b Шта је Љубица Маји и Дејану?
c Шта је Дејан Маји?
d Шта је Биљана Марку?
e Шта је Маја Марку?
f Шта је Марко Стевану?
g Шта су Ана и Јелена Стевану?

6 You are having a conversation with a friend whom you have met during your stay in Serbia. What can you tell the person about yourself, the place where you live and your family? Try to answer some of the following questions: Колико имаш година? Где живиш? Шта радиш? Да ли си ожењен/удата? Како се зове твој муж/твоја жена? Да ли имаш сина или ћерку? Колико има година?

7 Put the nouns in brackets into the correct case (nouns are given in the nom. case: apply sing. or pl. endings as indicated):

a Морам да пишем (сестра и брат).
b Маја је купила хлеб и млеко (родитељи).
c Вера иде на ручак са (пријатељице).
d Говоримо о (хотели) у Београду.
e Марко је послао поруку (отац).
f Купили су лепе поклоне (ћерке).

Test yourself

Here you can check some of the things you have learnt in this unit. Look at the questions below and choose the right answer:

1 You want to ask your Serbian friend for his/her age. Which form of the word would you use in the question **Колико имаш** ....?

   a година   **b** године   **c** годину

2 How would you say that you are thirty-four years old: **Имам тридесет четири** ....?

   a година   **b** годину   **c** године

3 What is the meaning of the word **ћерка?**

   a sister   **b** daughter   **c** grandmother

4 What is your mother's sister to you?

   a тетка   **b** ујна   **c** стрина

5 **Новинар** is a person who works:

   a in a bank
   b for a newspaper
   c in a post office

6 If someone tells you **Још нисам ожењен** he wants to say that:

    a he is still married
    b he is not married yet
    c he is not married any more

7 What is **трпезарија?**

    a living room   **b** bedroom   **c** dining room

8 Which form of the word would you use to complete the sentence **Морам да пишем . . . .?**

    a брату   **b** брата   **c** брат

9 How would you say that you want to go shopping: **Хоћу да идем у . . . . . .?**

    a куповини   **b** куповину   **c** куповина

10 **Посластичарница** is a place where we can:

    a have lunch
    b have a glass of wine or beer
    c have a cake and a soft drink

11

Planning a holiday

In this unit you will learn:

- Phrases for discussing holiday plans
- Expressions for planning a journey
- About places to go in Serbia and Montenegro
- How to form the future tense
- Accusative and genitive pronouns
- Endings for accusative and genitive adjectives

Going to Kopaonik

Activity A

◀) CD 2, TR 1

The summer holidays are approaching and Vesna is planning to go away with her friend, Ana, to Kopaonik, a mountain resort in southern Serbia. Here she is telling Robert about it. Listen to the recording and answer the questions below before reading the text:

i How are Vesna and Ana going to Kopaonik?
ii Where are they going to stay?

Vesna	Ana i ja ćemo ići na letovanje na Kopaonik.
Robert	Kako ćete ići?
Vesna	Uzećemo autobus. Ići ćemo iz Beograda preko Kruševca. Postoji i drugi put, ali nije tako dobar.

Robert	Gde ćete boraviti?
Vesna	Iznajmićemo apartman jer su hoteli na Kopaoniku za nas skupi. U apartmanu ćemo imati kuhinju i moći ćemo da spremamo svoju hranu.
Robert	Moraćete da kuvate?
Vesna	Ne, ponekad ćemo jesti u restoranu. Bićemo blizu glavnog turističkog naselja, gde ima dobrih restorana. Ja ih već znam, bila sam tamo prošle godine.

QUICK VOCAB

letovanje	*summer holiday*
preko	*via, across* (preposition with gen.)
postojati, postojim	*to be, to exist*
put	*road, way*
tako	*so*
boraviti	*to stay*
jer	*because, for*
za nas	*for us*
spremati; spremiti	*to prepare*
kuvati; skuvati	*cook*
ponekad	*sometimes*
blizu glavnog turističkog naselja	*near the main tourist settlement/ area*
ima dobrih restorana	*there are some good restaurants*
ja ih već znam	*I already know them*
prošle godine	*last year*

For holidays Serbia has mountain resorts and relaxing spas offering a broad range of accommodation from luxury-class hotels to self-catering bungalows. The two largest resorts are at the mountains (**planina**): Kopaonik and Zlatibor. They are much frequented for both summer holidays (**letovanje**) and winter holidays (**zimovanje**). There are many spa towns (**banja**): Vrnjačka banja and Soko banja being amongst the more famous. Besides its natural beauty Serbia also offers the tourist many examples of fine medieval monasteries with the influences of Byzantine culture evident in their architecture and frescos.

How it works

Forming the future tense

The future tense in Serbian is formed by using the short form of the verb **hteti** as an auxiliary verb with the infinitive (or alternative infinitive construction):

HTETI		
short form	long form	negative
ja ću	hoću	neću
ti ćeš	hoćeš	nećeš
on će	hoće	neće
mi ćemo	hoćemo	nećemo
vi ćete	hoćete	nećete
oni će	hoće	neće

Ja ću ići.	*I shall go.*
Ja ću da idem.	
Vesna će uzeti autobus.	*Vesna will take a bus.*
Vesna će da uzme autobus.	

As you are already aware, word order sometimes needs to be changed when using short forms since they cannot come at the beginning of a sentence or clause. They tend to follow the first word or phrase:

Gde ćete boraviti?	*Where will you stay?*
U apartmanu ćemo imati kuhinju.	*We'll have a kitchen in the apartment.*

When there is no such introductory word, the auxiliary form follows the infinitive. In this case, if the infinitive ends in **-ti**, remove the ending and form a single word by adding the auxiliary verb to the infinitive stem. If the infinitive ends in **-ći**, keep the full form of the infinitive and write the auxiliary verb separately:

Uzećemo autobus . . .	*We shall take a bus . . .*
. . . moći ćemo da spremamo svoju hranu.	*. . . we shall be able to prepare our own food.*

Insight

Remember that if there is no introductory word the future tense has to be shortened into one word:

Mi ćemo imati kuhinju.
Imaćemo kuhinju.

However, if the infinitive ends in -ći there is no such shortening but the infinitive precedes the auxiliary verb:

Mi ćemo ići autobusom.
Ići ćemo autobusom.

Verbal aspect in the future

As with the past tense, it is important to use the correct aspect of the verb to express the type of action which is intended in the future. Imperfective verbs indicate frequent or incomplete actions, perfective verbs indicate actions to be undertaken and completed on one occasion:

Uzećemo autobus iz Beograda. *We shall take a bus from Belgrade.*

(perfective verb to show the intention to take it just once to get to Kopaonik)

Ponekad ćemo jesti u restoranu. *Sometimes we'll eat at a restaurant.*

(imperfective verb to show the intention that this will be a repeated occurence and not just a single action in the future)

Activity B

◆) **CD 2, TR 1, 01.19**

Vesna and Robert are continuing chatting. Listen to the recording, read the dialogue below and then answer the questions:

Robert	Šta ćete raditi na letovanju?
Vesna	Priroda je tamo na planini vrlo lepa. Ceo kraj je pun gustih šuma, polja i livada, potoka i reka. Ja ću šetati po šumi i ići na izlete do planinskih vrhova. Ima do njih divnih staza. Ana ne voli da šeta. Ona će se, valjda, sunčati i čitaće knjige. Ne razumem je. Može to da radi i u Beogradu.

Robert	Da li ćete ići same?
Vesna	Nećemo. Vodićemo i Aninog brata Uroša.
Robert	Zašto?
Vesna	Zato što njihovi roditelji ove godine neće ići na odmor. On ne može da ide sam jer je još mali. Neko mora da ga čuva. Ali, što se nas tiče, nema problema. Njega zanima samo sport i hoće samo da igra fudbal ili košarku. Na Kopaoniku organizuju razne sportove. Za njega će tamo biti dobro. Naći će svoje društvo. A da li ti imaš planove za raspust, Roberte?

priroda	*nature, countryside*
planina	*mountain*
ceo	*whole*
pun gustih šuma	*full of thick forests*
pun (with gen.)	*full of*
polje	*field*
livada	*meadow*
potok	*stream*
po	*around* (preposition with dat.)
izlet	*excursion*
do planinskih vrhova	*to the mountain peaks*
ima divnih staza	*there are some wonderful paths*
do njih	*to them, up to them*
valjda	*probably*
sunčati se	*to sunbathe*
čitati; pročitati	*to read*
sam	*alone*
voditi; povesti, povedem, poveo	*to take, to lead*
zašto	*why*
zato što	*because*
ove godine	*this year*
odmor	*holiday, rest*
mali	*small, young* (for a child)
Neko mora da ga čuva.	*Someone has to look after him.*
što se nas tiče	*as far as we are concerned*
nema problema	*there are no problems*
Njega zanima samo sport.	*He is only interested in sport.*
igrati	*to play*

QUICK VOCAB

fudbal	*football*
košarka	*basketball*
za njega	*for him*
organizovati, organizujem	*to organize*
razni	*various, different*
raspust	*school holidays, vacation*

Questions

i Does Ana like walking?
ii Are there opportunities to play sport on Kopaonik?

How it works

Forming questions and negative statements in the future tense

The simplest way to form a question using the future tense is to use **da li** as the introductory question phrase followed by the auxiliary verb and then the infinitive:

Da li ćete ići same?   *Will you go alone?*

The other possibility is to use the long form of the verb **hteti** followed by **li**:

Hoćete li ići same?

To make a negative statement in the future tense simply use the negative of **hteti** followed by the infinitive. These negative forms are not short forms:

Njihovi roditelji neće ići na odmor.   *Their parents will not go on holiday.*

Using *hteti* to want

You have already used the verb **hteti** *to want*. Remember that in this meaning you always use the long form usually with the alternative infinitive expression as in:

Uroš hoće samo da igra fudbal ili košarku.   *Uroš wants only to play football or basketball.*

Accusative and genitive pronouns

Pronouns have different forms for the cases as do nouns. As with the verbs **biti** and **hteti**, some of these pronouns have long and short forms. These are the patterns for the acc. and gen. cases:

nom.	acc.		gen.	
	short	long	short	long
ja	me	mene	me	mene
ti	te	tebe	te	tebe
on/o	ga	njega	ga	njega
ona	je/ju	nju	je	nje
mi	nas	nas	nas	nas
vi	vas	vas	vas	vas
oni	ih	njih	ih	njih

There are minimal differences between the acc. and gen. of the personal pronouns. The long forms of **mi** and **vi** are stressed and the short forms unstressed. The forms for **on** and **ono** in cases other than the nominative are always the same.

In the plural, the forms for **oni** are the same as for fem. **one** and neut. **ona**.

The short form is preferred. However, it may not be put as the first word of a sentence or clause. The long form is used for emphasis and after prepositions.

Short form examples:

Ne razumem je.	*I do not understand her.*
Neko mora da ga čuva.	*Someone has to look after him.*

Long form examples:

Njega zanima samo sport. *Only sport interests him.*
(acc. long form for direct object of verb used for emphasis)

Za njega će tamo biti dobro. *It will be fine for him there.*
(acc. long form after preposition)

The form **je** is the preferred acc. short form of **ona**. The form **ju** is only used when the short form **je** from **biti** as part of the past tense is also present:

Ne razumem je.	*I don't understand her.*
	(je acc. from **ona**)
Razumela ju je.	*She understood her.*
	(je short form from **biti**)

There is/are . . . is not/are not . . .

To express *there is/are* use **ima** followed by the gen. singular or plural:

ima dobrih restorana	*there are some good restaurants*
ima dobrih staza	*there are some good paths*
Da li ima vode na stolu?	*Is there (any) water on the table?*
Ima vode na stolu.	*There is (some) water on the table.*

In these examples the noun after **ima** refers to an undefined quantity often expressed in English by *some* or *any*. When wishing to state *there is a . . .* (i.e. a single item) use the verb **postojati** *to exist*:

| Postoji i drugi put. | *There is also another road.* |
| | (lit. *Another road exists.*) |

Ima is sometimes used and often qualified by the addition of **jedan** or **neki**:

| Ima li neki autobus u | *Is there a bus at seven in the* |
| sedam sati ujutro? | *morning?* |

To express *there is not/are not* use **nema** followed by the gen. singular or plural:

Nema problema.	*No problem.* (lit. *There aren't any problems.*)
Nema dobrih restorana.	*There are not any good restaurants.*
Nema vode na stolu.	*There isn't any water on the table.*
Nema autobusa u sedam sati ujutro.	*There are no buses at seven in the morning.*

Practice

1 Put the following sentences into the future tense:

  a Ana i Vesna su iznajmile udoban apartman.
  b Čitala sam knjigu.

c Uroš nije igrao fudbal.
d Da li ste gledali taj film?
e Kako je išla u grad?
f Nismo imali kuhinju.
g Nisam ga videla.
h Mogli ste da putujete autobusom.

2 Put the pronoun given in brackets into the appropriate case and form. First look at the example:

e.g.   Znam (on).
       Znam ga.

a Videla sam (oni).
b Ovaj poklon je za (ona).
c Vesna (on) voli.
d Živećemo blizu (vi).
e Oni (ti) ne znaju.
f Kupio je kuću od (ona).
g Ne razumeš (ja).
h Autobuska stanica nije daleko od (mi).

3 Here you have some information about accommodation available on Mount Kopaonik. Read the text, find the meanings of the new words and then answer the questions that follow:

Hotel *Grand*

Ovaj moderan hotel sa pogledom na guste šume se nalazi 100 m od centra turističkog naselja. U hotelu su dva restorana, picerija, poslastičarnica i aperitiv bar. Hotel ima bazen, jakuzzi, saunu, terene za tenis, terene za rukomet, odbojku i košarku i fitnes centar sa teretanom.

Polupansion po osobi i danu	
Period	Dvokrevetna soba
27.4–28.6.	4800 din.
29.6–19.7.	5600 din.
20.7–16.8.	6000 din.

17.8–30.8.	5600 din.
31.8–15.10.	4800 din.

- Doplata za jednokrevetnu sobu je 40%.
- Popust 30% za dete od 2–12 godina.
- Dete do 2 godine ima besplatan boravak.

Hotel *Olga Dedijer*

Ovaj moderan hotel nalazi se u centru turističkog kompleksa. Ima 300 kreveta u komfornim sobama, restoran, aperitiv-bar, disko-klub, TV salon, teretanu i prodavnicu.

Pun pansion po osobi i danu				
soba	do 21.6.	22.6-12.7.	13.7-16.8.	17.8-30.10.
dvokrevetna	1700 din.	2200 din.	3000 din.	2200 din.
trokrevetna	1600 din.	2100 din.	2900 din.	2100 din.
četvorokrevetna	1400 din.	1900 din.	2700 din.	1900 din.

Apartmansko naselje *Konaci*

Ovo atraktivno apartmansko naselje u centru turističkog kompleksa ima 393 apartmana. Svaki apartman ima kuhinju, kupatilo, satelitsku TV i telefon. U naselju se nalaze i samoposluga, pošta, banka, apoteka, restorani, prodavnice, ski-servis.

Period	Usluga	Najam apartmana dnevno (za ceo apartman)			
		za 2 osobe	za 3 osobe	za 4 osobe	za 5 osoba
27.4–28.6.	NAJAM	1800 din.	2000 din.	2200 din.	2300 din.
29.6–19.7.	NAJAM	2000 din.	2400 din.	2600 din.	3000 din.

20.7–16.8.	NAJAM	2300 din.	2800 din.	3100 din.	3500 din.
17.8–30.8.	NAJAM	2000 din.	2400 din.	2600 din.	3000 din.
31.8–15.10.	NAJAM	1800 din.	2000 din.	2200 din.	2300 din.

pogled na (with acc.)	*view of*
bazen	*swimming pool*
sauna	*sauna*
teren	*pitch, court* (for sports)
tennis	*tennis*
rukomet	*handball*
odbojka	*volleyball*
teretana	*gym*
polupansion	*half board*
osoba	*person*
dvokrevetna soba	*double room*
doplata	*additional payment*
jednokrevetna soba	*single room*
popust	*discount*
besplatan	*free (of cost)*
boravak	*stay*
krevet	*bed*
komforan	*comfortable*
pun pansion	*full board*
usluga	*service*
najam	*hire, rent*
dnevno	*daily*

a Which hotel is the most expensive?

b Which hotel offers full board?

c Which hotel has the best sport facilities?

d How much would you have to pay for a double room at the *Grand* at the beginning of July?

e How much would you have to pay for children there?

f What kind of rooms do they offer at the *Olga Dedijer*?

g Where is it possible to rent a holiday flat?

h Is there a pharmacy in the tourist complex?

A holiday in Montenegro

Activity C

◀) CD 2, TR 1, 02.36

Vesna has asked Robert if he has any plans for the holidays. Listen to his plans on the recording, read the text and then answer the questions that follow:

> Idem sa Ričardom na more. Ići ćemo u Crnu Goru. Kupićemo karte za voz i putovaćemo preko noći do Bara. Rezervisaćemo mesta u spavaćim kolima. Nećemo ostati u Baru. Ja hoću malo da putujem po Crnoj Gori, da posetim Cetinje i Kotor. Ričard će provesti celo letovanje u Budvi. On je pravi čovek za more. Ja nisam. Ja ne volim da provodim vreme na plaži, mislim da je to dosadno. Ali ću i ja doći u Budvu. Provešću tamo drugu nedelju odmora. Našli smo privatan smeštaj preko putničke agencije. Soba je jeftina i nalazi se u centru starog grada.

more	sea
Crna Gora	Montenegro
preko noći	overnight
rezervisati, rezervišem	to reserve
mesto	place, space
u spavaćim kolima	in a sleeping car
ostajati, ostajem; ostati, ostanem	to stay, to remain
posećivati, posećujem; posetiti	to visit
provoditi; provesti, provedem, proveo	to spend (time)
pravi	right, correct
vreme	time
plaža	beach
misliti	to think
dosadan	boring
provešću	I'll spend
nedelja	week
privatan smeštaj	private accommodation
putnička agencija	travel agency
jeftin	cheap
star	old

QUICK VOCAB

Questions

i How are Robert and Richard travelling to Montenegro?

ii What kind of accommodation have they found in Budva?

Montenegro (**Crna Gora** lit. *Black Mountain*) is a small country of about half a million inhabitants next door to Serbia. Montenegro and Serbia were both parts of Yugoslavia and continued to be joined in a state union until 2006 when Montenegro declared its independence following a referendum. The two countries are traditionally close and share many aspects of their history and culture. The language spoken in Montenegro is very similar to the idiom adopted in this book, with some local variations which are unique but shouldn't hinder comprehension. The capital of Montenegro is Podgorica, but in the 19th century the capital was Cetinje, high in the mountains. The country has a coastline on the Adriatic Sea with tourist resorts around the Bay of Kotor and Budva further south. Contact with Belgrade is by road and rail, with the main railway station located at the large commercial port of Bar. The quickest connection, although more expensive than the land options, is by air. The flight from Belgrade to Podgorica only takes about 30 minutes. There is another airport at Tivat which is more convenient for the tourist resorts on the Adriatic.

How it works

Subgroups of nouns, adjectives and verbs

kola

This word is used in this unit as **spavaća kola** *sleeping car* (on a train). It is also a common term to mean *automobile* or *car*. It is always used in this form as a noun in the neut. plural, therefore, verbs used with it are plural too:

Moja kola su ispred kuće.   *My car is in front of the house.*

There are some other words which are always used in the plural although they refer to a singular object: **vrata** *door* (neut. plural), **novine** *newspaper* (fem. plural).

vreme

This word is neut. meaning both *time* and *weather* and takes an extra syllable -en- before adding case endings singular and plural:

	singular	plural
nom.	vreme	vremena
acc.	vreme	vremena
gen.	vremena	vremena
dat.	vremenu	vremenima
ins.	vremenom	vremenima
loc.	vremenu	vremenima

Some other words follow this same pattern, such as **ime** *name* (gen. singular **imena**), **prezime** *surname* (gen. singular **prezimena**).

ceo

You are aware that in certain words the final **-o** was once **-l** and that the consonant reappears in some parts of the word as in **posao** but **na poslu; on je bio** but **ona je bila**. So it is with the final letter of **ceo** *whole* and some other adjectives:

	singular			plural		
	masc.	fem.	neut.	masc.	fem.	neut.
nom.	ceo	cela	celo	celi	cele	cela

Verbal patterns

Verbs like **putovati** which end in **-ovati** and **posećivati** which end in **-ivati** all take the same **-ujem** ending in the first person singular of the present tense:

ja	putujem	ja	posećujem
ti	putuješ	ti	posećuješ

Verbs like **rezervisati** which end in **-isati** are borrowed from foreign sources and all take the same **-išem** ending in the first person singular of the present tense:

ja	rezervišem
ti	rezerviješ

Verbs like **provesti** and **jesti** which end in **-sti** all take the same **-šću** ending in the first person singular of the future tense:

provešću	ješću
provešćeš	ješćeš

Accusative and genitive adjective endings

Singular

	masc.	fem.	neut.
nom.	nov	nova	novo
acc.	as nom. or gen.	novu	novo
gen.	novog(a)	nove	novog(a)

Singular (adjective ending in a soft consonant)

	masc.	fem.	neut.
nom.	naš	naša	naše
acc.	as nom. or gen.	našu	naše
gen.	našeg(a)	naše	našeg(a)

Plural (soft adjective endings are the same)

	masc.	fem.	neut.
nom.	novi	nove	nova
acc.	nove	nove	nova
gen.	novih	novih	novih

Masc. acc. singular is the same as the nom. when the noun is inanimate and the same as the gen. when the noun is animate.

A journey by car

Activity D

◀) CD 2, TR 1, 03.29

Listen to the recording and read the text in order to find out about the journey Zoran and Vera Petrović undertake. Trace their journey on the road map and find out where they are at the moment of their conversation:

Zoran i Vera Petrović su planirali putovanje kolima u Niš i Vrnjačku Banju. Niš je prilično veliki grad na jugu Srbije. Tamo živi Zoranov brat. Idu kod njega jer ga dugo nisu videli. Iz Niša će voziti do Vrnjačke Banje, gde će boraviti kod Verine sestre od tetke i njenog muža. Oni imaju vilu i izdaju sobe turistima. Iz banje će ići na izlete u brda i u obilazak starih manastira. Sada putuju autoputem od Beograda prema jugu. Usput hoće da posete manastir Ravanicu.

Vera	Da li znaš koliko je daleko izlaz za Ravanicu?
Zoran	Nisam siguran. Ti imaš mapu. Možeš li da nađeš na mapi gde smo?
Vera	Mislim da smo blizu Jagodine.
Zoran	Onda nismo daleko. Skretanje za Ravanicu će biti u Ćupriji.
Vera	Iz Ćuprije ćemo skrenuti prema istoku, zar ne?
Zoran	Tako je. Odatle neće biti daleko do manastira. Ali prvo moramo da nađemo benzinsku pumpu. Nemamo mnogo benzina.
Vera	Vidim nešto sa desne strane puta. Vozi malo sporije. Jeste, to je pumpa. Stani ovde. Možeš ovde da parkiraš.
Zoran	Odlično. Pored pumpe je i kafana, možemo da popijemo kafu i da se odmorimo.

planirati; isplanirati	*to plan*
putovanje	*journey, trip*
prilično	*quite, rather*
jug	*south*
voziti	*to drive*
vila	*villa*
izdavati, izdajem; izdati	*to rent (out)*
brdo	*hill*
obilazak	*visit*
manastir	*monastery*
autoputem	*along the motorway*
prema	*towards* (preposition with dat.)
usput	*on the way*
siguran	*sure, certain*
mapa	*map*
mislim da...	*I think that . . .*
skretanje	*turn*
istok	*east*

QUICK VOCAB

odatle	*from there*
benzinska pumpa	*petrol station*
mnogo	*much, many* (with gen. case)
benzin	*petrol*
sporije	*slower*
stajati, stajem; stati, stanem	*to stop*
parkirati	*to park*
odmarati se; odmoriti se	*to rest*

Questions

i Why are Vera and Zoran going to Niš?

ii Where are they going to stay in Vrnjačka Banja?

Activity E

◀) CD 2, TR 1, 05.20

Vera and Zoran are sitting in the café, looking at the map and talking about their journey. Listen to the recording, read the dialogue and find the places which they mention on the map. Then answer the questions below:

Vera	Kako možemo brzo da stignemo od Niša do Vrnjačke Banje?
Zoran	Mislim da treba da idemo natrag autoputem, a onda da skrenemo prema jugozapadu u pravcu Kruševca i Kraljeva.
Vera	Ostaćemo kod moje sestre pet dana. Jesi li siguran da ćemo imati vremena da vidimo manastire?
Zoran	Siguran sam. Manastir Žiča je vrlo blizu, samo četiri kilometra od Kraljeva. Za Studenicu i Sopoćane treba da idemo iz Kraljeva prema jugu. Skretanje za Studenicu nije daleko. Sopoćani su malo dalje, moramo da prođemo kroz Rašku i Novi Pazar.
Vera	Ja baš želim da vidim Sopoćane. Znam da su freske tamo vrlo lepe.
Zoran	Da, biće to prijatan izlet.

QUICK VOCAB

natrag	*back*
jugozapad	*south-west*
pravac	*direction*
kilometar	*kilometre*
dalje	*further*
ja baš želim ...	*I really want ...*
freska	*fresco*

Questions

i Is the road they are taking from Niš the only possible way to get to Vrnjačka Banja from there?

ii Which monastery is the closest to Vrnjačka Banja and which is the furthest?

Vera and Zoran will visit a number of towns and monasteries in central and southern Serbia (see map given in Activity D where the names are given in the nom. case). When they discuss their journey they, of course, put the names of places in the appropriate case. In English the names of places (and people) are put in the nom.:

u pravcu Kruševca	*in the direction of Kruševac*
skretanje za Studenicu	*the turning for Studenica*
Želim da vidim Sopoćane.	*I want to see Sopoćani.*
	(masc. plural ending)

How it works

Points of the compass

The basic points of the compass are:

sever	*north*	**istok**	*east*
jug	*south*	**zapad**	*west*

To say *in the north*, etc. use the preposition **na** (and loc. case):

Mi smo na severu.	*We are in the north.*
Mi smo na zapadu.	*We are in the west.*

To say *to the north*, etc. use the preposition **na** (and acc. case):

Idemo na sever.	*We are going to the north.*
Idemo na zapad.	*We are going to the west.*

To say *towards the south*, etc. use the preposition **prema** (and dat. case):

prema jugu	*towards the south*
prema istoku	*towards the east*

The forms of the adjectives *northern*, etc. are:

severni	*northern*	**istočni**	*eastern*
južni	*southern*	**zapadni**	*western*

Compound forms such as *south-west* or *south-western* are made by interposing **-o-** between the parts:

jugozapad	*south-west*	**jugozapadni**	*south-western*

Expressions of quantity

Words and phrases to express a quantity of something tend to be followed by the gen. case as in the examples:

mnogo benzina	*much (a lot of) petrol*
litar mleka	*a litre of milk*
malo vode	*a little water*
Koliko imaš godina?	*How old are you?*

Phrases and expressions

- The gen. case is used in expressions of quantity meaning *some* or *any*:

  Nemam vremena.   *I haven't any time.*

- Serbian has an intensifying particle **baš** *quite, really* which is used with verbs, adjectives and adverbs:

  Nisam baš siguran.   *I am not quite sure.*
  Ja baš želim da vidim Sopoćane.   *I really want to see Sopoćani.*

- To say *by motorway* or *along the street* use the ins. case of the noun:

  Idemo natrag autoputem.*   *We go back by the motorway.*
  Idu ulicom.   *They are going along/down the street.*

*The word **put** is treated as if it has a soft ending in the ins. singular and the plural: **putem** and **putevi**.

Practice

4 You are working in Belgrade and are planning to spend your summer holiday on Kopaonik. How would you tell your plans to your Serbian friend? Try to answer some of the following questions: Kuda ideš na letovanje? Kako ćeš putovati? Gde ćeš boraviti? Koliko ćeš ostati tamo? Šta ćeš raditi?

5 Study the road map given in Activity D and find out which of the following statements are true (**istina**) and which are false (**neistina**):

   a Kraljevo se nalazi na jugu od Beograda.
   b Kruševac je na jugozapadu od Kraljeva.
   c Iz Beograda možemo stići do Kraljeva preko Kragujevca.
   d Kopaonik je na severu od Kraljeva.
   e Put od Beograda do Niša ide preko Kruševca.
   f Kragujevac nije na putu za Niš.

6 You have been asked by some tourists how to get from Belgrade to Vrnjačka Banja by car. Look at the map in Activity D again and explain to them two possible options.

7 Listen to the conversation between Milan and Branka. Find out how they plan to spend their summer holiday and answer the questions below:

🔊 **CD 2, TR 1, 06.15**

a Kuda će Branka ići na letovanje?
b Da li će ići sama?
c Kako će putovati?
d Koliko će ostati?
e Da li će Milan ići na more?
f Hoće li on putovati autobusom?
g Da li je već rezervisao hotelsku sobu?

8 Put the nouns and adjectives in brackets into the genitive case, singular or plural as appropriate, as required after **ima/nema** or after the expressions of quantity:

a Nema (hleb).
b Mogu li dobiti malo (voda)?
c Nemamo mnogo (vreme).
d U Beogradu ima (dobri restorani).
e U turističkom naselju nema (jeftine sobe).
f Ima li na plaži mnogo (ljudi)?
g Blizu hotela ima (lepe šume).
h Na pumpi nema (benzin).

Test yourself

Here you can check some of the things you have learnt in this unit. Look at the questions below and choose the right answer:

1 How would you tell your Serbian friend that you and your family will rent a flat in Belgrade: **Mi . . . . iznajmiti stan u Beogradu?**

    a ću   **b** ćete   **c** ćemo

2 Which word would you use if you want to say that you will not eat in the hotel: **Ja . . . . jesti u hotelu?**

    a neće   **b** nećeš   **c** neću

3 Which of the two options would you use to complete the question **Da li . . . . vozom?**

   a ćeš ići   **b** ići ćeš

4 How would you say *There are no problems*: **Nema . . . . ?**

   a problem   **b** problemi   **c** problema

5 What does **Volim te** mean?

   a I love her.   **b** I love you.   **c** I love him.

6 How do you say that you are interested in sport?

   a Zanima me sport.
   b Zanima te sport.
   c Zanima je sport.

7 **Košarka** is one of the most popular sports in Serbia. What is this game called in English?

   a handball   **b** volleyball   **c** basketball

8 How do you say *cheap* in Serbian?

   a skup   **b** jeftin   **c** udoban

9 You are told **Treba da vozite na sever.** Which direction should you drive?

   a to the north   **b** to the west   **c** to the south

10 Where is Serbia situated?

   a na jugozapadu Evrope
   b na jugoistoku Evrope
   c na severozapadu Evrope

12

Buying travel tickets

In this unit you will learn:

- How to buy travel tickets
- Phrases for travelling by train, bus and air
- Days of the week
- How to express dates
- Dative, instrumental and locative pronouns
- Endings for dative, instrumental and locative adjectives

Travelling by bus

Activity A

◀) CD 2, TR 2

Listen to the passenger buying a bus ticket from Niš to Novi Sad, read the passage below and then answer the questions which follow:

Путник	Молим вас, једну карту за петак ове недеље за Нови Сад.
Службеник	За колико сати?
Путник	Има ли неки аутобус око седам сати ујутро?
Службеник	Има један. Полази у седам и петнаест.
Путник	И када стиже у Нови Сад?
Службеник	У петнаест до дванаест.
Путник	Добро. Дајте ми карту за тај аутобус.
Службеник	Хоћете повратну карту или у једном правцу?
Путник	Повратну.
Службеник	Када хоћете да се вратите?

Путник	У недељу увече.
Службеник	Имате један аутобус у пола осам увече из Новог Сада.
Путник	У реду.
Службеник	Изволите, осамсто десет динара.

за петак	*for Friday*
ове недеље	*this week*
За колико сати?	*For what time?*
ујутро	*in the morning*
полазити, поћи, пођем, пошао	*to set off*
повратна карта	*return ticket*
карта у једном правцу	*one-way ticket*
враћати се, вратити се	*to return*
у недељу	*on Sunday*

Questions

i At what time does his bus leave Niš?

ii How much does he pay for his ticket?

Serbia has a comprehensive and relatively inexpensive bus service linking towns and villages. It is a good idea to check on times and routes as some services are express buses going directly between major urban centres while others call at many more stops. Look at times of departure (**полазак**) and times of arrival (**долазак**) on the timetable (**ред вожње**) and you may need to ask times for a connection (**веза**). When buying a ticket you ask for **карта за . . .** giving the name of your destination in the acc. case.

How it works

Days of the week

The days of the week in Serbian are written with a small letter:

понедељак	*Monday*
уторак	*Tuesday*
среда	*Wednesday*
четвртак	*Thursday*
петак	*Friday*

| субота | Saturday |
| недеља | Sunday |

When you want to say *for a day* use **за** with the acc. case:

Молим вас, једну карту   *A ticket for Friday, please.*
   за петак.

When you want to say *on a day* use **у** with the acc. case:

Враћам се у недељу увече.   *I am returning on Sunday in the evening.*

When you want to say *on Mondays* etc. use the ins. singular ending:

| понедељком | *on Mondays* |
| средом | *on Wednesdays* |

The word **недеља** means *week* as well as *Sunday*, so you have to listen to the context in which the word is used to get the correct meaning (also **недељно** *weekly*).

Expressions of time are often put in the gen. case in Serbian:

ове недеље	*this week*
прошле недеље	*last week*
идуће недеље	*next week*
једног дана	*one day*
ове године	*this year*

Times of day

You need to be able to specify whether you want tickets for six o'clock in the morning or the evening. Look at the following for how to express this in Serbian:

morning	**јутро**	*evening*	**вече**
this morning	**јутрос**	*this evening*	**вечерас**
in the morning	**ујутро**	*in the evening*	**увече**

(the form **ујутру** *in the morning* is also used)

day	**дан**	*night*	**ноћ**
today	**данас**	*tonight*	**ноћас**
by day	**дању**	*by night*	**ноћу**

(**ноћ** is a fem. noun and is only used to refer to times after midnight)

at midday	**у подне**
before noon	**пре подне**
afternoon	**после подне**
at midnight	**у поноћ**

yesterday	**јуче**	*tomorrow*	**сутра**
day before yesterday	**прекјуче**	*day after tomorrow*	**прексутра**

Serbian also has a special form for saying *last night* or *yesterday evening* **синоћ**.

Activity B

🔊 **CD 2, TR 2, 01.10**

Vesna is in the travel agency arranging travel to Kopaonik for herself, Ana and Ana's brother. Listen to the recording and answer the following questions before reading the passage:

Questions

i How many buses go to Kopaonik in the morning?
ii At what time do they leave?
iii When does the train to Kopaonik leave?

Весна	Добар дан.
Службеница	Добар дан, изволите?
Весна	Желим да купим карте за Копаоник. Кажите ми, молим вас, какав превоз постоји до тамо.
Службеница	Можете да идете аутобусом или возом. Из Београда имате два аутобуса. Један полази у седам часова, а други мало касније, у седам часова и седамнаест минута.
Весна	Да ли они иду истим путем?
Службеница	Не. Први аутобус иде преко Крушевца и Бруса, други преко Краљева и Ибарском долином.
Весна	А у колико сати иде воз?
Службеница	Има само један воз дневно. Полази у четрнаест часова и четрдесет пет минута.
Весна	Њиме ћемо стићи тек увече. То је сувише касно. Колико кошта карта за тај аутобус који иде аутопутем преко Крушевца?

Службеница	У једном правцу кошта четиристо двадесет динара.
	Повратна карта је шестсто деведесет.
Весна	Дајте ми три повратне карте, молим вас.
Службеница	За када?
Весна	За седми август. Враћамо се двадесет првог августа.
Службеница	У тим аутобусима је обавезна резервација седишта.
Весна	У реду.
Службеница	Изволите ваше карте. Хвала вам.

QUICK VOCAB

службеница	*clerk* (woman)
превоз	*transport*
мало касније	*a little later*
истим путем	*by the same road*
Ибарском долином	*along the Ibar valley*
њиме	*by it* (ins. of **он**, **оно**)
тек	*as late as, not until*
сувише касно	*too late*
август	*August*
у тим аутобусима	*in those buses*
обавезан	*obligatory*
резервација	*reservation*
седиште	*seat*

There are two main road routes going south towards the mountain resort of Kopaonik. One goes via Kruševac and Brus using the main motorway for some of the way. The other route is slower via Kraljevo and then following the road down the valley of the River Ibar. There is only one train daily, which does not run at a convenient time for Vesna and her friends.

How it works

Dative, instrumental and locative pronouns

nom.	dat.		ins.	loc.
	short	long		
ja	ми	мени	мном(е)	мени
ти	ти	теби	тобом	теби

он/о	му	њему	њим(е)	њему
она	јој	њој	њом(е)	њој
ми	нам	нама	нама	нама
ви	вам	вама	вама	вама
они	им	њима	њима	њима

The dat. and loc. forms of the personal pronouns are the same except that the loc. has no short form as it is only ever used with prepositions. The ins. forms of the personal pronouns also have no short form, but sometimes an extra **e** is added at the end when the pronoun is used without a preposition:

| Идем њиме. | *I am going by it* (e.g. *by that train*). |
| Идем са њим. | *I am going with him.* |

Dative, instrumental and locative adjective endings

Singular

	masc.	fem.	neut.
nom.	нов	нова	ново
dat.	новом(е)	новој	новом(е)
ins.	новим	новом	новим
loc.	новом(е)	новој	новом(е)

Singular (adjective ending in a soft consonant)

	masc.	fem.	neut.
nom.	наш	наша	наше
dat.	нашем(у)	нашој	нашем(у)
ins.	нашим	нашом	нашим
loc.	нашем(у)	нашој	нашем(у)

Plural (soft adjective endings are the same)

	masc.	fem.	neut.
nom.	нови	нове	нова
dat.	новим(а)	новим(а)	новим(а)
ins.	новим(а)	новим(а)	новим(а)
loc.	новим(а)	новим(а)	новим(а)

The rule relating to soft adjective endings (when -o- changes to -e-) applies only to masc. and neut. forms and does not apply to fem. ins. singular endings. Plural endings are identical for all adjectives. Additional vowels are added when the adjective is used without a noun.

Dates

The word for *month* in Serbian is **месец** (also **месечно** *monthly*). The names of the months are written with a small letter:

јануар	*January*	**јул**	*July*
фебруар	*February*	**август**	*August*
март	*March*	**септембар**	*September*
април	*April*	**октобар**	*October*
мај	*May*	**новембар**	*November*
јун	*June*	**децембар**	*December*

To state a date use the ordinal form of the number and the nom. case:

Данас је први јануар.	*Today is 1 January.*
Сутра ће бити осамнаести мај.	*Tomorrow will be 18 May.*

In compound numbers only the last word is expressed as an ordinal number:

Двадесет осми август	*28 August*
Тридесет први децембар	*31 December*

To state *on* a date use the gen. case:

Враћамо се двадесет првог августа.	*We are coming back on 21 August.*
Идемо шестог јула.	*We are going on 6 July.*

To say *in* a month use **у** with the loc. case:

у фебруару	*in February*
у децембру	*in December*

When writing a date in Serbian, ordinal numbers written in figures are followed by a full stop:

Данас је 1. јануар.	*Today is 1 January.*
Враћамо се 21. августа.	*We are coming back on 21 August.*

Insight

Remember that to say *on a day of the week* you use the preposition **у** with the accusative case:

Путујем у среду.

To say that you want a ticket *for a particular day* use the preposition **за** followed by the accusative case:

Дајте ми карту за среду.

To say *on a date* use the genitive case:

Путујем првог фебруара.

To say *for a date* use **за** with the accusative case:

Дајте ми карту за први фебруар.

When saying a year use the formula *(one)thousand nine hundred ninety fifth year* with the acc. case for *thousand* (i.e. **хиљаду** without a word for *one*).

Only the last numeral is an ordinal, which is then put in the gen. case to say *in* a year. When writing the year in figures put a full stop after the ordinal number:

хиљаду деветсто деведесет пете године	*in 1995*
две хиљадите	*in 2000*
две хиљаде десете године	*in 2010*
23. јануара 1997.	*on 23 January 1997*

Practice

1 You are in a travel agency looking for information about the times of the buses from Subotica in north Serbia, through Belgrade, to Niš in south Serbia. From Niš you and your travel companion intend to take a connection (**веза**) to Skopje (Serb. **Скопље**), the capital of Macedonia. Check the timetable and answer your partner's questions:

Ниш Експрес
Полазак

02.00	Суботица
03.30	Нови Сад
04.45	Београд
06.35	Ћуприја
06.50	Параћин
08.00	Ниш

Веза из Ниша у
08.10^h за Скопље.

a Колико дуго траје пут аутобусом од Суботице до Ниша? (*How long does the journey last . . . ?*)

b У колико сати полази аутобус из Суботице?

c Када стиже у Ниш?

d Колико дуго треба да чекамо на везу за Скопље?

2 Jelena is at the ticket office at the bus station. She wants to buy two return tickets to Budva in Montenegro. Fill in her part of the conversation.

◄)) **CD 2, TR 2, 02.34**

Јелена	*How much does a ticket to Budva cost, please?*
Службеник	Повратна карта или у једном правцу?
Јелена	*Return.*
Службеник	Хиљаду петсто динара.
Јелена	*Give me two return tickets for Saturday 15 July.*
Службеник	Када желите да путујете, ујутро или увече?
Јелена	*In the evening.*
Службеник	Имам два седишта у аутобусу који полази у десет и двадесет.
Јелена	*Does that bus go via Kraljevo?*
Службеник	Не, преко Ужица.
Јелена	*At what time does it arrive in Budva?*
Службеник	У једанаест пре подне.
Јелена	*All right.*
Службеник	Када желите да се вратите?
Јелена	*On 30 July.*
Службеник	Добро. То је три хиљаде динара.
Јелена	*Here you are. Thank you.*

3 Milan is trying to arrange to meet his old friends Mira and Janko after he comes back from his summer holiday. Listen to their conversation, find out when they are going to be away on holiday and fill in the grid below with the dates of their departure and arrival. When will they all be back in Belgrade and able to meet?

🔊 **CD 2, TR 2, 04.30**

a Милан	
b Мира	
c Јанко	

4 Add the correct case ending to the adjectives in the sentences below:

a Путовали смо велик _____ аутобусом.
b Изнајмио је јефтин апартман у леп _____ крају града.
c Била сам на одмору са стар _____ пријатељима.
d Данас ћемо вечерати у нов _____ ресторану.
e Хоћеш ли да идемо у град мој _____ колима?
f Све собе у наш _____ хотелу имају купатило.
g Туристичко насеље се налази у густ _____ шуми.
h Да ли сте писали њен _____ родитељима?

5 Put the pronoun given in brackets into the appropriate case and form. First look at the example:

e.g. Дајте (ја) једну карту.
Дајте ми једну карту.

a Купила сам (ви) хлеб и млеко.
b Бићемо са (они) сутра увече.
c Можете ли да (ја) дате њену адресу?
d Дајте (ми) три карте.
e Хоћеш ли да идеш са (ја) на море?
f Писала сам (он) јуче.
g Да ли је био са (ти) на летовању?
h Треба да (она) пишемо.

Travelling by train

Activity C

🔊 **CD 2, TR 2, 05.27**

Martin is a Czech working in Belgrade. His company has called him urgently to Prague for a business meeting. He could not get a plane ticket in time and has to travel by train. Listen to what happened at the railway station and answer the questions below:

> Мартин је Чех. Ради у Београду. Он је представник једне чешке фирме. Фирма увози из Србије воће и производи џемове и сокове. Продају своје производе свим европским земљама, чак извозе и у Азију и Аустралију. Мартин обично путује између Београда и Прага авионом, али сада мора хитно да се врати на пословни састанак. Није могао да купи авионску карту. Ишао је на железничку станицу да тражи информације о међународним возовима. Рекли су му да један воз полази у десет увече сваког дана. Може да иде тим возом. Стићи ће у Праг сутрадан у један сат после подне. То му одговара јер састанак почиње у четири сата. Одмах је купио повратну карту првог разреда и те вечери се вратио на станицу да путује у Праг.

QUICK VOCAB

Чех	*Czech* (man)
представник	*representative*
увозити	*to import*
воће	*fruit*
производити	*to produce*
производ	*product*
европски	*European*
извозити	*to export*
Азија	*Asia*
обично	*usually*
хитно	*urgently*
састанак	*meeting*
међународни	*international*
рећи, рекао (followed by dat.)	*to say, to tell*
сваки	*every*
сутрадан	*tomorrow, the next day*

одговарати	to suit
почињати, почињем,	to begin
почети, почнем	
карта првог разреда	first-class ticket
те вечери	on that evening

Questions

i When does Martin's train arrive in Prague?
ii What kind of ticket does he buy?

How it works

Nouns: monosyllabic masc. nouns and *вече*

Most masc. nouns with one syllable take an extended stem in the plural before adding case endings such as **џемови** and **сокови**. Some, however, do not:

Чех	plural	Чеси
Грк	plural	Грци
дан	plural	дани

and some other fairly common words including **зуб** *tooth*, **гост** *guest*, **коњ** *horse*.

Вече *evening* is an unusual noun in that it is considered a neut. noun in the nom. voc. and acc. singular cases but in all others is considered to be a fem. noun ending in **-р** like **ствар** with the endings **вечери** (gen. dat. ins. loc. singular and nom. voc. acc. gen. plural) and **вечерима** (dat. ins. loc. plural). The word is used in Activity C in the gen. as an expression of time: **те вечери** *that evening*.

Endings for adjectives *сав, овај* and *мој*

сав

	Singular			Plural		
	masc.	fem.	neut.	masc.	fem.	neut
nom.	сав	сва	све	сви	све	сва

The endings for **сав** are regular except that it is treated as a soft adjective in the masc. and neut. with the gen. and dat. singular forms **свег(а)** and **свем(у)**.

Also, remember that **сви** (masc. plural) means *everyone* and **све** (neut. singular) means *everything*.

| Сви су стигли. | *Everyone has arrived.* |
| Све је било на столу. | *Everything was on the table.* |

овај

	Singular			Plural		
	masc.	fem.	neut.	masc.	fem.	neut
nom.	**овај**	**ова**	**ово**	**ови**	**ове**	**ова**

The stem for **овај** is **ов-** and adjective endings are added to this. The stem for **тај** is **т-** and for **онај** is **он-**.

мој

	Singular				Plural		
	masc.	fem.	neut.		masc.	fem.	neut.
nom.	**мој**	**моја**	**моје**	nom.	**моји**	**моје**	**моја**
acc.	nom. or gen.	**моју**	**моје**	acc.	**моје**	**моје**	**моја**
gen.	**мог(а)** **мојег(а)**	**моје**	**мог(а)** **мојег(а)**	gen.		**мојих**	
dat.	**мом(е)** **мојем(у)**	**мојој**	**мом(е)** **мојем(у)**	dat.		**мојим(а)**	
ins.	**мојим**	**мојом**	**мојим**	ins.		**мојим(а)**	
loc.	**мом(е)** **мојем(у)**	**мојој**	**мом(е)** **мојем(у)**	loc.		**мојим(а)**	

The shorter forms for the gen., dat. and loc. in masc. and neut. singular are preferred.

The endings for gen., dat., ins., and loc. in the plural are the same for all genders.

The adjectives **твој** and **свој** follow the same pattern as **мој**.

To say, tell

The verb **рећи, рекао** is a perfective used in the past tense, the future tense and in the imperative but not in the present tense. To express *to say, tell* in the present tense use another verb **казати, кажем** which may be used both as imperfective and perfective aspect:

Кажем ти да ћу доћи сутра.	*I am telling you that I shall come tomorrow.*
Морам да ти кажем.	*I have to tell you.*
Рекао ми је.	*He told me.*
Рекли су да воз полази у 7 сати.	*They said that the train leaves at seven o'clock.*
Реците ми . . .	*Tell me . . .* (imperative **ви** form)

The word **да** means *that* in these expressions:

Рекао је да . . .	*He said that . . .*
Мислим да . . .	*I think that . . .*
Знали смо да . . .	*We knew that . . .*

Reflexive verbs

A reflexive verb is one which expresses an action done to oneself, e.g. *I washed myself.* Many verbs in Serbian can take this form with the addition of **се** although it may not always be apparent from an English translation why this is so. The expression **зовем се** means literally *I call myself* (i.e. my name is). The verb **враћати, вратити** in Serbian means *to give back, return something* whereas when used reflexively **враћати се, вратити се** means *to go back* (i.e. to return oneself).

In the past and future tenses reflexive verbs continue to include the reflexive pronoun **се** after the auxiliary verb:

Вратићемо се.	*We shall go back.*
Вратили смо се.	*We went back.*

Except that the auxiliary verb is omitted in the third person singular of the past tense:

Вратио се.	*He went back.*
Вратила се.	*She went back.*

Travelling by air

Activity D

🔊 **CD 2, TR 2, 06.40**

Роберт је последњи пут био код куће у Енглеској у јануару. Сада је мај и он хоће да купи карту да иде кући током распуста. Свратио је у ЈАТ-ову агенцију на Булевару краља Александра.

Роберт	Добар дан.
Службеник	Изволите?
Роберт	Молим вас, тражим информације о летовима за Енглеску.
Службеник	Да . . . шта вам треба?
Роберт	Да ли ЈАТ лети у Енглеску сваког дана?
Службеник	Летимо из Београда сваког дана осим среде.
Роберт	Добро. Желим да путујем крајем следећег месеца, двадесет трећег јуна.
Службеник	Само тренутак, да видим . . . Не, жао ми је, али тај авион је већ пун. Хоћете ли да вас ставим на листу чекања?
Роберт	Није потребно. Могу и после тога да путујем. Да ли имате слободно место двадесет петог јуна?
Службеник	На жалост, све је пуно до почетка јула. Могу одмах да вам резервишем карту за лет другог јула.
Роберт	У реду. То ми одговара.
Службеник	Да ли желите отворен или фиксиран повратак?
Роберт	Морам да се вратим до краја јула. Могу ли да путујем натраг двадесет осмог јула?
Службеник	Можете, господине. Једна повратна карта, полазак другог јула у десет и четрдесет пет. Долазак у Лондон у дванаест и четрдесет. Повратак је двадесет осмог јула у тринаест и четрдесет из Лондона, долазак у Београд у седамнаест и двадесет.

QUICK VOCAB

последњи пут	*last time*
у Енглеској	*in England*
код куће	*at home*
кући	*to home*
током распуста	*during the vacation*

свраћати, свратити	*to drop in, call at*
лет	*flight*
Шта вам треба?	*What do you need?*
летети	*to fly*
осим	*except* (preposition with gen.)
крајем следећег месеца	*at the end of next month*
тренутак	*moment*
да видим	*let me see*
жао ми је	*I am sorry*
стављати, ставити	*to put, place*
листа чекања	*waiting list*
потребан	*necessary*
слободан	*free, vacant*
на жалост	*unfortunately*
почетак	*beginning*
отворен повратак	*open return*
фиксиран	*fixed*
до краја	*by the end of* (followed by gen. case)

Question

What are Robert's departure and return dates?

The national airline is **JAT** which is the acronym from **Југословенски аеротранспорт**. It has offices (**JAT-ове агенције**) in the centre of Belgrade on Булевар краља Александра, Краља Милана and at the hotel *Славија*. JAT operates regular flights to many European capitals and beyond. The flight time from London to Belgrade is about 2 hours 30 minutes.

How it works

Names of countries

The names of some countries in Serbian are adjectives and they take adjective case endings. All such names end in **-ска, -шка** or **-чка** and they are all fem.:

Енглеска *England*	у Енглескoj	из Енглеске
	in England	*from England*
Француска *France*	у Француској	из Француске
Немачка *Germany*	у Немачкој	из Немачке
Хрватска *Croatia*	у Хрватској	из Хрватске

But note:

Америка *America*	у Америци	из Америке
Аустралија *Australia*	у Аустралији	из Аустралије
Јапан *Japan*	у Јапану	из Јапана
Русија *Russia*	у Русији	из Русије
Србија *Serbia*	у Србији	из Србије

Some states have compound names formed with both adjectives and nouns:

Сједињене Америчке Државе (САД)	*United States of America (USA)*
у Сједињеним Америчким Државама	*In the United States of America*
Велика Британија	*Great Britain*
из Велике Британије	*from Great Britain*

Expressions of time

The dialogue in Activity D contains a number of useful expressions of time. These are prepositions or prepositional phrases followed by the gen. case:

током or у току	*during*
током распуста	*during the vacation (school or university)*
крајем or на крају	*at the end of*
крајем идуће недеље	*at the end of next week*
почетком or на почетку	*at the beginning of*
почетком деведесетих	*at the beginning of the 90s (the 1990s)*
средином or у средини	*in the middle of*
средином октобра	*in the middle of October*
до краја	*by the end of*

| до краја фебруара | *by the end of February* |

As an expression of time **до** means *by*:

до почетка августа	*by the beginning of August*
до јануара	*by January*
до два сата	*by two o'clock*

Saying what you need

To say that you need something use **треба** with the dat. case for the person concerned and the nom. case for the thing needed:

Шта вам треба?	*What do you need?*
Шта Роберту треба?	*What does Robert need?*
Треба ми авионска карта.	*I need an aeroplane ticket.*
Роберту треба авионска карта.	*Robert needs an aeroplane ticket.*

Saying 'sorry'

The phrase **жао ми је** *I am sorry* is an expression of regret that you are unable to comply with a request or that you feel sympathy for someone's misfortune, in which case *I am sorry for him* is **жао ми га је** (i.e. the dat. pronoun for yourself and the gen. for the other person).

The phrase **извините** is the equivalent of saying *pardon me* or *excuse me* if you want to attract someone's attention or to excuse yourself if you inconvenience someone else by dialling a wrong telephone number or bumping into someone in the street. For the latter occasion the word **пардон** is also used.

Using *код* meaning 'at home' or 'to see someone'

To say you are *at home* use the phrase **код куће** and for going *to home* use **кући**:

| Ја сам код куће. | *I am at home.* |
| Идем кући. | *I am going home.* |

To say that you are either *at the house* of someone or going *to the house* of someone use **код** followed by the gen. case of the person:

| Ја сам код брата. | *I am at my brother's.* |
| Идем код брата. | *I am going to my brother's.* |

This same construction is also used for saying that you are *going to see someone* such as a doctor:

Треба да идеш код лекара.   *You should go and see a doctor.*

Practice

6 Look at the timetable for flights from Belgrade to Montenegro (destinations Podgorica and Tivat) and answer the questions below:

Ред летења: 25. март–27. октобар							
Подгорица: Број летова ЈY 662, ЈY 666, ЈY 668							
Тиват: Број летова ЈY 680, ЈY 686, ЈY 690							

ЛЕТ	ПОН	УТО	СРЕ	ЧЕТ	ПЕТ	СУБ	НЕД
JU 662	9.15	7.15	7.15	7.15	7.15	7.15	
JU 666	18.10	18.10	18.10	18.10	18.10	14.45	14.45
JU 668	20.50	20.50	20.50	20.50	20.50	20.50	20.50
JU 680	7.20	6.30	7.20	8.25	8.25	7.20	7.20
JU 686	13.20	14.15	13.20	14.15	13.20	14.15	
JU 690					20.10	20.10	20.10

a У колико сати је први лет за Подгорицу средом?

b У колико сати су летови за Подгорицу суботом и недељом?

c Да ли има летова за Тиват увече?

7 You are at one of the JAT offices in Belgrade. You want to travel to Podgorica where you have a business meeting on Monday 14 March, at 12 o'clock. Look at the timetable above to see which flight suits you best and fill in your part of the conversation:

◀) CD 2, TR 2, 08.29

Ви	*I want to buy a ticket to Podgorica, please.*
Службеник	Када желите да путујете?

Ви	*On 14 March.*
Службеник	Ујутро или увече?
Ви	*In the morning.*
Службеник	Четрнаести је понедељак. Понедељком ујутро имамо лет у девет и петнаест.
Ви	*All right. That suits me.*
Службеник	Хоћете ли повратну карту или у једном правцу?
Ви	*Return.*
Службеник	Желите ли фиксиран или отворен повратак?
Ви	*Fixed. Is there an evening flight to Belgrade on the 14th?*
Службеник	Понедељком увече има два лета из Подгорице. Први је у деветнаест и двадесет, а други у двадесет два часа.
Ви	*Give me a ticket for the first flight, please. How much does a return ticket cost?*
Службеник	Шест хиљада динара. Аеродромска такса је двеста динара.
Ви	*All right. I'll take the ticket.*

Test yourself

1 Which day of the week comes after **уторак**?

    a петак   **b** недеља   **c** среда

2 You want to travel on Saturday. Which word would you use to fill the gap in the sentence **Хоћу да резервишем карту . . . . . суботу**?

    a за   **b** у   **c** на

3 Which word means *this evening*?

    a вече   **b** увече   **c** вечерас

4 How would you tell your friend that you will write to him: **Писаћу . . . . . .**?

    a те   **b** ти   **c** тобом

5 What is the meaning of the phrase **идуће недеље**?

    a last week   **b** next week   **c** this week

6 How would you say that you will arrive by the first bus: **Стићи ћу** . . . .

   a првом аутобусу   **b** први аутобус   **c** првим аутобусом

7 What is the Serbian word for *departure*?

   a полазак   **b** долазак   **c** улазак

8 What does **са њим** mean?

   a with him   **b** with her   **c** with them

9 How would you say that you live in England: **Живим у** . . . .?

   a Енглеска   **b** Енглеску   **c** Енглеској

10 How would you say that you are travelling home: **Путујем** . . . . . .?

   a кући   **b** код куће   **c** у кућу

13

Daily routine

In this unit you will learn:

- How to describe your daily routine
- Phrases for discussing future plans
- Expressions for talking about the weather
- How to form adverbs and impersonal expressions
- About word order and short forms
- How to form the future exact tense

Miloš talks about a normal day

Activity A

◄ CD 2, TR 3

Listen to Miloš describing his daily routine on the recording, read the text and answer the questions that follow:

Moj budilnik zvoni u šest sati i budi me. Odmah ustajem, idem u kupatilo i brzo se tuširam. Za doručak uvek jedem malo, možda kiflu ili neko voće, i pijem kafu. Svi tada još spavaju. Tiho je u kuhinji dok se spremam za polazak. Izlazim iz našeg stana u pola sedam. Jedan moj prijatelj radi u istoj firmi i on me čeka na kraju ulice u kolima. Ja mu kažem da ne treba, da nije daleko. Mogu da idem i autobusom. Ali on kaže da mu nije teško. To mu je usput. Mora da prođe pored moje ulice na putu prema poslu.

Stižemo na posao za dvadesetak minuta i počinjemo da radimo u sedam sati. U podne imamo pauzu. Ta pauza traje pola sata. Idemo u menzu, gde možemo da popijemo kafu ili nešto pojedemo. Završavamo posao u tri kada idemo kući. Kod kuće Biljana i ja ručamo u četiri i posle toga se odmaramo. Maja ponekad ruča s nama, a ponekad je nema kod kuće. Kada je bila mala, volela je da nam za stolom ispriča šta se toga dana desilo u školi. Bilo nam je zabavno da slušamo njene priče o učiteljima i školskim drugaricama.

Uveče gledamo televiziju, ali više volimo da idemo u bioskop ili u pozorište. Ako je vreme lepo, idemo u šetnju i svraćamo u neku kafanu da popijemo čašu vina. Volimo društvo i često zovemo prijatelje u goste. Lepo nam je da sedimo sa njima i razgovaramo. Idemo na spavanje oko ponoći.

budilnik	*alarm clock*
zvoniti; zazvoniti	*to ring*
buditi; probuditi	*to wake*
ustajati, ustajem; ustati, ustanem	*to get up*
tuširati se; istuširati se	*to shower*
uvek	*always*
tada	*at that time*
spavati	*to sleep*
tih	*quiet*
spremati se; spremiti se	*to get ready*
izlaziti; izići, iziđem, izišao	*to go out*
teško je	*it is difficult*
dvadesetak	*around 20*
pauza	*pause, break*
menza	*canteen*
završavati; završiti	*to finish*
ponekad je nema kod kuće	*sometimes she is not at home*
za stolom	*at the table*
pričati; ispričati	*to tell, to talk*
dešavati se; desiti se	*to happen*
zabavno	*amusing, entertaining*
slušati	*to listen*
priča	*story*
televizija	*television*
više volimo . . .	*we prefer . . .*
ako	*if*
često	*often*
zovemo prijatelje u goste	*we invite friends for a visit*

sedeti, sedim	*to be sitting*
razgovarati	*to talk, to chat*
idemo na spavanje	*we go to bed*

Questions

i At what time does Miloš get up?
ii How does he go to work, by bus or by car?
iii What are his working hours?

How it works

Adverbs and impersonal expressions

Adverbs are words which qualify other words like verbs or adjectives: **brzo se tuširam** *I shower quickly*. In English these words are usually formed by adding -ly to an adjective. In Serbian they are usually taken from the neut. singular form of the adjective: **brz – brzo** *quick – quickly*. There are adverbs which are not formed according to these simple rules, such as **vrlo** or **veoma** *very*; **odmah** *immediately*. These are best learnt separately. The adverbs from adjectives which end in -**ski** are taken from the masc. form of the adjective.

Adverbs are also used in Serbian with the third person singular of the verb *to be* as impersonal expressions. These are the equivalent of saying in English *it is . . .*:

| Tiho je u kuhinji. | *It is quiet in the kitchen.* |
| Bilo je tiho u kuhinji. | *It was quiet in the kitchen.* |

The person concerned is expressed in the dat. case as in the following examples:

| Kaže da mu nije teško. | *He says that it is not difficult for him.* |
| Bilo nam je zabavno. | *It was fun for us.* |

There are further examples later in this unit such as:

lako mi je da vozim	*it is easy for me to drive* (I find it easy to drive)
hladno je	*it is cold*
dosadno im je	*it is boring for them* (they find it boring)

More about verbal aspects

In Activity A most verbs are in the imperfective aspect as Miloš is recounting what he does every day as a matter of daily routine. Verbs used in the present tense in order to express current, i.e. unfinished, or general actions are used in the imperfective aspect. In Activity B most verbs are in the perfective aspect since Maja is telling what happened yesterday when actions were performed once and completed.

All verbs which follow **počinjati; početi** *to begin* are automatically put into the imperfective aspect:

> **Počinjemo da radimo u**   *We begin working at*
> **sedam sati.**   *seven o'clock.*

Some verbs only possess one form for both aspects: e.g. **ići**; verbs which are connected with meal times **doručkovati, ručati, večerati;** verbs which are borrowed from foreign languages **telefonirati, rezervisati;** verbs to do with the senses **videti, čuti.**

There is not . . ./There are not . . . **Nema . . .**

You are already aware that the expression **nema** with the gen. case means *there is not . . ./there are not . . .* It is also used to express that someone is not there, not at home, or not in the office:

> **Ponekad Maja ruča sa**   *Sometimes Maja has lunch*
> **nama, a ponekad je**   *with us and sometimes she*
> **nema kod kuće.**   *is not at home.*

Maja's day at the university

Activity B

◀) CD 2, TR 3, 01.40

Listen to Maja recounting what happened to her yesterday at the university, read the text and then answer the questions that follow:

> Juče sam se probudila u pola devet. Istuširala sam se, doručkovala i brzo izišla iz kuče. Vreme nije bilo dobro. Padala je kiša i duvao je vetar. Čekala sam autobus. Uskoro je došao. Ušla sam u njega i sela. Put do centra grada

je trajao otprilike petnaest minuta. Sišla sam na Studentskom trgu, prešla ulicu i ušla u zgradu Filološkog fakulteta. Katedra za anglistiku se nalazi na drugom spratu. Moje prvo predavanje je počelo u deset sati.

Posle predavanja, u jedanaest, išla sam sa prijateljima u bife, gde smo naručili kafu. Rekla sam Neveni, jednoj svojoj drugarici, da sam zaboravila svoj udžbenik za sledeći čas. Ona je imala drugo predavanje, ali je nosila taj udžbenik sa sobom u torbi. Dala mi ga je i ja sam otišla na čas. Kasnije sam joj ga vratila.

Naše poslednje predavanje se završilo u četiri posle podne. Neki studenti su išli kući, ali ja sam morala da ostanem još malo u biblioteci. Studiram englesku književnost i spremam esej o Šekspiru. Dogovorila sam se sa drugaricama da se nađemo u poslastičarnici na Trgu Republike. Vreme je tada bilo lepo, sunce je sijalo, i mi smo mogle da sedimo napolju. Ispričala sam im kako je moj brat od ujaka iz Engleske bio kod nas. Nevena me je dosta pitala o njemu. Kaže da želi da ga upozna.

buditi se; probuditi se	*to wake up*
padala je kiša	*it was raining*
duvao je vetar	*the wind was blowing*
uskoro	*soon*
sesti, sednem, seo	*to sit down*
otprilike	*approximately*
trajati, traje	*to last*
zgrada	*building*
Filološki fakultet	*Faculty of Philology*
katedra za anglistiku	*English department*
predavanje	*lecture*
naručivati, naručujem; naručiti	*to order*
zaboravljati; zaboraviti	*to forget*
udžbenik	*textbook*
sa sobom	*with oneself*
torba	*bag*
odlaziti; otići, odem, otišao	*to leave, go away*
vraćati, vratiti	*to return, give back*
književnost	*literature*
esej	*essay*
Šekspir	*Shakespeare*
dogovoriti se	*to agree*

QUICK VOCAB

nalaziti se; naći se	to meet
sunce sija	the sun is shining
napolju	outside
dosta	much, enough
pitati	to ask

Questions

i How did Maja get to the university?

ii At what time did she have her first lecture?

iii Why did she have to stay in the library in the afternoon?

How it works

Word order and enclitics

For most purposes word order in Serbian is fairly free. The ending of a noun will tell you whether it is the subject of the verb or the object of the verb. Whereas in English word order is fixed *Vesna saw Robert* **Vesna je videla Roberta**, in Serbian we can change the order of words **Roberta je videla Vesna** without changing the basic meaning of the sentence. **Vesna** is nom. case and must be the subject of the verb, while **Roberta** is acc. case and must be the object of the verb, wherever you put them in the sentence. However, there is a strict order and position for the short forms of verbs and personal pronouns. These short forms are called enclitics. They are the short forms of **biti** and **hteti** (auxiliary verbs to form the past and future tenses), the short forms of personal pronouns in the acc. gen. and dat. cases **me/mene** or **te/tebe**, and the form **se** used to make a reflexive verb.

Enclitics may not be placed as first word in a sentence or a clause. They do not come after a pause in speaking or following a comma or full stop in writing. They usually come after the first introductory word or phrase (note that for these purposes **i** and **a** do not count). In Activity A you saw the following examples:

| dok se spremam | *while I get ready* |
| i on me čeka | *he waits for me* |

200

There is also a strict order for the enclitics, particularly important when using the past or future tense:

- in first place: the verbal enclitic except for the third person singular je
- in second place: the pronoun enclitics in the order dat./gen./acc.
- in third place: either the reflexive particle se or the third person singular je

Look at the following examples from Activity B:

i	Juče sam se probudila u pola devet.	*Yesterday I woke up at 8.30.*
ii	Dala mi ga je.	*She gave it to me.*
iii	Kasnije sam joj ga vratila.	*Later I returned it to her.*

In (i) the enclitics follow the introductory word juče with the verbal enclitic first (sam) followed by the reflexive particle (se).

In (ii) the enclitics follow the order: dat. pronoun (mi); acc. pronoun (ga); third person singular verbal enclitic of biti (je).

In (iii) the verbal enclitic is in first place (sam); the dat. pronoun enclitic is in second place (joj); the acc. pronoun enclitic is in third place (ga).

The position and order of enclitics always follow these fixed patterns.

Insight

Remember that the enclitics should not be put after a full stop, comma or the words i and a:

Došli smo u bife,/naručila sam kafu . . .
Došli smo u bife/i naručila sam kafu.

However, if there is another word (NOT i or a) at the beginning of the clause, the enclitics come immediately after it:

Došli smo u bife,/gde sam naručila kafu.

More about reflexive verbs

Some verbs may be used with or without a reflexive pronoun se in certain specific circumstances:

Budilnik zvoni u šest sati i budi me.	*The alarm clock rings at six o'clock and wakes me.*
Juče sam se probudila u pola devet.	*Yesterday I woke up at 8.30.*

The difference is between *to do something* and simply *to do* (i.e. the verb in the first example is followed by an object and does not take the reflexive pronoun which grammatically functions as the object of the verb: *Yesterday I woke myself at 8.30.*).

Compare the following examples:

Završavamo posao u tri.	*We finish work at three o'clock.*
Predavanje se završilo u četiri.	*The lecture finished at four o'clock.*
Spremam esej o Šekspiru.	*I am preparing an essay on Shakespeare.*
Spremam se u kuhinji.	*I get ready in the kitchen. (lit. prepare myself)*
Vratila sam joj udžbenik.	*I returned the textbook to her.*
Vratila sam se kući.	*I returned home.*
Oni igraju fudbal.	*They are playing football.*
Oni se igraju.	*They are playing.*

Some verbs aquire a different meaning when used reflexively: e.g. **nalaziti; naći** *to find*. When used with a reflexive pronoun this verb means *to be situated* or *to meet* (by arrangement):

Katedra za anglistiku se nalazi na drugom spratu.	*The English Department is situated on the second floor.*
Dogovorila sam se sa drugaricama da se nađemo u poslastičarnici.	*I arranged with my (girl) friends that we meet in the cake shop.*

Practice

1 Robert has been given a language task by one of his teachers. He has to interview two people about their daily routine. He asks Zoran Petrović and Jelena Jovanović the questions given on the

grid below. Listen to the recording and tick the boxes to show the correct answers:

◀ CD 2, TR 3, 03.40

a U koliko sati ustajete?	u 6.00	u 7.00	u 8.00	u 9.00	posle 9.00
Zoran					
Jelena					
b Kako idete na posao?	peške	kolima	autobusom	tramvajem	vozom
Zoran					
Jelena					
c Kada počinjete da radite?	u 7.00	u 8.00	u 9.00	u 10.00	posle 10.00
Zoran					
Jelena					
d Gde ručate?	kod kuće	na poslu	u menzi	u restoranu	ne ručam
Zoran					
Jelena					
e Kada završavate posao?	u 2.00	u 3.00	u 4.00	u 5.00	posle 5.00
Zoran					
Jelena					

2 You have been asked to describe your own daily routine. Give as much information as possible, using the interview above and the previous activities in this unit as a model.

3 Replace the nouns and adjectives in bold with the appropriate pronouns. Take care to use the correct word order. First look at the example:

e.g. Vratila sam Vesni **knjigu.**
      Vratila sam je Vesni.

a Sutra ću videti **Roberta.**
b Ispričali su **Barbari** gde su bili.
c Vesna je zaboravila **udžbenik** kod kuće.
d Obično zovemo **prijatelje** u goste subotom.
e Mnogo je voleo **svog sina.**
f Kupiće **Ričardu kartu.**
g Bili su juče u biblioteci i videli su tamo **Nevenu.**
h Nisam dala **rečnik** Veri i Zoranu.

Biljana will look after the grandchildren

Activity C

🔊 CD 2, TR 3, 04.40

Listen to Biljana talking about and planning her visit to Dejan and his wife the next day. Read the text, then answer the questions:

Sutra ujutro moram da budem kod Dejana, našeg sina. Praznik je, ali on i njegova žena Ivana treba da idu na posao. Pošto obdanište ne radi, ja ću čuvati decu. Kao i obično, Milošev prijatelj dolazi po njega kolima, tako da ću imati naš auto. Lako mi je da vozim kod Dejana i Ivane jer stanuju nedaleko od nas i ne moram da vozim kroz centar grada. Tamo je uvek gužva.

Dejan i Ivana odlaze zajedno na posao svojim kolima oko pola osam. Tada ću i ja stići kod njih. Kad budem tamo, daću deci doručak. Posle doručka ćemo izići u šetnju. Imaju u blizini divan park, gde sam već bila s decom. Deca su se tada lepo igrala. U parku je jedna prijatna kafanica pored malog jezera. Sešćemo tamo i naručiću kafu za sebe i sok ili sladoled za decu. Naravno, mora da bude lepo vreme. Ako bude padala kiša, nećemo moći da iziđemo. Šta da radimo ako vreme bude loše? Moraćemo da ostanemo kod kuće. Čitaću deci priče, ili će se oni igrati u dnevnoj sobi. Suviše su mali da ih vodim u bioskop, ali će moći da gledaju kod kuće neki video ako im bude dosadno. Moram večeras da gledam vremensku prognozu na televiziji.

moram da budem . . .	*I have to be . . .*
praznik	*holiday* (public)
pošto	*since, because*
obdanište	*nursery school*

QV

204

deca	*children*
kao i obično	*as usually*
prijatelj dolazi po njega	*a friend comes to pick him up*
lako	*easy*
gužva	*traffic jam*
kad budem tamo . . .	*when I am there . . .*
igrati se	*to play*
kafanica	*a small café*
jezero	*lake*
sešćemo	*we shall sit down*
mora da bude lepo vreme	*it has to be nice weather*
Ako bude padala kiša . . .	*If it rains . . .*
loš	*bad*
. . . ako im bude dosadno	*. . . if they are bored*
vremenska prognoza	*weather forecast*

Questions

i Does Dejan live far from his parents?

ii Where is Biljana going to take the children if the weather is nice?

How it works

To be *budem, budeš, bude*

There is another present tense form of the verb *to be* in Serbian:

ja	budem	mi	budemo
ti	budeš	vi	budete
on	bude	oni	budu

This form of the verb is not an enclitic and follows the regular pattern of other -e verbs. It is used specifically to express the alternative infinitive form:

moram da budem . . . (moram biti . . .)	*I have to be*
mora da bude lepo vreme (mora biti lepo vreme)	*it has to be nice weather*

Future exact

This form of the present tense of the verb *to be* is also used to form a future tense after expressions like *if, when, while, until, as soon as*. This tense is formed by combining **budem, budeš**, etc. as an auxiliary verb with the verbal adjective which you have used already in the past tense. In these constructions English does not use a future tense:

Ako bude padala kiša, nećemo moći da iziđemo.	*If it rains, we shall not be able to go out.*

English uses a present tense of the verb after *if* but its meaning is a reference to a future time, which is registered in the future tense of the following verb. In Serbian, use the future exact of the verb after *if* (or *when, while, until, as soon as*) and the ordinary future for the next verb.

When this construction occurs with the verb *to be*, the verbal adjective is omitted:

Kad budem kod njih, daću deci doručak.	*When I am at their house, I shall give the children their breakfast.*

You are not yet at their house but you are intending to be there sometime in the future. Using the ordinary short form of **biti** in this sentence would not be a reference to the future but would mean *whenever*:

Kad sam kod njih, dajem deci doručak.	*Whenever I am at their house, I give the children their breakfast.*

Noun agreement

Sometimes a phrase or word is linked to another simply by being put in the same case. These are often nouns used in the way that Biljana does when she speaks about her intention to visit their son, Dejan: **Sutra idem kod Dejana, našeg sina.**

Both nouns are here in the gen. case. In such constructions, the two nouns refer to the same person or thing.

Noun subgroups

deca children

This noun is grammatically fem. singular and its case endings are those of a regular fem. singular noun in -a, although its meaning is obviously plural:

Čuvam decu.	*I am looking after the children.*
Čuvam dobru decu.	*I am looking after the good children.*

When **deca** is used as the subject of a verb, the verb concerned is plural. In the past tense the auxiliary verb is plural, and the verbal adjective is fem. singular to agree with the grammatical subject:

Deca se igraju.	*The children are playing.*
Deca su bila sa mnom.	*The children were with me.*

There are two other words which also take similar plural forms:

dete	*child*	deca	*children*
brat	*brother*	braća	*brothers*
gospodin	*gentleman*	gospoda	*gentlemen*

Moja braća žive u Engleskoj.	*My brothers live in England.*
Gospoda su čekala u sobi.	*The gentlemen were waiting in the room.*

Foreign borrowings

Nouns which are borrowings from foreign languages and which end in -o are masculine:

auto	*car*
video	*video*
radio	*radio*

Adjective agreements with these words are masculine as in: **naš auto**, **neki video**.

Oneself

There are a number of words in English like *myself, yourself, oneself,* etc., used as objects. Serbian has just one word to cover them all and it changes case according to the following pattern:

acc.	**sebe**
gen.	**sebe**
dat.	**sebi**
ins.	**sobom**
loc.	**sebi**

The precise meaning of the word depends on the context in the sentence:

Nevena je nosila
taj udžbenik sa sobom
u torbi.

Nevena was carrying
(lit. with herself) the
textbook in her bag.

Naručiću kafu za sebe i
sok ili sladoled za decu.

I'll order a coffee for myself
and a juice or ice cream for
the children.

What's the weather like?

Activity D

◀) CD 2, TR 3, 06.29

Listen to Dragan telling Robert about the seasonal weather in Belgrade, read the text and then answer the questions:

Pitate me kakvo je vreme u Beogradu? Zimi je veoma hladno. Pada sneg i temperatura je često ispod nule. Sneg ostaje na ulicama nekoliko dana. Duva jak vetar i taj hladni period obično traje do marta. Onda dolazi proleće. U proleće je vreme ponekad veoma prijatno i toplo, a ponekad kišovito i sveže. Leti je uvek lepo. Dani su dugi i sunčani. Kiša ne pada kao u proleće, ali imamo pljuskove. Moram da kažem da u avgustu ponekad dolazi velika vrućina, sparno je i nije prijatno. Ljudi napuštaju grad i idu u planine ili na more. Jesen je, po mom mišljenju, najlepše godišnje doba u Beogradu. Letnja vrućina prolazi i vreme se polako menja. Svi znamo da će biti još dosta lepih dana dok ne bude došla prava zima.

QUICK VOCAB

Kakvo je vreme?	*What's the weather like?*
zimi	*in winter*
veoma	*very*
hladan	*cold*
period	*period*

pada sneg	*it is snowing*
temperatura	*temperature*
ispod nule	*below zero*
nekoliko	*a few*
jak	*strong*
proleće	*spring*
topao	*warm (like* ceo*)*
kišovit	*rainy*
svež	*fresh, cool*
leti	*in summer*
sunčan	*sunny*
pljusak	*shower*
vrućina	*heat*
sparno	*muggy*
napuštati; napustiti	*to leave*
jesen	*autumn*
po mom mišljenju	*in my opinion*
najlepše godišnje doba	*the nicest season of the year*
polako	*slowly*
dok ne	*until*
pravi	*real*

Questions

i What is spring like in Belgrade?

ii What do Belgrade people usually do in August?

How it works

More about the future exact

Another example of the future exact can be found in Activity D:

Svi znamo da će biti još dosta lepih dana dok ne bude došla prava zima.	*We all know that there are still going to be a lot of nice days until the real winter comes.*

The future exact form of **doći** is used after **dok ne** meaning *until* as the action refers to something which will happen in the future. It is also possible to use the present tense instead of the future exact with a perfective verb.

The word **dok** means *while*, but when used with a negative verb as **dok ne**, it means *until*.

Seasons

The seasons of the year are:

zima	*winter*	zimi	*in winter*
proleće	*spring*	u proleće	*in spring*
leto	*summer*	leti	*in summer*
jesen	*autumn*	u jesen	*in autumn*

The word for *season* is **godišnje doba** (lit. *time of the year*) in which **doba** is a neut. singular noun: **ovo godišnje doba** *this season*.

Masc. nom. adjective ending in *-i* and voc. endings

Most masc. adjectives in the nom. singular end in a consonant like **dobar, star, hladan**. However, the nom. masc. ending is not always a consonant and may sometimes be **-i**. This ending adds the meaning of *the* to the adjective and is often found in conjunction with the adjective **taj**:

Duva jak vetar.	*A strong wind blows.*
Taj hladni period traje do marta.	*The cold spell lasts until March.*

When using the voc. case, the adjective ending is the same as the nom. with the **-i** form in the masc. singular. The pattern of endings is:

	Singular			Plural		
	masc.	fem.	neut.	masc.	fem.	neut.
nom.	**star(i)**	**stara**	**staro**	**stari**	**stare**	**stara**
voc.	**stari**	**stara**	**staro**	**stari**	**stare**	**stara**

Several adjectives only exist with this **-i** form, e.g. **prvi** (and other ordinal numbers), **neki**, etc. There are also a number of adjectives which may not add **-i** to make this form, e.g. **moj, naš** (and other possessive adjectives), **jedan**, etc.

The ending without -i is always used in the following type of simple construction using the verb *to be* saying *I am . . .* or *He is . . .*:

Tvoj prijatelj je ljubazan.   *Your friend is kind.*

Expressing approximate numbers

To say an approximate number you can add the word **otprilike** *approximately* in front, or the word **oko** *around, about*.

On je pojeo oko pet sendviča.   *He ate about five sandwiches.*

If saying *about* when using a round number such as 10, 20, etc. you may add the ending -ak instead to the whole number:

desetak   *about ten (a dozen)*
dvadesetak   *twenty or so*

Phrases and expressions

- To say that you have been somewhere or are going somewhere to visit someone as a guest use the preposition **u** followed by the word **gost** *guest* in the loc. or acc. plural:

  Bili smo kod njih u gostima.   *We were round at their house.*
  Idemo kod njih u goste.   *We are going to their house.*

- To say *prefer* use the verb **voleti** *like* with the comparative form **više** *more*:

  Više volimo da idemo   *We prefer to go to the cinema.*
     u bioskop.

- To say *in my opinion, in your opinion* use the preposition **po** followed by the dat. case of the possessive adjective and of the word **mišljenje** *opinion*:

  Po mom mišljenju . . .   *In my opinion . . .*
  Po tvom mišljenju . . .   *In your opinion . . .*

- To say *to come for someone* or *to fetch something* use the preposition **po** with the acc. case as in the following:

  Milošev prijatelj dolazi po njega. *Miloš's friend comes for him.*
  Idem po hleb.   *I am going for bread.*
                                       (to fetch bread)

- Expressions referring to the weather may use the verbs **padati** *to fall* or **duvati** *to blow* as in:

pada kiša	*it is raining*
pada sneg	*it is snowing*
duva vetar	*it is windy*

- To say that there is a traffic jam use the word **gužva**. The same word is used to refer to a *crowd* somewhere on the streets or in a room.

- Serbian often uses a diminutive form of a noun which adds the meaning of *little* or *small*. If it is a fem. noun replace the -a ending with **-ica,** or if it is a masc. noun add the ending **-ić:**

kafana	kafanica	*little café*
grad	gradić	*small town*

Diminutive endings often add a tone of emotional closeness.

- To say *to be sitting at a table* use **sedeti za stolom** and *to sit down to a table* **sesti za sto**. In the first phrase **za** (lit. *behind*) is followed by the ins. case and in the second phrase by the acc. case.

Practice

4 Replace the infinitive given in brackets with the alternative infinitive construction. First look at the example:

e.g. Želeli smo (ići) u bioskop.
Želeli smo da idemo u bioskop.

a Morala je (kupiti) kartu.
b Volim (biti) u Beogradu.
c Da li ćeš moći (doći) kod mene?
d Želeli su (pozvati) prijatelje u goste.
e Hteo je (biti) lekar.
f Nećemo (sedeti) napolju.
g Hoćete li (biti) na poslu?
h Nisam planirala (putovati) na odmor.

5 Put the verbs in brackets into the future exact tense. First look at the example:

e.g. Ako (padati) kiša, nećemo ići u šetnju.
     Ako bude padala kiša, nećemo ići u šetnju.

a Ako (biti) lepo vreme, Biljana će voditi decu u park.
b Ako (duvati) vetar, neću izlaziti u grad.
c Kad (završiti) posao, ići ćemo kući.
d Kad (biti) u Beogradu, telefoniraću ti.
e Ako Robert (znati) gde je restoran, on će mi reći.
f Dok (čitati), Vesna će slušati radio.
g Barbara će svratiti kod tebe kad (imati) vremena.
h Dok (biti) na moru, nećete misliti na posao.

6 Look at the map and listen to the recording of the weather forecast for 4 June. Then read the text of the forecast and answer the questions that follow.

🔊 **CD 2, TR 3, 07.27**

PROGNOZA VREMENA ZA 4. JUN

SRBIJA I CRNA GORA: Ujutro i pre podne pretežno sunčano i toplo. Posle podne u Crnoj Gori i zapadnim i jugozapadnim krajevima Srbije promenljivo oblačno sa pljuskovima i grmljavinom. Vetar slab, južni i jugozapadni. Jutarnja temperatura oko 15, a najviša dnevna oko 29 stepeni.

BEOGRAD: Tokom dana pretežno sunčano. Krajem dana oblačno, u toku noći pljuskovi sa grmljavinom. Vetar umeren. Jutarnja temperatura oko 15, a najviša dnevna oko 29 stepeni.

SUTRA: Oblačno i svežije sa kišom, pljuskovima i grmljavinom. Vetar slab, zapadni i severozapadni. Najviša dnevna temperatura od 17 do 24 stepena.

pretežno	*mostly*
promenljivo	*changeable*
oblačno	*cloudy*
grmljavina	*thunder*
slab	*weak*
jutarnji	*morning* (adj.)
najviši	*highest*
stepen	*degree* (gen. plural **stepeni**)
svežije	*fresher, cooler*
umeren	*moderate*

a Kakvo će vreme biti pre podne?
b Da li će posle podne biti u Crnoj Gori sunčano?
c Da li će duvati jak vetar?
d Koja će biti najviša dnevna temperatura?
e Kakvo će vreme biti sutra?

7 Look at the information about the weather in some European cities on 4 June. If you were there on that day, how would you answer the questions that follow?

London	Pariz	Madrid	Prag	Atina
KIŠA	OBLAČNO	GRMLJAVINA I PLJUSAK	PROMENLJIVO OBLAČNO	SUNČANO
15°	16°	22°	19°	35°

a Kakvo je vreme u Londonu?
b Kakvo je vreme u Parizu?
c Kakvo je vreme u Atini?

8 You have been asked to describe the weather in your country. Follow the model of Activity D and give as much information as you can using the vocabulary introduced in this unit.

Test yourself

Here you can check some of the things you have learnt in this unit. Look at the questions below and choose the right answer:

1 If **dolaziti** is the imperfective and **doći** the perfective aspect of the verb *to come* in Serbian, which option would a female choose to say that she used to arrive by taxi?

    a Dolazila sam taksijem.   **b** Došla sam taksijem.

2 You are arranging to see someone this evening. How would you ask: *Where shall we meet?*

    a Gde da se nađemo?   **b** Gde da se nalazimo?

3 How would you ask when the class finishes: **Kada . . . . čas?**

    a završava   **b** završava se   **c** se završava

4 What is the meaning of the word **uvek**?

    a sometimes   **b** always   **c** often

5 How would a female person say that she forgot her key?

    a Našla sam ključ.
    b Spremila sam ključ.
    c Zaboravila sam ključ.

6 Which word order would you choose to fill the gap in the sentence **On . . . . dao kartu?**

    a mi je   **b** je mi

7 How would you say *They have returned to England*: **Vratili . . . . u Englesku?**

    a se su   **b** su se

8 Fill the gap with the correct form of **sebe**: **Naručila je za . . . . . . kafu:**

    a sebi   **b** sobom   **c** sebe

9 The weather forcast is: **Pre podne pretežno sunčano sa slabim vetrom. Posle podne svežije i oblačno sa pljuskovima.** When would it be better to go for a walk?

    a in the morning   **b** in the afternoon

10 How would you say *in my opinion* in Serbian?

    a u mom mišljenju
    b po mom mišljenju
    c u moje mišljenje

14

....

Free time

In this unit you will learn:

- About sport and hobbies
- Phrases for talking about what you do in your free time
- Buying tickets for the theatre and cinema
- Comparative forms of adjectives
- Indefinite pronouns
- How to form the conditional

Talking about sport

Activity A

🔊 CD 2, TR 4

Robert and Vesna are talking about their hobbies. Listen to the recording, read the dialogue and then answer the questions:

Весна	Роберте, шта радиш када си слободан?
Роберт	Бавим се спортом. Играм тенис и фудбал. Волим и да гледам спорт на телевизији, нарочито кошарку. Морам да признам да нисам добар у кошарци, али ипак волим да је гледам. Шта ти радиш у слободном времену?
Весна	Допада ми се пливање. Зими, када је хладно, не радим ништа. Седим код куће, слушам музику или гледам телевизију. Али од маја идем на пливање. Када сам била мала, ишла сам на базен са старијом сестром. Она је пливала боље него ја. Била је виша и јача.
Роберт	Где ти је базен?
Весна	Има доста отворених и затворених базена у Београду. А куда ти идеш?

Роберт	Најлакше ми је да идем у спортски центар на Дунаву, близу моје куће. Имају напољу терене за све спортове. Унутра имају и велику салу, где можеш да играш ако пада киша, ако је хладно или нешто слично.
Весна	А шта радиш када затворе спортски центар?
Роберт	То се скоро никада не дешава. Он ради сваког дана, само га затварају за празник. Али шта да радиш? За празник нигде ништа није отворено. Нико ништа не ради.

бавити се	*to be engaged in* (with ins. case)
нарочит	*special*
признавати, признајем, признати	*to confess, recognize*
ипак	*nevertheless*
слободно време	*free time*
допада ми се пливање	*I like swimming*
ништа	*nothing*
музика	*music*
старији	*older*
пливати	*to swim*
бољи	*better*
него	*than*
виши	*taller*
јачи	*stronger*
отворен базен	*open-air swimming pool*
затворен базен	*indoor swimming pool*
најлакши	*easiest*
спортски центар	*sport centre*
унутра	*inside*
сала	*hall*
нешто	*something*
сличан	*similar*
затварати, затворити	*to close*
скоро	*almost*
никада	*never*
Шта да радиш?	*What are you to do?*
нигде	*nowhere*
нико	*nobody*

Questions

i Which sports does Robert like to play?

ii Where does he go to play sports?

How it works

Comparative form of adjectives

Adjectives may form their comparative (i.e. *tall* and comparative form *taller*) according to one of five patterns, taking the normal case endings which you already know. The comparative adjective endings are all soft:

1 To form the comparative add **-ији** to the adjective:

стар	old	стар+ији	старији	older	
хладан	cold	хладан+ији	хладнији	colder	
пријатан	pleasant	пријатан+ији	пријатнији	more pleasant	
свеж	fresh	свеж+ији	свежији	fresher	
топао	warm	топао+ији	топлији	warmer	

2 Add **-ји** to the adjective, but in this case the final consonant changes according to the following pattern д–ђ, г–ж, х–ш, к–ч, с–ш, т–ћ, ст–шћ, з–ж, н–њ, л–љ.

млад	young	млад+ји	млађи	younger
дуг	long	дуг+ји	дужи	longer
тих	quiet	тих+ји	тиши	quieter
јак	strong	јак+ји	јачи	stronger
густ	thick	густ+ји	гушћи	thicker

3 With adjectives which end in **-ак, -ек,** and **-ок** remove the last two letters and proceed as for 2 above:

сладак	sweet	слад+ји	слађи	sweeter
далек	far	дал+ји	даљи	further
висок	tall	вис+ји	виши	taller

4 Some adjectives which end in -б, -п, -м, -в add -љи:

скуп	expensive	скупљи	more expensive
сув	dry	сувљи	drier

5 Some adjectives form an irregular comparative including three which add the ending -ши to the adjective:

добар	good	бољи	better
лош	bad	гори	worse
		(also **лошији**)	
мали	small	мањи	smaller
велик	big	већи	bigger
лак	easy	лакши	easier
леп	nice	лепши	nicer
мек	soft	мекши	softer

Saying *more* and *less*

These words in Serbian are **више** *more* and **мање** *less*. Nouns which follow them are in the gen. case (as for **много** *many*, *a lot of* and **мало** *a little*):

Ово је мање занимљиво.	*This is less interesting.*
Он је пио много кафе, али је његов брат пио више.	*He drank a lot of coffee, but his brother drank more.*

These words are also used to form the comparative of those adjectives which end in -ски: **пријатељски** *friendly*, **више пријатељски** *more friendly*.

Saying *than*

There are two ways of saying *than*:

1 Use **него** with the same case endings or construction before and after:

Она је пливала боље него ја.	*She swam better than me.*
Време је у Београду лепше него у Лондону.	*The weather in Belgrade is nicer than in London.*

2 Use the preposition **од** followed by the gen. case (it is not always possible to use the gen. case, as in the second example above):

Моја сестра је била јача
    од мене.
	My sister was stronger than
	    me.

Ваш ауто је већи од нашег.	*Your car is bigger than ours.*

Superlative forms of adjectives

To form the superlative of adjectives (i.e. *tallest, strongest*) add **нај**
to the beginning of the comparative:

најстарији	*oldest*
најтоплији	*warmest*
најдужи	*longest*
најјачи	*strongest*
најскупљи	*most expensive*
најбољи	*best*
најлепши	*most beautiful*

Most and *least* are **највише** and **најмање**.

Serbian never uses double consonants except in the superlative form
of those adjectives which begin with ј such as **јак – најјачи** and
јефтин – најјефтинији.

Comparative of adverbs

For the comparative and superlative of adverbs use the neut. singular
form:

Она плива добро, али
    њена сестра плива боље.
	She swims well, but her sister
	    swims better.

На планинама је лепо, али
    је на мору лепше.
	It is nice in the mountains, but
	    it is nicer at the seaside.

Insight

When you want to say that you like someone or something
more than another person or thing use **више волим**:

Више волим тенис него
    кошарку.
	I like tennis more than
	    basketball.

When you want to say that you like something most of all, use
највише волим:

Највише волим фудбал.	*I like football most of all.*

Indefinite pronouns

You are already aware of the words **ко, шта, када** etc. for forming questions or for linking two parts of a sentence such as **Идем у спортски центар када сам слободан.** These words also form the basis for saying *somebody*, *nobody*, etc:

ко	who	шта	what
неко	somebody	нешто	something
нико	nobody	ништа	nothing
ико	anybody	ишта	anything
када	when	где	where
некада	once, formerly	негде	somewhere
никада	never	нигде	nowhere
икада	anytime	игде	anywhere
како	how	куда	(to) where
некако	somehow	некуда	somewhere
никако	no way	никуда	nowhere
икако	anyhow	икуда	anywhere

Да ли ико зна Весну?	*Does anybody know Vesna?*
Некако смо стигли.	*We got there somehow.*
Боље икада него никада.	*Better late than never.*

There are alternative forms for *anywhere, anything*, etc. formed with either **било** or **год** in the following way:

било ко	*anybody*	**било шта**	*anything*
кад год	*whenever*	**где год**	*wherever*

When you are using the negative forms *nobody, never*, etc. the whole phrase must be negative, including the verb. This practice differs from English where only one part of the phrase is made negative:

Нигде ништа није отворено.	*Nothing is open anywhere.*
Нико ништа не ради.	*Nobody does anything.*

When you use **ко** or one of its variants the gender agreement is masc. and when you use **шта** or one of its variants the gender agreement is neut.:

Ко је узео мој уџбеник?	*Who took my textbook?*
Нико није дошао.	*Nobody has come.*

Нешто црно је у реци.	*Something black is in the river.*
Ништа није било.	*Nothing happened.*

The final **a** is sometimes dropped from **када, куда** and their variants. The same happens with the word **сада** and the preposition **са**. The vowel is dropped particularly when the following word also begins with a vowel.

To like

You have used the verb **волети** meaning *to like* or *to love*. In this unit there is another expression **допада ми се пливање** *I like swimming*. Using this expression you are literally saying *swimming is pleasing to me*. The verb **допадати се** is in the third person and the person who likes swimming is in the dat. case. Compare these two sentences and in particular pay attention to the position of the subject of the verb in the nom. case at the end:

Весни се допада та књига.	*Vesna likes that book.*
Допадају јој се те књиге.	*She likes those books.*

In addition to this expression, there is also another verb used in the same way: **свиђа ми се пливање** *I like swimming*.

Весни се свиђа та књига.
Свиђају јој се те књиге.

Dative case to show possession

To show possession you have used the possessive adjectives **мој, твој, наш,** etc., the adjectives formed from personal names **Весна – Веснин** *Vesna – Vesna's*, or the gen. case as in **то је ауто мог оца** *that is my father's car* (lit. *the car of my father*). Another possibility is to use the dat. case of the personal pronoun:

Где ти је базен?	*Where is your swimming pool?*

This method is most frequently used when speaking about things or people emotionally close to you:

Сестра ми је у Аустралији.	*My sister is in Australia.*

Activity B

🔊 **CD 2, TR 4, 01.38**

Listen to the following recording of Dragan Jovanović talking to Robert about sport. Then read the text and answer the questions:

Кад сам био млађи, волео сам да играм фудбал, хокеј и ватерполо. Зими сам ишао на Копаоник на скијање. Још увек идем на планине зими и водим породицу. Сад учим своју децу да се скијају. На жалост, што се тиче других активности, ретко имам времена. Лакше ми је да идем у теретану два-три пута недељно или кад год могу.

Најпопуларнији спорт је код нас фудбал. Када југословенска фудбалска репрезентација има утакмицу, на улици нема никога. Сви гледају пренос на телевизији. Људи не говоре ни о чему другом. Нећу да кажем да их не разумем. Али има и других спортова и спортиста. О коме моја деца причају? Само о фудбалерима. Ја волим да гледам атлетику, а немам с ким да идем на стадион. Знам да није тако само код нас. И Енглези највише воле фудбал, зар не?

<table>
<tr><td>хокеј</td><td>hockey</td></tr>
<tr><td>ватерполо</td><td>water polo</td></tr>
<tr><td>још увек</td><td>still</td></tr>
<tr><td>скијање</td><td>skiing</td></tr>
<tr><td>скијати се</td><td>to ski</td></tr>
<tr><td>активност</td><td>activity</td></tr>
<tr><td>два-три пута</td><td>two or three times</td></tr>
<tr><td>недељно</td><td>weekly</td></tr>
<tr><td>популаран</td><td>popular</td></tr>
<tr><td>код нас</td><td>at our place, in our country</td></tr>
<tr><td>југословенски</td><td>Yugoslav</td></tr>
<tr><td>фудбалски</td><td>football (adj.)</td></tr>
<tr><td>репрезентација</td><td>national team</td></tr>
<tr><td>утакмица</td><td>match</td></tr>
<tr><td>нема никога</td><td>there is nobody</td></tr>
<tr><td>пренос</td><td>broadcast</td></tr>
<tr><td>ни о чему другом</td><td>about nothing else</td></tr>
<tr><td>спортист</td><td>sportsman</td></tr>
<tr><td>о коме</td><td>about whom</td></tr>
</table>

QUICK VOCAB

фудбалер	*football player*
атлетика	*athletics*
с ким	*with whom*
стадион	*stadium*

Questions

i Which sport does Dragan practise in winter?
ii Which sport is most popular in Serbia?

When Dragan is speaking about his country, he uses the expression **код нас**. The same expression is used with the meaning *at our house*. Dragan's usage of the plural pronoun is very common to mean *in our country*; **код вас** *in your country*. Dragan mentions the Yugoslav national team. He actually means the football team which represented the state union of Serbia and Montenegro. These days, of course, he would say **фудбалска репрезентација Србије**.

How it works

Case endings for *ко* and *шта*

The words **ко, шта** and their variants **неко нико нешто ништа** have case endings which resemble adjective endings:

nom.	ко	шта
acc.	кога	шта
gen.	кога	чега
dat.	коме	чему
ins.	ким(е)	чиме
loc.	коме	чему

Кога си видео?	*Whom did you see?*
С ким си ишао?	*With whom did you go?*
(e usually omitted)	
Немој да кажеш никоме.	*Don't tell anyone.*
О чему си говорио?	*What did you speak about?*

When using **нико** and **ништа** with a preposition, the word is divided as in:

Људи не говоре ни о чему другом.	People speak about nothing else.
Није дошла ни са ким.	She came with nobody. (She did not come with anyone.)

Once, twice, etc.

The word for *time/s* is **пут/а** in the phrases *twice* **два пута**, *three times* **три пута**, *five times* **пет пута**, etc.; *once* **једанпут** is one word.

_____

Practice

1 Listen to Barbara and Richard talking about their spare time and answer the following questions:

◄) **CD 2, TR 4, 02.47**

   a Which sports does Richard like?
   b Does he play football?
   c Which sport does Barbara like?
   d Does she like to watch television?

2 Put the adjectives in the sentences below into the required comparative forms with the correct case endings. They are given in brackets in the masc. nom. form. First look at the example:

   e.g. Весна је (млад) од своје сестре.
          Весна је млађа од своје сестре.

   a Време је данас (хладан) него јуче.
   b Ми смо били у (велик) хотелу.
   c Наш стан је (мали) од вашег.
   d Разговарала је са (стар) сестром.
   e Роберт је (висок) од Ричарда.
   f Ово је (дуг) пут.
   g Никада нисам видео (леп) девојку.
   h Немам (добар) пријатеља од њега.

3 Pick the most appropriate form of **неко, нешто**, etc. out of the box to fit the sentences. Use each word only once:

a Хоћу _____ да ти кажем.
b _____ није дошао.
c Не знам _____ о фудбалу.
d Да ли је _____ био јуче на утакмици?
e Њихова кућа је _____ близу центра.
f _____ нисмо били у Лондону.

ништа	ико	негде	нико	никад	нешто

4 Replace the words in brackets with their correct case form. First look at the example:

e.g. (Ко) си знао?
      Кога си знао?

a (Ко) треба да пишем?
b (Нико) нису видели.
c (Шта) си се бавио на одмору?
d Са (ко) си ишао на утакмицу?
e (Нико) нисам дала новац.
f Мислила сам о (нешто).

Hobbies: reading and the cinema

Activity C

🔊 **CD 2, TR 4, 03.25**

Listen to Richard talking to Vesna's friend Ana about what she does in her spare time. Then read the dialogue and answer the question that follows:

Ричард	Ана, шта волиш да радиш кад си слободна? Имаш ли неки хоби?
Ана	Знаш, Ричарде, ја нисам спортски тип. Више волим да читам неки добар роман, приповетку или поезију.
Ричард	Ко ти је омиљени писац?
Ана	Раније сам читала само страну књижевност. А онда, пре неколико година, почела сам да читам и наше писце, Андрића, Киша ... Баш сада сам још једном прочитала Андрићев роман *На Дрини ћуприја*.

Ричард	Не знам много о српској култури. О чему је тај роман?
Ана	То је роман о историји Вишеграда од шеснаестог до двадесетог века. Вишеград је град на реци Дрини, на граници између Србије и Босне.
Ричард	И шта још волиш да радиш?
Ана	Волим да идем у позориште и у биоскоп.
Ричард	Какви филмови ти се свиђају?
Ана	Гледам свашта – трилере, комедије, кримиће, љубиће. Али не волим хорор филмове.
Ричард	Слажем се с тобом. Ни ја не волим да их гледам. Мени се највише свиђају историјски и ратни филмови.

хоби	*hobby*
спортски тип	*sporty type*
роман	*novel*
приповетка	*short story*
поезија	*poetry*
омиљен	*favourite*
писац	*writer*
раније	*earlier*
пре неколико година	*a few years ago*
баш сада	*just now, right now*
још једном	*once more*
На Дрини ћуприја	*The Bridge over the Drina*
култура	*culture*
век	*century*
граница	*border, frontier*
Босна	*Bosnia*
какви филмови	*what kind of films*
свашта	*everything*
трилер	*thriller*
комедија	*comedy*
љубић	*love story*
хорор филм	*horror film*
ни	*neither*
ратни филмови	*war films*

228

Question

What is the novel *На Дрини ћуприја* about?

Ivo Andrić (1892–1975) and Danilo Kiš (1935–89) are two of Serbia's most celebrated writers of the twentieth century. Andrić won the Nobel prize for literature in 1961. His best-known work is *Na Drini ćuprija The Bridge over the Drina* (1945), which tells the story of the town of Višegrad and in particular events surrounding its spectacular bridge on the River Drina. Their works have been translated and published abroad.

How it works

What kind of?

The word **какав** *what kind of* is an adjective in Serbian. It is used to ask questions:

Какав ауто имаш?	*What kind of car do you have?*
Какве филмове они воле?	*What kind of films do they like?*

It is also used as an exclamation:

Какав човек!	*What a man!*
Каква је ово земља!	*What kind of a country is this!*

Phrases and expressions

- To say *ago* use **пре** as in the phrase **пре неколико година** *a few years ago*. When using the words **недеља, месец, година** on their own, you will find that the gen. plural of **дан** is added as in the following phrases:

Идем у Београд на недељу дана.	*I am going to Belgrade for a week.*
Био сам у Лондону пре месец дана.	*I was in London a month ago.*
Читам ту књигу већ годину дана.	*I have been reading that book for a year.*

- The intensifying particle **баш,** the meaning of which varies depending on the context, has the sense of *really, quite* or *just*:

Баш сада сам прочитала тај роман.	*I have just now read that novel.*
Он је баш слатко дете.	*He is a really sweet child.*

- To say *once more* use **још једном**. To say *one more* when you want to ask for one more of something which you already have use **још један**:

Дајте нам, молим вас, још једну кафу.	*Bring us, please, another coffee.*

- The particle **ни** means *neither* but because English does not use double negatives it often translates into English as *either*:

Ни ја не волим да их гледам.	*I don't like to watch them either.*

You repeat the **ни** for the phrase *neither . . . nor . . .* as you do with **или** for *either . . . or . . .* and with **и** for *both . . . and . . .*

Не волим ни њега ни њу.	*I like neither him nor her.*
Ја ћу пити или сок или кока-колу.	*I'll drink either fruit juice or a coke.*
Ја волим да читам и романе и поезију.	*I like reading both novels and poetry.*

Going to the cinema

Activity D

🔊 CD 2, TR 4, 04.53

Ana and Vesna are choosing which film to go and see. Listen to the recording, read the text and answer the questions that follow:

Весна	Иде ми се у биоскоп. Хајде да идемо вечерас да гледамо неки филм.
Ана	У реду. Шта се даје?
Весна	Да видим шта има у *Политици*. Хоћеш ли страни или домаћи филм?
Ана	Није важно.
Весна	У *Балкану* се даје *Америчка лепота*.
Ана	То је сувише озбиљан филм. Ја бих волела нешто забавно.

Весна	Да ли би волела нешто за децу? У *Јадрану* се даје *Хари Потер и камен мудрости*.
Ана	Супер. То је баш за мене. У колико сати?
Весна	Имају представе у четири, седам и десет сати. Да идемо у десет?
Ана	Не знам. Морам да чувам Уроша док се мама и тата не врате кући. Ако би дошли кући пре девет, могле бисмо да идемо.
Весна	Нема везе. Можемо да идемо на прву представу и да водимо и Уроша. После биоскопа свратићемо у Мекдоналдс, преко пута *Москве*. Урош ће бити задовољан.

Иде ми се у биоскоп.	*I feel like going to the cinema.*
да идемо	*let's go*
давати се, даје се	*to be showing* (of a film, or play)
да видим	*let me see*
домаћи филм	*home* (i.e. Serbian) *film*
лепота	*beauty*
озбиљан	*serious*
ја бих волела . . .	*I would like . . .*
Да ли би волела . . .	*Would you like . . .*
супер	*super*
представа	*performance*
Ако би дошли кући . . .	*If they were to come home . . .*
могли бисмо да идемо	*we could go*
нема везе	*it doesn't matter*
задовољан	*pleased, satisfied*

QUICK VOCAB

Questions

i What does Ana have to do in the evening?
ii What is Vesna's solution?

Политика is Serbia's main daily newspaper, published in Belgrade. **Балкан** and **Јадран** are two cinemas in the centre of Belgrade. Foreign films are shown subtitled with the original sound: *Америчка лепота American Beauty*; *Хари Потер и камен мудрости Harry Potter and the Philosopher's Stone*. In addition to the more traditional **кафана** there are many other kinds of restaurants in Belgrade such as

Italian, Chinese, Mexican, and McDonalds **Мекдоналдс**. There is a McDonalds in the centre of town opposite the hotel *Москва Moscow*.

How it works

I feel like . . .

You can say in Serbian that you *feel like* doing something by making the verb reflexive and putting it in the third person form. The one who *feels like* going to the cinema or a drink of tea in the examples below is expressed in the dat. case:

Иде ми се у биоскоп.	*I feel like going to the cinema.*
Пије му се чај.	*He feels like a (drink of) tea.*

Let me, let him, etc.

You have learnt how to tell someone to do something using the imperative form of the verb. If you want to say *let me* or *let us* do something, use the word **да** with the appropriate part of the verb in the present tense:

да видим	*let me see*
да идемо	*let us go (let's go)*

To say *let him*, *let her* or *let them* do something, use **нека** and add the appropriate part of the verb in the present tense:

Нека гледа телевизију.	*Let him watch TV.*
Нека иду у биоскоп.	*Let them go to the cinema.*

Conditional

The conditional part of a verb is expressed in English by *would*: *I would like to see a film*. In Serbian combine the verbal adjective taken from the infinitive (**волео, дошао**) with the following short forms used as an auxiliary verb:

ja	бих		ми	бисмо
ти	би		ви	бисте
он	би		они	би

| Ја бих волела . . . | *I would like . . .* |
| Они би дошли . . . | *They would come . . .* |

The conditional is often used in more formal and polite language. A waiter may well use it in a restaurant **Шта бисте желели, господине?** *What would you like, sir?* You used a shortened version of this kind of construction in Unit 4 **Ја бих једну кафу** (**Ја бих желео једну кафу**) *I would like a coffee.* In these circumstances (in a restaurant, ordering food and drink) Serbian uses the verb **желети** or **хтети** *to want* whereas English prefers the verb *to like.*

The short forms **бих, би,** etc. follow the same rules as other verbal short forms and do not come at the beginning of the sentence or phrase:

Волели бисмо . . .
Не бисмо волели . . .

Ако with the conditional

You have already used the word **ако** *if* with the future perfect or present tense:

Ако буду дошли пре девет,	*If they come before nine, we*
моћи ћемо да идемо	*shall be able to go to the*
у биоскоп.	*cinema.*

This is a simple statement of intention. However, we can qualify this statement by using the conditional, which makes the outcome seem less certain:

Ако би дошли пре девет,	*Should they come before nine,*
могле бисмо да идемо	*we could go to the cinema.* or
у биоскоп.	*Were they to come before nine,*
	we would be able to go to the
	cinema.

By using the conditional with **ако** Ana is showing some doubt that her parents will arrive home by nine o'clock, which is why Vesna suggests they go earlier and take Uroš with them.

In this construction **ако** may be replaced by **кад.**

Theatre programme

Activity E

Dragan and Jelena Jovanović want to go to the theatre next week. Dragan is looking at the theatre programme which is given below. Read the programme and find out what is on. Then listen to Dragan and Jelena discussing the options. Answer the following questions before reading the text of the dialogue:

Questions

i Why do they not want to see *Swan Lake* or *Carmen*?
ii Have they seen *Pygmalion* already?
iii Why can't they go to the theatre on Friday?
iv Which performance do they choose in the end?

Народно позориште
Београд, Трг Републике 1
тел. 620-946
Радно време благајне од 10 до 14
и од 15 до почетка представе

Велика сцена у 19.30:

16. мај	*Лабудово језеро*,	балет П.И. Чајковског
17. мај	*Кармен*,	опера Жоржа Бизеа
18. мај	*Пигмалион*,	комедија Б. Шоа
19. мај	*Травијата*,	опера Ђ. Вердија
20. мај	*Галеб*,	драма А.П. Чехова
21. мај	*Путујуће позориште Шопаловић*,	драма Љ. Симовића
22. мај	*Ричард трећи*,	драма Виљема Шекспира

Now read the dialogue and check if you have given the right answers:

Јелена	Шта је на програму у понедељак?
Драган	Чекај да видим . . . Понедељак је шеснаести . . . Даје се *Лабудово језеро*. У уторак је *Кармен*.

Јелена	Рекли смо да нећемо ни оперу ни балет. Шта имају после тога?
Драган	После тога је *Пигмалион*. То смо већ гледали. Деветнаестог је опет опера. Могли бисмо да идемо двадесетог. Даје се *Галеб*.
Јелена	Двадесети је петак, зар не? Не можемо у петак. Долазе нам твоји тата и мама на вечеру. А шта се даје у суботу?
Драган	*Путујуће позориште Шопаловић*.
Јелена	Чула сам да је то добра представа. Хајде да идемо то да гледамо.
Драган	У реду, купићу карте за ту представу.

благајна	*ticket office*
сцена	*stage*
програм	*programme*
лабуд	*swan*
галеб	*seagull*
драма	*drama*
путујући	*travelling*

QUICK VOCAB

Activity F

🔊 **CD 2, TR 4, 07.12**

Dragan has gone to the **Народно позориште** to buy tickets. Listen to the recording, read the dialogue and answer the questions:

Драган	Хтео бих карте за двадесет први мај, за *Путујуће позориште Шопаловић*.
Благајница	Колико карата хоћете, господине?
Драган	Дајте ми две карте.
Благајница	Партер или балкон?
Драган	Партер, молим вас. Негде напред, ако има слободних места.
Благајница	Хоћете ли у петом реду? Или мало даље?
Драган	Дајте ми пети ред.
Благајница	Изволите, господине, пети ред лево, седишта пет и шест.
Драган	Одлично. Када се завршава представа?
Благајница	Око пола једанаест.

благајница	*woman in the ticket office*
партер	*stalls*
балкон	*circle*
напред	*in front*

Questions

i Where are Dragan's and Jelena's seats?
ii When does the performance end?

Practice

5 In a survey, Milan and Vera have been asked to tick the things they like to do in their free time. Study the results and answer the questions below. Give your answers in Serbian:

i Који спорт вам се допада?	фудбал	тенис	хокеј	кошарка	друго
Вера		✓			пливање
Милан	✓		✓	✓	ватерполо
ви					

ii Куда волите да идете?	у биоскоп	у позориште	у оперу	на концерт	друго
Вера	✓	✓		✓	
Милан	✓	✓			на фудбалске утакмице
ви					

a Describe what sports Vera and Milan like using the verb **допадати се.**

b Describe where they like to go in their spare time.

c Now fill in the form yourself and then describe what sports you like and where you like to go.

6 Zoran Petrović is talking to a colleague from Niš who is visiting his company. The visitor's name is Ðorđe Pantić. Zoran has been asked to entertain him during his stay and is trying to find out what he would like to do. Fill in Ђорђе's part of the conversation:

◀) **CD 2, TR 4, 07.55**

Зоран	Шта волите да радите кад сте слободни, господине Пантићу?
Ђорђе	*When I have time, I like to go to the cinema and to the theatre. I like music too.*
Зоран	И мени се свиђа музика. Идете ли често на концерте?
Ђорђе	*Yes, I do.*
Зоран	У Београду имамо добар концертни програм. Могли бисмо да идемо заједно на неки концерт.
Ђорђе	*That would be good. I would also like to go to the National Theatre to see an opera.*
Зоран	Нема проблема. Погледаћу шта је ове недеље на програму. Шта још желите да видите док сте у Београду?
Ђорђе	*I like football very much. Could we go to a football match on Saturday?*
Зоран	У реду. Видећу ко игра ове суботе. А сада можемо да идемо у шетњу до Калемегдана. Да ли се слажете?
Ђорђе	*Yes, I feel like going for a walk.*

7 Put the verbs in brackets in the sentences below into the required conditional forms. First look at the example:

e.g.   Да ли бисте (хтети) партер или балкон?
       Да ли бисте хтели партер или балкон?

a Ми бисмо (волети) да гледамо неку комедију.
b (Желети) бих две карте за вечерас.
c Роберт не би (моћи) да дође сутра.
d (Морати) бисмо да га видимо.
e Да ли би ти (доћи) својим колима?
f Ако би (падати) киша, Весна би (остати) код куће.
g Да ли бисте (слушати) музику?
h Кад бих (имати) времена, (ићи) бих често на тенис.

8 You want to go to the cinema. Here is the programme for the Belgrade cinema *Kinoteka* for the next two days. *Kinoteka* specializes in showing films which are regarded as classic examples of cinema. Read the programme and answer the questions which follow:

(**режија** *direction* and **улога** *role*)

КИНОТЕКА
Косовска 11

петак 23. мај

4.00   *Грађанин Кејн*, амерички, драма, режија и главна улога Орсон Велс

6.00   *Неки то воле вруће*, амерички, комедија, режија Били Вајлдер, главне улоге Мерилин Монро, Тони Кертис и Џек Лемон.

8.30   *Апокалипса сада*, амерички, ратни, режија Франсис Форд Копола, главне улоге Марлон Брандо и Мартин Шин

субота 24. мај

3.00   *Тачно у подне*, амерички, вестерн, режија Фред Цинеман, главне улоге Гари Купер и Грејс Кели

5.30   *Психо*, амерички, трилер, режија Алфред Хичкок, у главној улози Антони Перкинс

8.00   *Кабаре*, мјузикл, ратни, режија Боб Фос, у главним улогама Лиза Минели и Мајкл Јорк.

---

a Which films are they showing?
b Who directed the film *Citizen Kane*?
c What kind of film is *Some Like It Hot*?
d Who star in that film?
e How would you ask for two tickets in the stalls to see *High Noon*?

Test yourself

Here you can check some of the things you have learnt in this unit. Look at the questions below and choose the right answer:

1 How would you ask your Serbian friend if he/she practises sport: **Бавиш ли се . . . .?**

   a спорт   **b** спорта   **c** спортом

2 What is the meaning of **бољи**?

   a bigger   **b** better   **c** worse

3 How would you say that the weather is nicer: **Време је** . . . . ?

   a лепши   **b** лепша   **c** лепше

4 How would you say that your sister is younger than you: **Моја сестра је млађа од** . . . . . . ?

   a мени   **b** мене   **c** мном

5 What is the meaning of the question **Када се затвара музеј?**

   a When does the museum open?
   b When does the museum close?

6 Which form would you use to complete the statement **Допадају ми се** . . . . ?

   a српски филмови   **b** српске филмове   **c** српских филмова

7 Which word would you choose to fill the gap in the sentence **Она** . . . . **није била у Београду?**

   a некада   **b** икада   **c** никада

8 How would you ask in Serbian *To whom should I write?* . . . . **треба да пишем?**

   a кога   **b** коме   **c** ким

9 What is the meaning of the question **Да ли вам се иде у шетњу?**

   a Are you going for a walk?
   b Do you like to go for a walk?
   c Do you feel like going for a walk?

10 How would you say that you and your friend would like to go to a football match: **Волели** . . . . . . **да идемо на фудбалску утакмицу?**

   a бих   **b** бисмо   **c** бисте

15

Celebrations

In this unit you will learn:

- Expressions when talking about celebrations
- How to describe flats and furniture
- How to describe people
- More about numbers
- How to express reported speech
- How to express **koji** *which*

Family lunch

Activity A

◀) CD 2, TR 5

Marko Pavlović is in Belgrade again and he has gone for lunch at his aunt Biljana's and uncle Miloš's house. Maja is there too. Biljana and Maja are preparing lunch. Listen to the recording, then read the dialogue and answer the questions that follow:

Biljana	Majo, molim te, pomozi mi da postavim sto.
Maja	Naravno, mama. Gde si stavila stolnjak?
Biljana	Stolnjaci su u kredencu, u gornjoj fijoci. Ja idem po viljuške, kašike i noževe. A ti donesi tanjire i salvete i stavi ih, molim te, na sto.
Maja	Nema problema. Koliko će nas biti?
Biljana	Nas troje i Marko, znači četvoro. Niko drugi ne dolazi.
Maja	Da li ti treba pomoć u kuhinji?

Biljana	Ne, hvala ti. Stavila sam meso u rernu da se peče. Supa se kuva na ringli, a salatu sam već napravila.
Maja	Dobro, ja ću onda posle ručka oprati sudove.
Biljana	Gde ti je tata? Rekla sam mu da treba da ide po hleb.
Maja	Valjda priča sa Markom.
Biljana	Da, vidim ih tamo pored prozora kako pričaju. On i Markov tata su bili školski drugovi. Ta dvojica su išla svugde zajedno.

pomagati, pomažem; pomoći, pomognem, pomogao	*to help* (with dat. case)
pomozi, pomozite	*help* (imperative)
postavljati; postaviti	*to set, place*
stavljati; staviti	*to put*
stolnjak	*tablecloth*
kredenac	*sideboard*
gornji	*upper*
fijoka	*drawer*
viljuška	*fork*
kašika	*spoon*
nož	*knife*
donositi; doneti, donesem, doneo	*to bring*
tanjir	*plate*
salveta	*serviette*
troje	*three* (men and women)
značiti	*to mean*
četvoro	*four* (men and women)
pomoć	*help*
rerna	*oven*
peći, pečem, peku (3rd person plural), **pekao; ispeći**	*to roast*
ringla	*hotplate* (on stove)
praviti; napraviti	*to make*
prati, perem; oprati, operem	*to wash*
sudovi	*dishes*
valjda	*probably*
prozor	*window*
kako pričaju	*talking* (lit. as they talk)

QUICK VOCAB

| ta dvojica | *those two* (men) |
| svugde | *everywhere* |

Questions

i How many of them will be there for lunch?

ii What has Biljana asked her husband to do?

How it works

More about numbers

In addition to the ones which you have already learnt there are two further sets of numbers. The first one refers to mixed groups of both men and women or to groups of children, and the second set refers to groups of men only.

Mixed groups/children

These numbers are formed as follows:

dvoje 2	petoro 5
troje 3	šestoro 6
četvoro 4	sedmoro 7

Higher numbers if required follow the same pattern adding the suffix **-oro** to the cardinal number. They may only be used when talking about a group of men and women or a group of chidren: **dvoje** means *a couple, one man and one woman*, or *two children*. When they are used as part of a subject, the verb is singular and the agreement in the past tense is neut. They are sometimes found in combination with a noun or pronoun in the gen. case:

| Video sam dvoje dece. | *I saw two children.* |
| Petoro ljudi je došlo. | *Five people came.* |

Groups of men

These numbers are formed as follows:

dvojica 2	petorica 5
trojica 3	šestorica 6
četvorica 4	sedmorica 7

Higher numbers if required follow the same pattern adding the suffix **-orica** to the cardinal number. They may only be used when talking about a group of men: **trojica** means *three men*. They are sometimes found in combination with a noun or pronoun in the gen. case:

Imam trojicu braće.	*I have three brothers.*
Njih dvojica idu svugde zajedno.	*The two of them go everywhere together.*

These numbers are, grammatically, fem. nouns with case endings like other fem. nouns which end in **-a**, and with fem. adjective agreements. When they are used as part of a subject, the verb is plural and the agreement in the past tense is fem.:

Ta dvojica su studirala zajedno.	*Those two studied together.*

Both

Both in Serbian is expressed by **oba** and **obe**. The former is used with masc. and neut. nouns and the latter with fem. nouns (like **dva/dve**) and they are followed by the genitive singular. They also have the forms **obojica** and **oboje** (like **dvojica** and **dvoje**):

Obojica su večerala u restoranu.	*They both had dinner in the restaurant.*

Numbers as part of a subject

When cardinal numbers appear as part of a subject, verbal agreements are as follows:

One

Verbs following subject **jedan, jedna, jedno** are always singular, including when used in compound numbers:

Jedan Englez je bio na ulici.	*One Englishman was on the street.*
Dvadeset jedan Englez je bio na ulici.	*Twenty-one Englishmen were on the street.*

Two, three, four

Verbs following subject **dva/dve, tri, četiri** are always plural and the past tense agreement is **-a** for masc. and neut. nouns and **-e** for fem. nouns, including when used in compound numbers:

| Dva stola su stajala u sobi. | *Two tables were standing in the room.* |
| Dvadeset tri žene su stigle. | *Twenty-three women arrived.* |

Five, six, etc.

Verbs following subject **pet**, **šest**, etc. are always singular, and the past tense agreement is neut. irrespective of the nouns involved, including when used in compound numbers:

| Pet stolova je stajalo u sobi. | *Five tables were standing in the room.* |
| Dvadeset devet žena je stiglo. | *Twenty-nine women arrived.* |

Adjectives in expressions with numbers

Adjectives used in expressions with **jedan** agree with the noun described in gender and case as usual:

| Video sam jednog visokog Engleza. | *I saw one tall Englishman.* |

Adjectives used in expressions with numbers followed by a noun in the gen. plural also take a gen. plural ending:

| Video sam pet visokih ljudi. | *I saw five tall people.* |

Adjectives used in expressions with numbers followed by a noun in the gen. singular take the ending -a for masc. and neut. nouns and the ending -e for fem. nouns:

| Gledao sam dva visoka čoveka. | *I watched two tall men.* |
| Gledao sam dve visoke žene. | *I watched two tall women.* |

More about imperatives

Note these three imperative forms which vary slightly from the usual rules:

pomozi	pomozite	from	**pomoći** *to help*
reci	recite	from	**reći** *to say, tell*
sedi	sedite	from	**sesti** *to sit down*

You are already aware of the rules for forming the negative imperative using **nemoj** and **nemojte**. It is also possible to express the negative imperative with **ne** followed by the imperative. This method can be used with imperfective verbs only to express a firm prohibition not to do something such as a parent might use to a child:

Ne prelazi ulicu!   *Don't cross the street!*
Ne gazi travu!   *Don't walk on the grass!*

Family celebrations

Activity B

◆ CD 2, TR 5, 01.15

Listen to Miloš and Marko talking together, read the dialogue and then answer the questions that follow:

Miloš	Marko, da li tvoj tata slavi slavu?
Marko	Retko. Teško je kod nas slaviti slavu. Tamo gde mi živimo nema mnogo Srba, a Englezi ne znaju šta je to.
Miloš	Da si bio ovde kad smo slavili prošle godine, bio bi to za tebe pravi doživljaj. Došlo nam je u goste više od pedeset ljudi. Možda ove godine, za Svetog Nikolu?
Marko	Nadam se da ću ove zime doći sa devojkom. Voleo bih da ona vidi Beograd i upozna moju beogradsku porodicu.
Miloš	Odlično, dođite u decembru. Da li možete da ostanete malo duže?
Marko	Zašto?
Miloš	Zato što Maja ima rođendan 23. decembra, a onda dolaze Nova godina i Božić.
Marko	Ne znam, bojim se da bi to bilo suviše dugo. Sumnjam da ćemo imati toliko vremena. Rekao sam Silviji da ćemo u Srbiji provesti desetak dana. Pitaću je da li hoće da ostane duže, ali čini mi se da neće moći. Već mi je rekla da je obećala mami da će biti kod kuće krajem decembra.

slaviti; proslaviti	*to celebrate*
slava	*slava* (family patron saint's day)
Da si bio ovde . . .	*If you had been here . . .*
doživljaj	*experience*
možda	*perhaps*
Sveti Nikola	*Saint Nicholas*

QUICK VOCAB

nadati se	to hope
rođendan	birthday
Nova godina	New Year
Božić	Christmas
bojati se, bojim se	to fear, to be afraid
sumnjati	to doubt
čini mi se	it seems to me
obećavati, obećati	to promise

Questions

i With whom does Miloš hope to come to Belgrade during winter?

ii Who has a birthday on 23 December?

Marko asks Miloš if his father celebrates the **slava** in England. This is a uniquely Serbian celebration for the whole family and, traditionally, the date represents the family's conversion to Christianity. A priest may come to bless the house in the morning, after which you can expect family and friends to visit at any time during the course of the day. Each **slava** is known by the name of the saint whose holiday falls on that date in the Orthodox Church calendar. There are some dates which are more popular than others, such as **Sveti Nikola** *Saint Nicholas* on 19 December, and **Sveti Jovan** *Saint John* on 20 January. Church holidays in the Orthodox calendar do not always coincide with dates in other churches; e.g. **Božić** *Christmas* falls on 7 January.

How it works

Reported speech

Reported (or indirect) speech is when you tell someone else what you have said or what you intend to say, or what someone else has said. Such constructions begin with expressions like *I said that . . .* or *he told me that . . .* Reported speech also includes other verbs which are not strictly what has been said but are associated; such verbs as *hope, think, doubt, suppose that*:

> **Nadam se da ću doći sa**   *I hope that I shall come with*
> **devojkom.**   *my girlfriend.*

The choice of the tense of the verb which comes after **da** is not always the same as in English. The tense used in Serbian is the same tense that the speaker would have used in the original statement:

Rekao sam Silviji da ćemo u Srbiji provesti desetak dana.	*I told Sylvia that we would spend about ten days in Serbia.*

In his original statement to Sylvia, Marko said, 'We shall spend about ten days in Serbia.' Therefore, when reporting this conversation with his girlfriend, Marko uses the future tense . . . **da ćemo u Srbiji provesti desetak dana.**

For reporting an imperative or command use the construction **da** followed by the present tense. Biljana told her husband to fetch some bread, so he might say:

Rekla mi je da idem po hleb.	*She told me to go for the bread.* (lit. *told me that I go . . .*)

Indirect questions

The same principle regarding choice of tense operates with indirect questions. These are sentences of the type:

Pitao sam ga da li će doći sa mnom.	*I asked him if he would come with me.*

The original question was 'Will you come with me?' using the future tense, so the future tense is incorporated when reporting the question.

In these constructions the second part of the sentence in English begins with *if*, and in Serbian the second part of the sentence begins with **da li . . .**

Pitaću je da li hoće da ostane duže.	*I shall ask her if she wants to stay longer.*

Alternatively, the second part of the sentence may be introduced by **li** placed after the verb:

Pitaću je hoće li da ostane duže.	*I shall ask her if she wants to stay longer.*

Question words may also be incorporated into such constructions:

| Pitao sam je ko će ići po hleb. | *I asked her who was going for the bread.* |

Insight

When reporting what you or someone else said to someone, remember that the verbs **reći** and **kazati** are followed by the dative case:

| Rekla sam vam ... | *I told you ...* |

However, the verb **pitati** is followed by the accusative case:

| Pitala sam vas ... | *I asked you ...* |

Masculine nouns ending in *-in*

Some masc. nouns in Serbian end in -in in the nom. singular. They often refer to people, their nationality or where they are from. The final syllable is dropped in the plural before case endings are added:

Singular		Plural	
Srbin	*Serb*	**Srbi**	*Serbs*
građanin	*citizen*	**građani**	*citizens*
Beograđanin	*Belgrader*	**Beograđani**	*Belgraders*

If you had been here ...

Constructions of the type *If you had been here ...* or *If I were you ...* are introduced in Serbian with **Da ...** These sentences express actions which did not or could not happen and the second part of the sentence is always in the conditional:

| Da si bio ovde, bio bi to za tebe pravi doživljaj. | *If you had been here, it would have been a real experience for you.* |

The first part of the sentence may be in the past or present tense:

| Da sam ja na tvom mestu, ja bih mu rekao da ode. | *If I were in your place, I would tell him to go away.* |

Practice

1 The previous day Biljana talked to her son Dejan on the phone about Marko's arrival in Belgrade. Now Dejan is reporting their conversation to his wife Ivana. Imagine that you are in his place and you have to put the following statements made by Biljana into indirect speech. Begin each answer with **Rekla je da . . .** *She said that . . .* Remember to take care with the order of short forms which have to come immediately after **da . . .** First look at the example:

e.g. Mi smo dobro.
      Rekla je da su oni dobro.

a Marko je juče došao u Beograd.
b Pozvali smo ga na ručak.
c Doći će sutra oko jedan sat.
d Biće i Maja na ručku.
e Sutra nema predavanja na fakultetu.
f Marko će imati u Beogradu mnogo posla.
g Mislim da ostaje do kraja nedelje.
h On bi voleo da vas vidi.

2 Here are the questions that Dejan asked Biljana on the phone and which he also reported to his wife. In this case you are again playing the role of Dejan, this time reporting to Ivana what you asked your mother. Change the questions below into indirect questions beginning with **Pitao sam je . . .** *I asked her . . .*

e.g. Da li si juče išla na posao?
      Pitao sam je da li je juče išla na posao.

a Da li Marko ima mnogo posla u Beogradu?
b Da li boravi kod vas ili u hotelu?
c Koliko dugo će ostati ovde?
d U koliko sati će doći na ručak?
e Da li vam je potrebna neka pomoć?
f Treba li nešto da vam kupimo?
g Da li možemo da svratimo posle ručka?
h Da li bi ti htela da nam čuvaš decu sutra uveče?

Dejan's flat

Activity C

🔊 **CD 2, TR 5, 02.28**

Biljana is describing to Marko the new flat which Dejan and his wife have recently bought. Listen to what she says on the recording and answer the questions on the next page:

> Dejan i Ivana imaju četvorosoban stan u novom bloku koji se nalazi u predgrađu. Stan je bio skup i zato oni oboje moraju da rade. Bez dve plate ne bi mogli da plaćaju kredit i da kupe nameštaj.
>
> Najveća soba u stanu im je dnevna soba, gde imaju trosed, fotelje, police za knjige i televizor. Trpezarija nije velika i u njoj su sto, stolice i kredenac. U kredencu drže čaše, servis i druge stvari koje koriste kad pozovu goste na večeru. Pored trpezarije je dosta velika kuhinja, u kojoj ima mesta za sve što je potrebno. Desno su stavili šporet, frižider i zamrzivač. Sa leve strane su sudopera i mali sto, a na zidu viseći elementi u kojima drže šerpe i drugo posuđe. Kupatilo je malo, u njemu imaju kadu sa tušem, wc, lavabo i mašinu za veš. Imaju dve spavaće sobe. Deca dele jednu sobu, a Dejan i Ivana koriste drugu. U njihovoj spavaćoj sobi su krevet, orman i komoda. Dejan je tamo stavio i radni sto da može da radi kod kuće.

QUICK VOCAB

blok	*block* (of flats)
predgrađe	*suburb*
zato	*for that reason, therefore*
plata	*pay, salary*
plaćati, platiti	*to pay*
kredit	*credit, mortgage*
nameštaj	*furniture*
trosed	*three-seater sofa*
fotelja	*armchair*
polica	*shelf*
televizor	*television set*
servis	*dinner service*
posuđe	*dishes* (neut. singular noun)
sudopera	*sink* (in kitchen)
šporet	*cooker*

frižider	*fridge*	
zamrzivač	*freezer*	
zid	*wall*	
viseći elementi	*wall cupboards*	
šerpa	*pan*	
kada	*bath*	
tuš	*shower*	
wc	*toilet, lavatory* (pronounced 've-tse')	
lavabo	*sink* (in bathroom)	
mašina za veš	*washing machine*	
deliti; podeliti	*to share*	
koristiti; iskoristiti	*to use*	
orman	*wardrobe*	
komoda	*chest of drawers*	
radni sto	*desk*	

Questions

i How big is Dejan's flat?
ii Where is the washing mashine kept?

How it works

Saying *which*

You have already come across **koji** *which, what* in questions:

Koja je vaša adresa?	*What is your address?*
Koju knjigu si kupio?	*Which book did you buy?*

The same word is used to join together two parts of a sentence:

Imaju četvorosoban stan u novom bloku koji se nalazi u predgrađu.	*They have a four-roomed flat in a new block which is situated in the suburbs.*

The word **koji** follows the same pattern of case endings as **moj** and so it has both long and short forms **kojeg/koga** and **kojem/ kome**. The short forms are used only when **koji** refers to people. It is an adjective and so its ending must conform to a particular gender, singular or plural, and to a particular case. The gender and number depend on the noun to which it refers. In the example above **koji** refers back to the *block of flats* **u novom bloku** and so its ending must be masculine and singular agreeing with **blok**. The case ending for **koji** depends on how it is being used in its part of the sentence. In the example above, the word is the subject of the verb *is situated* and therefore put in the nom. case.

Look at these examples:

To je čovek koji ima stan pored nas.	*That is the man who has the flat next to us.*
To je čovek koga sam juče video.	*That is the man whom I saw yesterday.*
To je pismo u kojem piše da ne dolazi.	*That is the letter in which he writes that he is not coming.*

The word for *which* after **to** *that* and **sve** *everything* is **što**:

Pored trpezarije je dosta velika kuhinja, u kojoj ima mesta za sve što je potrebno.	*Next to the dining room there is a kitchen, where there is enough space for everything which is necessary.*

Describing people

Activity D

◆ CD 2, TR 5, 04.08

Now listen to Maja and Marko's conversation about Vlada and Sylvia. Read the dialogue and answer the questions that follow.

Maja	Kako izgleda tvoja devojka, Marko?
Marko	Silvija je lepa i visoka devojka. Ima plave oči i dugu smeđu kosu. Imam njenu sliku, hoćeš da ti pokažem?
Maja	Naravno. Koliko dugo ste već zajedno?
Marko	Tri godine. Ali znamo se već godinama, od detinjstva. Evo, pogledaj. Silvija mi je rekla da ne pokazujem ovu fotografiju, njoj se ne dopada. A ja mislim da tu izgleda sjajno.
Maja	Jeste, vrlo je lepa. I kakvi su vam planovi? Nameravate li da se venčate?
Marko	Da, idućeg leta.

Maja	Hoće li biti velika svadba?
Marko	Moraće da bude. Mama i tata bi se ljutili ako ne bismo imali veliku svadbu. Oni se tome već sada raduju. Naravno, voleli bismo kad biste i vi svi došli.
Maja	Ako me pozoveš, ja ću sigurno doći na svadbu. Drago mi je što vidim da si srećan.
Marko	Kaži sad ti meni nešto o sebi. Tvoj dečko se zove Vlada, zar ne? Jesi li zaljubljena u njega?
Maja	Pa, rekla bih da jesam. Ali ne mislim još da se udajem. Treba prvo da završim fakultet.
Marko	Kako ste se upoznali?
Maja	Upoznali smo se na jednoj žurci pre pet meseci. Ja sam te večeri bila nešto tužna, a Vlada je vrlo duhovit i zabavan. I uvek je veseo.

izgledati	*to look, to appear*
plav	*blue, blonde*
oko, pl. **oči**	*eye*
smeđ	*brown*
kosa	*hair*
slika	*picture*
pokazivati, pokazujem; **pokazati, pokažem**	*to show*
zajedno	*together*
znamo se	*we have known each other*
godinama	*for years*
detinjstvo	*childhood*
fotografija	*photograph*
sjajan	*marvellous*
nameravati	*to intend*
venčavati se; venčati se	*to get married*
idući	*next*
svadba	*wedding*
ljutiti se	*to be angry*
radovati se, radujem se	*to look forward to* (with dat. case)
drago mi je što . . .	*I am glad that . . .*
srećan	*happy*
dečko	*boy, boyfriend*

QUICK VOCAB

zaljubljen	*in love*
udavati se, udajem se;	*to get married* (of a woman)
udati se, udam se	
završiti fakultet	*to graduate*
žurka	*party*
tužan	*sad*
duhovit	*witty*
veseo	*jolly, merry* (like **ceo**)

Questions

i How long have Marko and Sylvia been together?

ii When did Maja and Vlada first meet?

How do you say . . . ?

Activity E

◀) CD 2, TR 5, 05.38

The conversation between Maja and Marko turns towards language. Listen to the recording, read the text and answer the questions:

Marko	Majo, kako se zove ovo što vi imate na podu? Ne mogu da se setim kako se to kaže na srpskom.
Maja	Šta na podu? Tepih?
Marko	Ne, ne, ispod tepiha. Ovaj drveni pod.
Maja	To je parket. A kako se kaže na engleskom?
Marko	I na engleskom je slično, parquet. To je ista reč, iz francuskog, samo je izgovor malo drukčiji.
Maja	Stvarno? Čudno je što učim engleski već toliko godina, a nikad tu reč nisam čula.
Marko	To znači da ti nije bila potrebna. Kad negde živiš, treba da koristiš mnogo reči koje ne moraš da znaš ako učiš jezik samo iz knjiga. Da živiš u Engleskoj, naučila bi razne izraze za stvari iz kuće i svakodnevnog života koje nećeš naučiti na fakultetu.
Maja	U pravu si. Da bi dobro naučio jezik, moraš da budeš u zemlji i da govoriš sa ljudima. Ima mnogo reči i izraza koje ne možeš da naučiš iz rečnika.

QUICK VOCAB

pod	*floor*
sećati se; setiti se	*to remember* (with gen. case)
tepih	*carpet*
kako se kaže na srpskom?	*how do you say in Serbian?*
drven	*wooden*
reč	*word*
izgovor	*pronunciation*
drukčiji	*different*
stvarno	*really*
čudan	*strange*
toliko	*so many, so much*
izraz	*expression*
svakodnevni	*everyday*
život	*life*
u pravu si	*you are right*
da bi dobro naučio jezik	*in order to learn a language well*

Questions

i Has Maja heard the word *parquet* before?

ii What does she think is the best way to learn a language?

How it works

Phrases and expressions

- To say that you *see/hear someone doing something* use the construction **kako** followed by the present tense as in the example: **Vidim ih pored prozora kako pričaju** *I see them talking by the window*; also in the example: **Čuli smo kako ulaze u sobu.** *We heard them coming into the room.*

- To ask *what someone looks like* use the verb **izgledati** as in the example: **Kako izgleda tvoja devojka?** *What does your girlfriend look like?* When talking about appearances the adjective **plav** normally means *blue*, but when talking about hair it means *blonde*.

- A reflexive particle may be added to a verb to mean *each other* or *one another* as in the phrase **znamo se već godinama** *we have known each other for years*. The ins. plural form of other words like **godina** has the same meaning: **satima** *for hours*, **mesecima** *for months*, **vekovima** *for centuries*.

- You have used the word **da** to mean *that* in phrases like **Rekao mi je da** . . . The word **što** is used in certain expressions to mean *that* when what follows is a reason or explanation as in the phrase **Drago mi je što** . . . *I am glad that...*or **Čudno je što** . . . *It is strange that* . . . The word **što** is almost like *because*.

- You are already aware that there are different words to say *married*: **oženjen** (of a man); **udata** (of a woman). They are taken from different verbs: **on se ženi** *he is getting married* and **ona se udaje** *she is getting married*. When speaking of a man and woman getting married use the verb **venčati se**: **oni će se venčati** *they will get married*.

- To say *you are right* you can use the expressions **u pravu si** (**biti u pravu** lit. *to be in the right*) or **imaš pravo** (**imati pravo** lit. *to have the right*): **nisi u pravu** *you are wrong*, **bili smo u pravu** *we were right*.

- To say *in order to* you can use the alternative infinitive construction as in: **Išli smo da mu kažemo** . . . *We went to tell him.../We went in order to tell him* . . . If you want to be more emphatic about the purpose then use **da** followed by the conditional form of the verb as in: **Da bi dobro naučio jezik** . . . *In order to learn a language well* . . .

Practice

3 Milan Lukić has recently married and is moving with his wife Gordana into a new flat. They have already decided which room they will use for what purpose. Look at the plan of the flat (**radna soba** *study*, **hodnik** *corridor*) and the list of furniture given below. Help Milan to tell the removal men into which room they should put the furniture. Follow the model in the example:

e.g.   fotelja
       Fotelju stavite u dnevnu sobu.

a krevet
b kredenac
c frižider
d radni sto
e sto i stolice
f orman
g polica za knjige
h trosed

4 Describe Milan's new flat to Dragan, who has not yet seen it. There is more vocabulary for furniture given in this unit. Use Biljana's description of Dejan's flat in Activity C as a model.

5 Put the correct form of **koji** into the sentences below. First look at the example:

e.g.   Ovo je kuća o (koji) sam vam govorio.
       Ovo je kuća o kojoj sam vam govorio.

a To je najlepši stan (koji) sam ovde videla.
b Da li je to devojka s (koji) si išla u školu?
c Njegov brat, (koji) živi u Engleskoj, ima svadbu u junu.
d Ovo je najbolja drugarica (koji) imam.
e Ovo je nameštaj o (koji) sam ti pričala.

f Ona visoka devojka (koji) sedi pored Vere je njena sestra.

g Kuća u (koji) stanuje Robert je u centru grada.

h Da li je to konobar (koji) ste dali novac?

6 Robert is talking to Vesna about her flat and her family. Fill in his part of the conversation:

◀) **CD 2, TR 5, 07.05**

Robert	*What kind of flat do you have?*
Vesna	Imam mali stan u predgrađu.
Robert	*Do you live alone?*
Vesna	Ne, živim sa sestrom.
Robert	*Do you have your own room?*
Vesna	Ne, delim spavaću sobu sa sestrom. Imamo i trpezariju, koju koristimo i kao dnevnu i kao radnu sobu.
Robert	*And where do your parents live?*
Vesna	Oni stanuju u komšiluku.
Robert	*What does the word komšiluk mean? I don't know that word.*
Vesna	Stvarno još nisi čuo tu reč? Komšiluk znači neighbourhood.
Robert	*And how do you say 'a neighbour' in Serbian?*
Vesna	*A neighbour* je komšija. Za muškarca se kaže *komšija, moj komšija*. A za ženu se kaže *komšinica*. Moji roditelji imaju stan u istoj kući gde i ja. Oni su moje komšije.
Robert	*I have good neighbours. They are always kind and ask me if I need any help.*

Test yourself

Here you can check some of the things you have learnt in this unit. Look at the questions below and choose the right answer:

1 When would you use the word **troje**?

    a talking about a group of men
    b talking about a group of women
    c talking about a mixed group

2 A friend told you that he would come for dinner. Which option would you choose to complete the sentence **Rekao je da . . .** ?

a će doći na večeru
b bi došao na večeru
c je došao na večeru

3 What is the meaning of **Nadam se**?

   a I believe   **b** I hope   **c** I doubt

4 How would you say *She asked me:* **Pitala** . . . . ?

   a me je   **b** mi je

5 You and your family have just been told important information. How would you say *If we had known it* . . . ?

   a Da smo znali . . .
   b Kad bismo znali . . .
   c Ako budemo znali . . .

6 Into which room would you put your new **šporet**?

   a dining room   **b** bedroom   **c** kitchen

7 What do people normally do in **trpezarija**?

   a gledaju televiziju   **b** spavaju   **c** jedu

8 How would you ask the waiter to bring you another plate: **Donesite nam još jedan** . . . . ?

   a nož   **b** tanjir   **c** stolnjak

9 Which form would you use to fill the gap in the sentence **Ovo je pismo** . . . . **sam dobio od drugarice?**

   a koji   **b** koja   **c** koje

10 Which of the following is the most suitable response to the question **Kako ona izgleda?**

   a Studira medicinu.
   b Ima dvadeset godina.
   c Ima kratku crnu kosu.

16

Health matters

In this unit you will learn:

- How to call a doctor
- How to say what is wrong with you
- Expressions when at a pharmacy
- Parts of the body
- More about verbal aspect
- How to express *do not have to/must not*

Calling a doctor

Activity A

◀) CD 2, TR 6

Some foreign guests are staying in a hotel at Kopaonik. Two of them have to go to reception to ask for a doctor for some minor medical problem. Listen to their requests, read the dialogues and answer the questions that follow.

Госпођа	Извините, мој муж је болестан. Молим вас, позовите лекара.
Рецепционер	Одмах, госпођо. Да ли му треба хитна помоћ?
Госпођа	Не треба, хвала. Мислим да није ништа опасно, али за сваки случај, боље да га види лекар.
Господин	Извините, моја жена је повредила ногу. Да ли имате лекара у хотелу?

Рецепционер	Не, господине, на жалост, немамо. Али могу одмах да се јавим лекару који живи близу. Доћи ће за неколико минута.
Господин	Хвала лепо. Замолите га да дође што пре. Реците да је хитно. Ми ћемо га чекати код нас у соби.

QUICK VOCAB

болестан	*ill*
хитна помоћ	*emergency aid*
опасан	*dangerous*
за сваки случај	*just in case*
повређивати, повређујем, повредити	*to injure*
нога	*leg, foot*
јављати се, јавити се	*to get in touch, give someone a ring* (with dat.)
хитан	*urgent*
што пре	*as soon as possible*

Questions

i Is there a doctor in the hotel?

ii How quickly is the doctor going to come?

Explaining what is wrong

Activity B

🔊 **CD 2, TR 6, 01.11**

The doctor arrives at the hotel and the patients explain what is wrong with them. Listen to the two short dialogues on the recording, read the text and answer the questions that follow:

Лекар	Како се осећате, господине?
Господин	Не осећам се добро. Кашљем целу ноћ, имам кијавицу, боли ме грло . . .
Лекар	Да видим . . . Прехлађени сте. Имате и температуру. Дaћу вам рецепт. Идите, госпођо, у апотеку по ове лекове. А ви останите у кревету два-три дана. И немојте да бринете. Ускоро ћете се осећати боље.

Лекар	Шта се десило, госпођо?
Госпођа	Изишли смо јутрос у шетњу и ја сам пала и повредила ногу.
Лекар	Покажите ми где вас боли?
Госпођа	Овде, на десној нози. Боли ме све више.
Лекар	Да видим . . . Добро је, нисте сломили ногу. Ја ћу да вам дезинфикујем рану и да ставим завој. Морате да се одмарате дан-два и биће све у реду.
Госпођа	Да ли морам да лежим?
Лекар	Не морате, али морате неколико дана да пазите. Немојте много да ходате.

осећати се, осетити се	to feel
кашљати, кашљем	to cough
кијавица	head cold
боли ме грло	I have a sore throat
бити прехлађен	to have a cold
рецепт	prescription
лек	medicine
два-три дана	two or three days
бринути, бринем	to worry
падати, пасти, паднем, пао	to fall
све више	more and more
ломити, сломити	to break
дезинфиковати, дезинфикујем	to disinfect
рана	wound
завој	bandage
дан-два	for a day or two
лежати, лежим	to lie
пазити	to be careful
ходати	to walk

Questions

i For how long does the first patient have to stay in bed?

ii Does the lady who hurt her leg have to stay in bed?

How it works

Contacting someone

There are various expressions which may be used to say you will contact someone:

писати некоме	to *write to someone* (with dat.)
звати некога	to *call someone* (with acc.), which may be by telephone or by calling out loud
телефонирати некоме	to *telephone someone* (with dat.)
јављати се некоме	to *contact someone* (with dat.), usually by telephone but may also be in writing

You are already aware of the word **веза** *connection* when talking about travel connections. The same word may also be used for being in touch:

Бићемо у вези.	*We shall be in touch.*

Insight

The English verb *to ask* can mean either *to ask a question* (for information) or *to request* (someone to do something). In Serbian these meanings are expressed by two different verbs: **питати** and **молити**.

Питала је да ли имамо лекара.	*She asked if we had a doctor.*
Молила је да позовемо лекара.	*She asked us to call a doctor.*

As . . . as possible

The phrase **што пре** means *as soon as possible*. In order to make up other expressions of the type *as . . . as possible* use **што** followed by the relevant adverb or adjective in the comparative form:

| што брже | as quickly as possible |
| што лакше | as easily as possible |

Another expression using the comparative form of the adverb or adjective is in the example **све више** *all the more, more and more*. To say that something or someone is *all the more . . .* use **све** followed by the relevant adverb or adjective in the comparative form:

| **Она је све лепша.** | *She is all the more beautiful.* (getting more and more) |
| **Постаје све хладније.** | *It is getting colder and colder.* (all the more cold) |

To hurt, ache

The verb **болети** *to hurt, ache* is only used in the third person:

Боли ме нога.	*My leg hurts.* (lit. *The leg hurts me.*)
Боли га грло.	*He has a sore throat.*
Да ли те боле ноге?	*Do your legs hurt?*

The adjective **болестан** *ill*, and all others which have the endings -**стан** in the masc. nom. singular drop both the **т** and **а** when adding case endings: fem. **болесна**.

Two or three

To say *two or three* in Serbian just say the two numbers together as in the example:

| **Останите у кревету два-три дана.** | *Stay in bed two or three days.* |

In writing put a hyphen between the two numbers.

When using expressions like *a day or two* use a similar construction **дан-два** in which the word *one* **један** is understood:

| **Морате да се одмарате дан-два.** | *You have to rest for a day or two.* |

At the pharmacy

Activity C

🔊 **CD 2, TR 06, 02.23**

Sometimes for minor problems you do not need a doctor but a pharmacist (**апотекар**) may be able to help. Milan's wife Gordana works as a pharmacist in Belgrade. Listen to her conversations with a couple of customers and answer the questions before reading the text below:

Questions

i What problem does the first gentleman have?

ii What kind of medicine is the second gentleman asking for?

Гордана	Добар дан. Изволите?
Господин	Страшно ме боли зуб. Молим вас, да ли имате неке таблете против болова?
Гордана	Имам, господине. Ово су врло јаке таблете и брзо делују.
Господин	Хвала вам много. Узећу једну кутију.
Гордана	Изволите, господине. Да вам кажем, док узимате ове таблете, не смете да пијете алкохол.
Гордана	Добар дан. Изволите?
Господин	Повредио сам прст, овде, на левој руци. Сада ме много боли. Мора да је инфекција. Не знам шта да радим. Могу ли да купим неки антибиотик?
Гордана	Антибиотике не можете да добијете без лекарског рецепта, господине. Имамо ову маст, она делује против инфекције. Али, да сам на вашем месту, ја бих ишла код лекара, за сваки случај. Ако вам треба неки јачи лек, он ће вам дати рецепт.

страшно	*terribly*	
зуб	*tooth*	
таблета	*tablet*	
против	*against* (followed by gen.)	QUICK VOCAB
бол	*pain*	
деловати, делујем	*to take effect*	

кутија	*box*
не смете	*you must not*
алкохол	*alcohol*
прст	*finger, toe*
рука	*arm, hand*
инфекција	*infection*
антибиотик	*antibiotic*
лекарски	*doctor's*
маст	*ointment*

How it works

May not . . ./must not . . .

Note the use of the verbs **моћи** *to be able, can,* *смети* *may* and **морати** *to have to, must* in the following phrases:

Можеш да купиш те таблете.	*You can buy those tablets.* (e.g. you have the money)
Смем ли да отворим прозор?	*May I open the window?* (e.g. do I have permission?)
Јован мора да лежи у кревету.	*Jovan has to stay in bed.* (e.g. the doctor says so)

and in the negative:

Не можеш да купиш те таблете без рецепта.	*You are not able to buy those tablets without a prescription.* (e.g. I'll not sell them)
Не смеш да отвориш прозор.	*You may not/must not open the window.* (e.g. you do not have permission)
Не мораш да лежиш у кревету.	*You do not have to stay in bed.* (e.g. the doctor says it is not obligatory)

More about verbal aspect

Most of the verbs which you have met appear with both an imperfective and a perfective aspect. In effect, for one verb in English there are two in Serbian. The imperfective verb shows that the action was not completed, or that it is in progress, or that it is a frequent action. The perfective verb shows that the action has occurred and is over, or that it is intended that the action be completed. It is often possible to tell which verbs form these aspectual pairs.

By taking the imperfective verb which is always given first as the basic form, we can see three main trends in producing the perfective verb.

1 the perfective verb is formed by adding a prefix to the imperfective:

будити	пробудити	*to wake*
писати	написати	*to write*
пити	попити	*to drink*

2 the perfective verb is formed by changing to a different type, usually one with an **и** ending:

осећати се	осетити се	*to feel*
остављати	оставити	*to leave*
спремати	спремити	*to prepare*

3 the perfective verb is shorter than the imperfective by one syllable:

давати	дати	*to give*
почињати	почети	*to begin*
устајати	устати	*to get up*

Parts of the body

Activity D

Look at the picture on the next page showing parts of the body. Fill in the names which are missing, indicated by the letters of the alphabet, and then answer the following questions:

Questions
  i How would you say in Serbian: 'I have a headache'?
  ii How would you say 'He has a stomachache'?
  iii How would you say 'I injured my knee'?

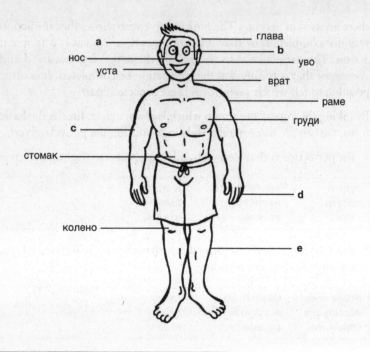

a ——— глава
b
нос ———
уво
уста ———
врат
раме
груди
c ———
стомак ———
d
колено ———
e

How it works

Parts of the body: nouns

A number of words which refer to parts of the body do not follow
standard patterns for case endings.

око, уво
These words follow regular neut. patterns in the singular (gen. **ока,
ува**) but the plural forms are fem. with nom. **очи** *eyes* and **уши**
ears:

nom.	очи	уши
acc.	очи	уши
gen.	очију	ушију
dat.	очима	ушима
ins.	очима	ушима
loc.	очима	ушима

рука, нога, прст

These words follow regular fem. or masc. patterns except for the gen. plural forms which are as follows:

рука	gen. plural	руку
нога	gen. plural	ногу
прст	gen. plural	прстију

The word **рука** means both *hand* and *arm*.
The word **нога** means both *foot* and *leg*.
The word **прст** means both *finger* (**прст на руци**) and *toe* (**прст на нози**).

раме

The word **раме** *shoulder* follows the same pattern of neut. noun endings as **време** with the additional syllable **-ен-** before case endings: gen. singular **рамена**.

уста, леђа

These are neut. nouns which are always in the plural (like **кола** *car*; **врата** *door*):

Боле ме леђа.	*I have backache.*

Some of these words are used in common idioms:

далеко од очију, далеко **од срца** (**срце** *heart*)	*out of sight, out of mind*
заљубљен до ушију	*head over heels in love*
остати празних руку	*to be left empty-handed*
од малих ногу	*from a tender age*

Practice

1 On her way to the language school Vesna meets Barbara and they continue walking together. Barbara does not feel well and Vesna suggests that she should see a doctor. Fill in Barbara's part of the conversation:

Весна	Здраво, Барбара. Како си? Нисам те јуче видела у школи.
Барбара	*I didn't go to school yesterday. I didn't feel well.*
Весна	Зашто? Шта ти је било?
Барбара	*I had a terrible headache.*
Весна	Да ли је то прошло? Како се сад осећаш?
Барбара	*I don't feel well. Everything hurts me. I think I have a cold.*
Весна	Имаш ли температуру?
Барбара	*I don't know. But I've taken an aspirin.*
Весна	Да видим . . . Врућа си. Чини ми се да имаш температуру. Треба што пре да идеш код лекара. Не смеш да чекаш.
Барбара	*All right. I agree. Can you tell Mr Lukić that I am ill and that I shall not come to the class?*
Весна	Наравно. Немој да бринеш. Иди одмах код лекара.
Барбара	*Thank you. I'll give you a ring in the afternoon.*

2 You will hear a conversation between a patient and a Serbian doctor. Listen to the dialogue and answer these questions:

◆ CD 2, TR 6, 05.41

a What does the patient say is wrong with him?
b Does he have a cough?
c Does he have a high temperature?
d What medicine does the doctor prescribe?
e Does he have to take anything else?
f How long should the patient stay in bed?
g When does he have to see the doctor again?

Test yourself

In this and in later units you will be able to check your knowledge of new points and of points learnt earlier in the book. Look at the questions below and choose the right answer:

1 You arrive in a hotel at 9pm. How would you greet the receptionist?

a Лаку ноћ.   **b** Добро вече.   **c** Здраво.

2 How do you say in Serbian *Go right and then turn left*?

   a Идите право и онда скрените лево.
   b Идите десно и онда скрените лево.
   c Идите лево и онда скрените десно.

3 How would you ask for a bottle of water: **Дајте нам флашу** . . . . ?

   a вода   **b** воде   **c** воду

4 How would you say that you are going for dinner: **Идем** . . . . ?

   a по вечеру   **b** на вечеру   **c** за вечеру

5 If *to be late* is **каснити** how would you say *You must not be late*?

   a Не смете да касните.
   b Не морате да касните.
   c Не можете да касните.

6 Match the questions with answers:

   I Да ли ти треба помоћ?   **a** Моја сестра.
   II Како се осећате?   **b** Није.
  III Ко најбоље зна српски?   **c** Сто десет динара.
  IV Колико коштају таблете?   **d** Боли ме глава.
   V Да ли је он ожењен?   **e** Не, хвала.

17

Buying clothes

In this unit you will learn:

- Phrases when buying clothes
- Expressions for using hotel services
- How to form gerunds
- How to say *from*

Buying clothes

Activity A

🔊 CD 2, TR 7

Listen to the recording, read the text and answer the questions that follow:

Robert i Ričard uskoro putuju na letovanje u Crnu Goru. Misleći o letovanju, Robert dolazi do zaključka da mora da kupi novu odeću. Nikad nije kupio odeću u Beogradu i sada razgovara sa Ričardom.

Robert	Hteo bih da kupim neke stvari za letovanje. Nemam kupaće gaćice i nemam ni sandale ni patike.
Ričard	Treba da ideš u neki butik. Pogledaćemo u jednom od tržnih centara. Možemo da odemo u onaj u Nušićevoj.
Robert	Dobro. Moram da nabavim i nove farmerke, šorc i dve-tri majice.
Ričard	Nema problema, sve ćemo naći u tržnom centru.
U butiku	
Prodavačica	Dobar dan, izvolite?

Robert	Dobar dan. Tražim majice. Hteo bih jednu crvenu i jednu zelenu.
Prodavačica	Koji broj vam treba?
Robert	Ja nosim broj četrdeset dva.
Prodavačica	Da vidim koje boje imamo. Broj četrdeset dva ... imamo bele, crvene i žute majice, ali ne vidim zelene. Hoćete li da probate broj četrdeset?
Robert	Ne, to je za mene suviše malo. Čije su ovo majice, domaće ili strane?
Prodavačica	Italijanske, gospodine.
Robert	U redu, uzeću jednu crvenu i jednu žutu majicu.

QUICK VOCAB

misleći	*thinking*
zaključak	*conclusion*
odeća	*clothes*
kupaće gaćice	*swimming trunks* (fem. plural)
sandale	*sandals*
patike	*training shoes*
butik	*boutique*
tržni centar	*shopping centre*
nabavljati; nabaviti	*to acquire, purchase*
farmerke	*jeans* (fem. plural)
šorc	*shorts* (masc. singular)
majica	*T-shirt*
crven	*red*
zelen	*green*
nositi	*to wear*
Ja nosim broj ...	*My size is ...*
boja	*colour*
žut	*yellow*
probati	*to try*
čiji	*whose*

Questions

i What is Robert's size?

ii What colour T-shirts does he finally buy?

Activity B

🔊 **CD 2, TR 7, 01.34**

Listen to the recording and read the text below. Can you say what Vesna is doing?

> Vesna se odavno vratila sa Kopaonika. U Beogradu polako dolazi kraj leta i ona gleda stvari u svom ormanu. Vreme je da menja garderobu, da spakuje letnju odeću i da izvadi zimsku. Vadi iz ormana letnju jaknu, tanke pantalone, svilene haljine, suknje i bluze. Mora da proveri da li ima sve što joj treba za jesen i zimu. Stavlja u orman kišni mantil, zimski kaput, topao kostim, debele pantalone, vunene haljine i džempere.

sa Kopaonika	*from Kopaonik*
garderoba	*wardrobe* (choice of clothes)
pakovati, pakujem; spakovati	*to pack*
letnji	*summer* (adj.)
vaditi; izvaditi	*to take out*
zimski	*winter* (adj.)
jakna	*jacket*
tanak	*thin*
pantalone	*trousers* (fem. plural)
svilen	*silk* (adj.)
haljina	*dress*
suknja	*skirt*
bluza	*blouse*
proveravati; proveriti	*to check*
kišni mantil	*raincoat*
zimski kaput	*winter coat*
kostim	*suit*
debeo	*fat, thick* (like **ceo**)
vunen	*woollen*
džemper	*jumper*

274

How it works

Present gerund

This form of the verb is not used very often in Serbian, especially in the spoken language. It is associated with a formal or bookish style. It is easily formed and is the equivalent of that part of the verb which ends in -*ing* in English as in the example:

Misleći o letovanju, Robert dolazi do zaključka da mora da kupi novu odeću.	*Thinking about the summer holiday, Robert comes to the conclusion that he has to buy some new clothes.*

It is formed in Serbian by adding -ći to the third person plural of the present tense (the **oni** form):

oni misle	misleći	*thinking*
oni čitaju	čitajući	*reading*
oni slušaju	slušajući	*listening*

It is often expressed in English as *while doing something, by doing something* or *in doing something*. Such introductory words are not expressed in Serbian:

Slušajući radio, pisao je pismo bratu.	*While listening to the radio, he was writing a letter to his brother.*

This form of the verb is only used when referring to two actions performed at the same time and by the same subject, and it is made from imperfective verbs only.

One of . . .

To express the phrase *one of . . .* in Serbian, use **jedan** followed by the preposition **od** and the gen. case. Remember that **jedan** is an adjective and has to agree with the noun to which it refers. When Richard suggests that they look for a boutique in one of Belgrade's shopping centres he says:

Pogledaćemo u jednom od tržnih centara.	*We'll have a look in one of the shopping centres.*

Here the word **jednom** is masc. and loc. as the sense of the sentence is *We'll have a look in one (shopping centre) of the shopping centres.*

Compare with:

Pogledaćemo u jednoj od tih kafana.	*We'll have a look in one of those cafés.*

where **jednoj** is fem. and loc. to convey the sense of **u jednoj kafani**.

Street names and case endings

Richard suggests looking in the shopping centre which is in **Nušićeva ulica** *Nušić Street*. Branislav Nušić (1864–1938) was a famous Serbian playwright and **Nušićeva** is an adjective formed from his surname, *Nušić's,* which has a fem. adjective ending to agree with the noun **ulica**. Making adjectives from surnames is a common way of naming streets. When talking about them, it is usual to use just the name with the appropriate case ending, as Richard does when he says **u Nušićevoj** *in Nušić Street* using the loc. case.

Another common way of making a street name is with the gen. case as in **Ulica Kneza Miloša** *Street of Prince Miloš*. With these names put a preposition in front but do not change the gen. ending, the word **ulica** is then often understood:

Radnja je u (ulici) Kneza Miloša.	*The shop is in Prince Miloš (street).*

Whose

The word to express *whose* **čiji** is an adjective and adds the regular case endings for adjectives with a soft consonant:

Čije je ovo dete?	*Whose is this child?*
U čiju sobu ste ušli?	*Whose room did you enter?*

From …

There are three prepositions which are used to mean *from*: **od, iz** and **sa**, all of which are followed by the gen. case.

1 **od** is used to mean *from* with those nouns for which you also use the preposition **kod** + gen.:

Jovan je kod lekara.	*Jovan is at the doctor's.*

276

Jovan ide kući od lekara.	*Jovan is going home from the doctor's.*
Jovan je kod brata.	*Jovan is at his brother's.*
Jovan ide u grad od brata.	*Jovan is going to town from his brother's house.*

It is also used to mean *from* a person:

Jovan je dobio pismo od brata.	*Jovan received a letter from his brother.*

. . . and to mean *from* in certain phrases:

Od Beograda do Novog Sada putujem autobusom.	*I travel by bus from Belgrade to Novi Sad.*
Njegov stan nije daleko od centra grada.	*His flat is not far from the centre of town.*

2 iz is used with those nouns for which you would say **u** with the loc. case to mean that you are there:

Jovan je u školi.	*Jovan is in school.*
Jovan ide iz škole.	*Jovan is going from school.*
Bili smo u gradu.	*We were in town.*
Stigli smo kući iz grada.	*We arrived home from town.*

Insight

Use од when saying that you received something from a person and из when saying that you received something from a place:

Dobila sam pismo od Roberta.	*I received a letter from Robert.*
Dobila sam pismo iz Londona.	*I received a letter from London.*

3 sa is used to mean *from* or *off* and with all those nouns for which you would say **na** with the loc. case to mean that you are there:

Vesna je bila na brdu.	*Vesna was on the hill.*
Sišla je sa brda.	*She came down off the hill.*

Dragan je bio na poslu.	*Dragan was at work.*
Došao je kući sa posla.	*He came home from work.*
Mi se odmaramo na Kopaoniku.	*We are on holiday on Kopaonik.*
Vraćamo se sa Kopaonika.	*We are returning from Kopaonik.*

(As Kopaonik is a mountain, you say that you are **na** *on* it.)

Getting a suit cleaned

Activity C

◀) CD 2, TR 7, 02.30

Read the text, listen to the recording of Marko's conversation with the receptionist and answer the questions:

Marko Pavlović se pažljivo spremio za put u Beograd. Spakovao je odeću koju će nositi na poslu, jedno braon i jedno tamnoplavo odelo, tri košulje i dve kravate. U kofer je stavio i donje rublje, pidžamu, papuče i sportsku odeću koju će nositi kada je slobodan. Stigavši u hotel, odlučio je da se odmah raspakuje. Primetio je da njegovo braon odelo nije sasvim čisto. Našao je u sobi informacije o uslugama u hotelu:

> Hotelske usluge:
>
> sobni servis 24 časa, pranje i peglanje, hemijsko čišćenje, individualni sefovi za čuvanje dragocenosti, menjačnica, foto-kopiranje, besplatno čuvanje prtljaga, lekarske usluge, prodavnica štampe i cigareta, radnja sa suvenirima, muški i ženski frizerski salon, garaža za parkiranje 100 vozila.

Zvao je recepciju.

Marko	Halo, ovde Marko Pavlović, soba trista osamdeset.
Recepcioner	Dobar dan, gospodine Pavloviću. Izvolite?
Marko	Vidim da imate servis za hemijsko čišćenje. Hteo bih da dam jedno odelo na čišćenje, ali mi je vrlo hitno. Moram već sutra da ga nosim.

Recepcioner	Ne brinite, gospodine. Odmah ću poslati sobaricu po odelo. Biće vam vraćeno večeras.
Marko	Dobro. Hvala vam lepo.
Recepcioner	Nema na čemu, gospodine. Prijatno.

braon	*brown*
tamnoplav	*dark blue*
odelo	*suit*
košulja	*shirt*
kravata	*tie*
donje rublje	*underwear*
pidžama	*pyjamas*
papuče	*slippers*
stigavši	*having arrived*
odlučivati, odlučujem; odlučiti	*to decide*
raspakovati se, raspakujem se	*to unpack*
primećivati, primećujem; primetiti	*to notice*
sasvim	*completely*
čist	*clean*
sobni servis	*room service*
pranje	*washing*
peglanje	*ironing*
hemijsko čišćenje	*dry cleaning*
sef	*safe*
čuvanje	*looking after*
dragocenosti	*valuables*
prtljag	*luggage*
štampa	*press, newspapers and magazines*
cigareta	*cigarette*
suvenir	*souvenir*
muški	*male*
ženski	*female*
frizerski salon	*hairdressing salon*
vozilo	*vehicle*

QUICK VOCAB

sobarica	*maid*
biće vraćeno . . .	*it will be returned . . .*

Questions

i When does Marko want to wear his suit?
ii When is it going to be returned to him?

How it works

Colours

When using **braon** *brown* remember that its ending never changes. There are very few such adjectives in Serbian:

braon odelo	*brown suit* (neut.)
braon jakna	*brown jacket* (fem.)

The way of saying a *dark* colour is to add **tamno-** to the colour and to say a *light* colour is to add **svetlo-**

tamnocrvena kravata	*dark-red tie*

Past gerund

This form of the verb like the present gerund is not used very often in the spoken language in Serbian. It is associated with a very formal style and is the equivalent of saying *having done something*, as in the example:

Stigavši u hotel, odlučio	*Having arrived at the hotel,*
je da se raspakuje.	*he decided to unpack.*

In English these constructions are sometimes expressed with *after* or *when*: *When he had arrived at the hotel, he decided to unpack.*

In Serbian the past gerund is formed by replacing the **-o** at the end of the masc. verbal adjective with **-vši**:

stigao	*arrived*	**stigavši**	*having arrived*
pročitao	*read*	**pročitavši**	*having read*

Pročitavši novine, ustao	*After he read the newspaper,*
je i izišao.	*he stood up and went out.*

The past gerund is used when referring to two actions, the first one completed before the second takes place (Marko arrived at the hotel and then decided to unpack). The subject of the two verbs must be the same. It is only formed from perfective verbs.

Practice

1 Ana has made a list of clothes which she has decided to take to Kopaonik. Her mother has offered to help her pack but she needs to know the colours of the items on Ana's list. Listen to their conversation and fill in the grid below with the appropriate colours.

(spisak *list*; kupaći kostim *ladies' swimming costume*)

◀ CD 2, TR 7, 04.39

a	haljina
b	pantalone
c	bluza
d	košulja
e	šorc
f	jakna
g	kupaći kostim

2 Maja goes to a boutique to buy a shirt. Fill in her part of the conversation:

◀ CD 2, TR 7, 05.40

Prodavačica	Izvolite, šta želite?
Maja	*I would like to buy a shirt. What kind of shirts do you have?*
Prodavačica	Košulje su ovde levo, gospođice. Pogledajte. Da li vam se sviđa ova svilena?
Maja	*Yes, I like it. What colours do you have?*
Prodavačica	Imamo belu, tamnocrvenu i crnu.
Maja	*Can I see the white one, please?*
Prodavačica	Odmah ću vam pokazati. Koji broj želite?

Maja	*My size is 38.*
Prodavačica	Evo, izvolite.
Maja	*Can I try it?*
Prodavačica	Naravno, gospođice.
Maja	*It's fine. I'll take it. Where can I pay?*
Prodavačica	Platićete na kasi.

3 Look at the information about hotel services in Activity C and answer the questions below:

  a Can you get a drink or a snack in your room after midnight?
  b Is there an exchange office in the hotel?
  c Do you have to pay to store your luggage?
  d Can you have your hair cut in the hotel?
  e Does the hotel have a garage?

4 You are now at the hotel reception. Try to use some of these services by asking the following questions in Serbian:

◀) **CD 2, TR 7, 07.08**

  a I would like to change some money. Where is the exchange office?
  b Can I buy a newspaper in the hotel?
  c Do you have a hairdressing salon?
  d Where can I park my car?
  e Do you have a doctor in the hotel?

Test yourself

Here you can check some of the things you have learnt in this unit. Look at the questions below and choose the right answer:

1 A woman is looking for some winter clothes for herself. Which of the following would she choose?

  a svilena haljina   **b** vunene pantalone   **c** kupaći kostim

2 How would you say *It is urgent*?

  a Važno je.   **b** Strašno je.   **c** Hitno je.

3 If *at the faculty* is **na fakultetu,** which preposition would you use in the sentence **Dolazim . . . . . . fakulteta?**

   a sa   **b** iz   **c** od

4 Which colour is **zelena boja?**

   a yellow   **b** green   **c** brown

5 Put the correct form of **koji** into the following question: **U . . . . sobi je gospođa Ilić?**

   a kojoj   **b** koju   **c** koja

6 Match one part of the sentence to another:

   I Počela je da me boli   **a** ratni filmovi.
  II Putovao je na odmor   **b** prijatnih ljudi.
 III Najviše nam se sviđaju   **c** slobodnog vremena.
 IV Upoznali smo mnogo   **d** leva ruka.
  V Oni nisu imali   **e** novim kolima.

18

Meeting in Novi Sad

In this unit you will learn:

- About writing letters
- How to make a hotel booking
- Phrases for arranging meetings
- About passive constructions

Formal letter

Activity A

Marko Pavlović is making another business trip to Belgrade. This section contains information about the arrangements for his trip. Read the texts and answer the questions that follow:

Марко Павловић долази опет послом у Београд. Његова секретарица је послала писмо у хотел *Парк* да резервише собу. У фирми је одлучено да њихов пословни партнер из Новог Сада, Душан Поповић, буде позван на састанак са Марком. Секретарица му је послала електронску поруку.

Хотел *Парк*
Његошева 4
11000 Београд

2. 9. 2002.

Поштована господо,

Хтели бисмо да резервишемо једну једнокреветну собу са купатилом од 22. до 27. септембра ове године (ноћење са доручком)

284

за нашег представника, господина Марка Павловића. Били бисмо вам захвални ако бисте нам доставили фактуру на име 'London Holdings plc', а господин Павловић ће сам платити рачун на крају боравка кредитном картицом.

Са поштовањем,
Гђа Павковић
секретарица компаније 'London Holdings plc'

Драги господине Поповићу,

Марко Павловић ће боравити у Београду од 22. до 27. септембра. Ваш састанак са њим је заказан за 24. септембар у 9.00 часова. Молимо Вас да будете у то време на рецепцији хотела *Парк*. Састанак ће трајати цело пре подне. Јавите нам се што пре ако Вам то време не одговара.

Срдачно Вас поздравља
Ема Павковић

долази послом	*comes on business*
одлучено је	*it was decided*
позван	*invited*
позивати, позвати, позовем	*to invite*
Поштовани . . .	*Dear/Respected . . .*
захвалан	*grateful*
доставати, доставити	*to deliver*
фактура	*invoice*
на име	*in the name*
кредитна картица	*credit card*
Са поштовањем	*Yours sincerely*
заказан	*arranged*
Срдачно Вас поздравља . . .	*Cordially greets you . . .*

Questions

i Who booked a hotel room for Marko?
ii When are Marko and Dušan to meet and where?

How it works

Formation of passive

This form of the verb is the equivalent of saying *something is done* in English. In Serbian these forms are adjectives and agree accordingly; you have already come across some of these forms, such as the passive *opened* **отворен**. They are formed from the infinitive of both imperfective and perfective verbs with the most common patterns given below:

1 Infinitives which end in **-ати**, replace that ending with **-ан** in order to form the nom. masc. singular:

читати	читан
позвати	позван
заказати	заказан

2 Infinitives which end in **-ити** or **-ети**, replace the ending with **-јен** or with **-ен** for the nom. masc. singular. Consonants preceding the ending **-јен** change according to the pattern seen for comparative adjectives ending in **-ји** (see Unit 14):

видети	виђен
затворити	затворен
одлучити	одлучен

3 Infinitives which end in **-нути**, replace the ending with **-нут** in order to form the nom. masc. singular:

окренути   окренут
(**окретати, окрећем, окренути, окренем** *to turn*)

4 Infinitives which end in **-ети** but have a present tense ending in **-мем** or **-нем**, replace the infinitive ending with **-ет** in order to form the nom. masc. singular:

узети   (узмем)   узет

Using the passive

The passive form in Serbian is an adjective and agrees with the noun which it describes, as in the examples:

Душан Поповић је био позван у Београд.	*Dušan Popović was invited to Belgrade.*
Одлучено је.	*It is decided.*
Радња је отворена.	*The shop is open.*

Writing letters

Formal letters

Formal letters often open with:

Поштовани господине ...	*Dear Sir/Dear Mr* ... (with name in voc. case)
Поштована госпођо ...	*Dear Madam/Dear Mrs* ... (with name in voc.)
Поштована господо,	*Dear Sirs,*

The word **Поштовани** ... means lit. *Respected* ... for which the term **Драги** ... *Dear* ... may be substituted in letters which are not quite so formal.

In a formal letter, the pronoun **Ви** (in all cases) is spelt with a capital letter when used to address one person but with a small letter when intended as a plural form addressing more than one person.

In formal letters phrases are often expressed in the conditional as in the hotel booking above. Such statements and requests in the conditional are less demanding and convey a more polite tone. E-mail messages do not easily carry the very formal style of more traditional letters.

Formal letters often close with one of the following expressions which correspond to English *Yours sincerely*:

Са поштовањем	lit. *With respect*
Срдачно вас/Вас поздравља	lit. *Cordially greets you*
Срдачан поздрав	lit. *Cordial greetings*

Informal letters

You may open informal letters with:

Драги ...
Драга ...

and the name of the person addressed in the voc. case, and close them with:

| Много поздрава | lit. *Many greetings* |
| Воли те . . . | lit. *Loves you . . .* |

Arranging a meeting

Activity B

🔊 **CD 2, TR 8**

Marko and Dušan meet as arranged. Listen to their dialogue on the recording, read the text and answer the question that follows:

> Душан и Марко су се нашли у хотелу и сада разговарају у малој кафани близу хотела. Душан убеђује Марка да посети његову канцеларију у Новом Саду.
>
> **Марко**   Душане, да имам више времена, дошао бих са задовољством, али имам пуне руке посла овде.
>
> **Душан**   Марко, мислим да је ово прилика да заједно прегледамо наше планове за развој бизниса у Војводини. Нови Сад није далеко, могу да вам пошаљем кола.
>
> **Марко**   Добро, јавићу се шефу да га питам. Ако долазим код вас, морао бих да одложим повратак за један дан и да заменим авионску карту.
>
> **Душан**   Нема проблема. Моја колегиница може одмах да вам замени карту и организује смештај у Новом Саду. Послаћемо кола по вас двадесет седмог и сутрадан идете директно на аеродром.
>
> **Марко**   Добро, ја ћу се вратити у хотел да позовем Енглеску. Оставићу вам на рецепцији поруку да вас обавестим шта кажу за моју посету Новом Саду.

QUICK VOCAB

убеђивати, убеђујем, убедити	*to persuade*
задовољство	*satisfaction*
имам пуне руке посла	*I have my hands full*
прилика	*opportunity*
заједно	*together*
прегледати	*to examine*
развој	*development*
бизнис	*business*

Војводина	*Vojvodina* (northern part of Serbia)
шеф	*boss*
одлагати, одлажем, одложити	*to delay, postpone*
повратак	*return*
замењивати, замењујем, заменити	*to exchange*
колегиница	*colleague* (woman)
смештај	*accommodation*
сутрадан	*the day after*
остављати, оставити	*to leave (behind)*
обавештавати, обавестити	*to inform*
посета	*visit*

QUICK VOCAB

Question

How is Marko going to travel to Novi Sad?

Leaving a message

Activity C

Read Marko's message and answer the question that follows:

Порука за господина Душана Поповића

Драги Душане,
Све је у реду. Одобрили су моју посету Новом Саду. Пошаљите, молим вас, кола, и нека ме чекају испред хотела у 2.00. Морамо да почнемо састанак у вашој канцеларији у Новом Саду најкасније у 3.30. Бићу вам захвалан ако можете да ми замените авионску карту за Енглеску. Веома сам заузет. Јавите ми се ако постоји неки проблем. Ако не, видећу вас у Новом Саду.

Срдачан поздрав,
Марко

одобравати, одобрити	*to permit*
заузет	*busy*

QV

Question

At what time should the meeting in Novi Sad begin?

Serbian tends to adopt foreign words readily into its vocabulary. You will find many words relating to business practice or modern technology such as **бизнис** *business* or **бизнисмен** *businessman*, **компјутер** *computer* or **вебсајт** *web site* in use. Sometimes a foreign word and a Serbian word are used with the same meaning, such as **менаџмент** or **управа** for *management*. Alternatively, you may find in Serbian translations of some terms such as a computer mouse, called **миш** *mouse*.

Insight

The word **заузет** means *busy* (occupied) in the following senses of the word:

Он је заузет.	*He is busy* (has a lot of work to do).
Тоалет је заузет.	*The toilet is occupied.* (**заузет** occupied; **слободан** vacant)
Телефон је заузет.	*The telephone is busy/occupied.*

If you want to say that a street is busy, use:
Улица је прометна. (from **промет** meaning traffic)

Telephone call

Activity D

◀) CD 2, TR 8, 01.20

Dušan telephones Novi Sad to make the necessary arrangements for Marko's visit with his colleague Kristina Jovanović. Listen to the recording, read the text and answer the question that follows:

Душан	Хало, добар дан, Душан Поповић овде. Могу ли да добијем госпођу Кристину Јовановић?
Централа	Само тренутак. Останите на вези. Нико се не јавља, господине.
Душан	Да ли сте пробали њен локал?
Централа	Јесам, нема је тамо.

Душан	Пробајте и локал 634.
Кристина	Хало, овде Кристина Јовановић.
Душан	Добар дан, Кристина, Душан овде. Хтео бих нешто да вас замолим. Господин Павловић долази двадесет седмог у Нови Сад. Резервишите му, молим вас, хотелски смештај за ту ноћ и јавите се ЈАТ-у да му замените авионску карту. Он има лет двадесет седмог који треба одложити за двадесет осми. Требаће нам и ауто да га пребаци у Нови Сад и да га сутрадан вози на аеродром.
Кристина	Без бриге, све ће то бити данас завршено.
Душан	Хвала вам. Кажите шоферу да треба да буде у Београду испред хотела *Парк* у два сата. Не сме да касни. Наш састанак мора да почне у пола четири. Хоћете ли ви моћи да присуствујете?
Кристина	Наравно.
Душан	Предлажем да после састанка одемо са господином Павловићем негде на вечеру.
Кристина	Добра идеја. Знам један одличан рибљи ресторан на Дунаву.

централа	*telephone switchboard*
останите на вези	*hold the line*
локал	*telephone extension*
требаће нам . . .	*we shall need* (future tense of треба нам . . .)
пребацивати, пребацујем, пребацити	*to transfer*
без бриге	*don't worry*
завршен	*completed*
шофер	*driver*
каснити, закаснити	*to be late*
присуствовати, присуствујем	*to be present*
предлагати, предлажем, предложити	*to suggest*
рибљи ресторан	*fish restaurant*

QUICK VOCAB

Question
What instruction does Kristina have to give to the driver?

How it works

Personal names and cases

People's names have been seen to change case according to the demands of each sentence. Most Serbian surnames end in **-ић** and they change cases when they refer to a male, but not to a female since the final consonant would require masc. endings which do not feel appropriate when the name refers to a woman:

Могу ли да добијем Марка Павловића?	*Can I get Marko Pavlović?*
Могу ли да добијем Кристину Јовановић?	*Can I get Kristina Jovanović?*

Foreign names are adapted as far as possible into Serbian. Foreign men's names which end in a consonant like *Charles* or *John* are simply transcribed as **Чарлс** and **Џон** and treated like ordinary men's names. Women's names which end in **-a** receive similar treatment such as *Moira* **Мојра** or *Sylvia* **Силвија**. The Christian names of women which end in a consonant are transliterated but do not change endings according to normal rules. They remain indeclinable:

Видео сам Чарлса.	*I saw Charles.*
Дали смо књигу Мојри.	*We gave the book to Moira.*
Ишла сам у биоскоп са Џејн.	*I went to the cinema with Jane.*

Practice

1 Marko Pavlović is arranging to meet his Belgrade business partner Stevan Marić. Listen to the recording of their telephone conversation and tick the right answers to the questions below:

◀)) CD 2, TR 8, 02.50

  a Where is Marko Pavlović?

   i In town.
   ii At the railway station.
   iii In the hotel.

b Where have they arranged to meet?

   i In front of the cinema *Jadran*.
   ii In Stevan's office.
   iii In front of the National Theatre.

c At what time have they arranged to meet?

   i At 11.00.
   ii At 12.30.
   iii At 11.30.

2 You are now planning to spend a week in Belgrade. Using Activity A as a model, write a short letter to book accommodation in the hotel *Park* from 10 May until 17 May this year. You want to book a double room with a bathroom.

3 You have arrived in Belgrade and have to arrange a meeting with a Serbian colleague, Milan Bojić, whom you met briefly during your previous visit. Leave a note for him at his office saying that you are in Belgrade, in the hotel *Park*, room number 203. Tell him that you will be in the hotel in the afternoon. Ask him to phone you or to leave a message for you at the hotel reception.

Test yourself

Here you can check some of the things you have learnt in this unit. Look at the questions below and choose the right answer:

1 There are two short letters given below. What is the most appropriate way for each of them to begin? Choose from the following options:

a Драга мама,
b Драги господине Матићу,
c Поштована господо,

   i Резервисао сам једнокреветну собу у вашем хотелу од 4. до 8. фебруара. На жалост, мораћу да одложим свој боравак у Београду. Да ли бих могао да заменим резервацију за период од 10. до 14. фебруара?

ii Стигла сам јуче на Копаоник. Имам лепу собу са великим балконом. Време је сјајно, сунце сија и има много снега. Скијаћу се сваки дан!

2 How should these letters finish? Choose the most appropriate option:

a Са поштовањем, ...

b Срдачно те поздравља . . . . . .

c Воли те . . . . .

19

On the telephone

In this unit you will learn:

- Expressions when using the telephone
- More about reflexive verbs
- About the aorist and pluperfect

___

In Novi Sad

Activity A

◀ CD 2, TR 9

Marko Pavlović has arrived in Novi Sad and is greeted by Dušan Popović in his office. Someone has telephoned Marko. Listen to the recording and try to answer the following questions before reading the text:

Questions

i Who phoned Dušan's office leaving a message for Marko?
ii Did that person try to find him on his mobile?

Dušan	Dobar dan, Marko. Dobro došli.
Marko	Dobar dan, Dušane. Kako ste?
Dušan	Dobro, hvala. Izvolite, sedite. Neko vas je tražio.
Marko	Ko je to bio?
Dušan	Jedna gospođa. Ostavila je poruku na sekretarici. Zapisao sam ovde negde . . . Da, zvala je gospođa Biljana Zorić. Zamolila je da joj se javite.
Marko	To je moja rođaka. Probaću sad da joj se javim ako vam to ne smeta.

Dušan	Ne, ne, samo izvolite.
Marko	(*govori u mobilni telefon*) Zdravo, tetka, Marko ovde. Čujem da si me tražila.
Biljana	Zdravo, Marko. Izvini što te prekidam u poslu. Zvala sam na mobilni, ali te nisam našla. Maja kaže da iz Novog Sada ideš pravo na aerodrom. Htela sam da se pozdravimo.
Marko	Nema problema. Mislio sam i ja da se javim pre polaska.
Biljana	Žao mi je što već ideš. Mnogo pozdravi mamu i tatu, a mi ćemo se videti kad sledeći put budeš u Beogradu.
Marko	Hvala ti. Pozdravi i ti sve svoje od mene.
Biljana	Zdravo, Marko, i srećan put.

QUICK VOCAB

dobro došli	*welcome*
sekretarica	*answer machine*
zapisivati, zapisujem; zapisati, zapišem	*to write down*
rođaka	*relative* (female)
smetati	*to bother* (with dat. case)
prekidati; prekinuti, prekinem	*to interrupt*
pravo	*directly*
pozdraviti se	*to say 'goodbye' to each other*
polazak	*departure*
pozdravi . . .	*give my regards to . . .*
videti se	*to see each other*
srećan put	*have a good journey*

Marko's firm writes to Dušan

Activity B

Marko reports on his talks with Dušan when he gets back to his office in England and a letter is sent to Novi Sad. Read the letter and answer the questions that follow:

Poštovani gospodine Popoviću,

Gospodin Pavlović nas je obavestio o svojim razgovorima sa Vama u Novom Sadu. Što se tiče dalje saradnje, predlažemo da nastavimo pregovore u

Engleskoj da bismo sakupili sve zainteresovane stranke iz kompanije. Da li biste mogli da odvojite dva-tri dana za takve razgovore krajem oktobra ili početkom novembra? Koji datumi Vam najviše odgovaraju? Snosićemo sve putne troškove, a biće Vam plaćen i hotelski smeštaj.

Zahvaljujemo na saradnji i želimo Vam sve najbolje.

Srdačno Vas pozdravlja
Džon Smit
direktor kompanije "London Holdings plc"

razgovor	*talk, conversation*
saradnja	*co-operation*
nastavljati; nastaviti	*to continue*
pregovori	*negotiations*
sakupljati; sakupiti	*to gather*
zainteresovan	*interested*
stranka	*party*
odvajati; odvojiti	*to set aside*
snositi putne troškove	*to cover travel expenses*
zahvaljivati, zahvaljujem; zahvaliti (na with loc. case)	*to thank for*
sve najbolje	*all the best*

QUICK VOCAB

Questions

i Where are the negotiations to continue?
ii At what time of the year?

Making telephone calls

Activity C

🔊 **CD 2, TR 9, 01.44**

You are already aware of some of the phrases used when making telephone calls. Listen to the recordings of the following dialogues for more expressions. Marko is phoning his business partner Nada Stanković in her office in order to arrange a meeting with her.

Službenik	Dobar dan, izvolite?
Marko	Dajte mi, molim vas, gospođu Nadu Stanković.
Službenik	Ja se izvinjavam, gospodine. Ona trenutno nije ovde. Ko je traži?
Marko	Marko Pavlović.
Službenik	Imate li neku poruku?
Marko	Recite joj, molim vas, da sam je tražio. Zovem u vezi sa pismom koje mi je poslala. Predložila je da se danas sastanemo.
Službenik	Javite se, molim vas, za petnaest minuta. Sigurno će se do tada vratiti.
Marko	Dobro, javiću se. Hvala i prijatno.
Marko	Halo, ovde Marko Pavlović. Mogu li da govorim sa gospođom Nadom Stanković? Zvao sam je malopre, ali nije bila u kancelariji.
Službenik	Žao mi je, gospodine, ona je bila ovde, ali je morala opet da iziđe. Rekla je da vam kažem da će biti slobodna posle dva. Ako možete tada da dođete, sigurno će vas primiti.
Marko	U redu, hvala lepo, biću kod nje u dva. Do viđenja.

QUICK VOCAB

izvinjavati se; izviniti se	*to apologize, to be sorry*
trenutno	*at the moment*
u vezi sa	*in connection with* (with ins. case)
sastajati se, sastajem se; sastati se, sastanem se	*to meet*
malopre	*a little while ago*
primati; primiti	*to receive*

Questions

i How does Marko ask to speak to Mrs Stanković?

ii How is he asked if he wants to leave a message?

Calling friends

Activity D

◀) CD 2, TR 9, 03.37

Vesna calls Ana. Ana's father picks up the phone. Ana is not at home, so Vesna has to phone later. First listen to the recording without looking at the text. Can you tell where and when Ana and Vesna have arranged to meet?

Vesna	Dobar dan. Ovde Vesna. Molim vas Anu.
Anin tata	Zdravo, Vesna. Ana nije kod kuće.
Vesna	A kad će doći?
Anin tata	Ne znam tačno. Imaš li neku poruku?
Vesna	Ne, hvala. Javiću se kasnije.
Later	
Vesna	Ćao, Ana. Ovde Vesna.
Ana	Ćao. Tata mi je rekao da si me tražila. Šta je bilo?
Vesna	Ništa naročito. Ide mi se u grad. Hoćeš da idemo na kafu?
Ana	Hoću. Kuda ćemo?
Vesna	Ne znam jesi li videla, otvorili su u Knez Mihailovoj novu poslastičarnicu. Da odemo tamo?
Ana	Važi. Znam gde je to. Čula sam da imaju dobre kolače.
Vesna	Hajde da se nađemo u pola pet na trgu, kod pozorišta. Tamo mi staje autobus.
Ana	Okej. Ćao, Vesna.
Vesna	Ćao.

ćao	*hi, hello, bye*
naročit	*special, particular*
otvarati; otvoriti	*to open*
važi	OK (colloquial)
kod pozorišta	*at the theatre*

Activity E

◀)) **CD 2, TR 9, 04.57**

Vlada calls Maja and talks to her mother first. Listen to the recording without looking at the text. Can you tell at what time Maja has told Vlada to come to pick her up?

Biljana	Halo.
Vlada	Dobar dan. Ovde Vlada. Da li je Maja kod kuće?
Biljana	Zdravo, Vlado. Jeste, tu je Maja. Sad ću da je zovem.
Maja	Zdravo, Vlado.
Vlada	Ćao. Šta misliš da iziđemo na večeru?

Maja	Kuda?
Vlada	Zavisi od tebe. Da li ti se ide u neku baštu na ćevape?
Maja	Da, ali nemoj da idemo negde gde se samo jede i pije. Htela bih neku muziku.
Vlada	Dobro. Hajdemo u Skadarliju. Tamo se slušaju starogradske pesme. Ti to voliš.
Maja	Okej. Dođi po mene u osam. Možemo prvo malo da prošetamo po gradu.

zavisiti (**od** with gen. case)	*to depend on*
ćevapi	shortened from **ćevapčići**
gde se samo jede i pije	*where one just eats and drinks*
slušati se	*to be listened to*
starogradske pesme	*old-town songs*
šetati; prošetati	*to walk, go for a walk*

Skadarlija is a street in the centre of Belgrade which once housed the city's bohemian quarter but is today well-known for its cafés. The **starogradske pesme** represent a tradition of urban songs from the nineteenth century which are still popular today.

Activity F

◀) CD 2, TR 9, 05.59

Dragan has just come back from a visit to England. His friend Pavle phones to invite him over to watch an international sports match on TV between Yugoslavia and Greece. This match took place a few years ago and today, of course, he would say Serbia instead of Yugoslavia. Listen to the recording. Can you tell what they are going to watch?

Pavle	Zdravo, Dragane. Ovde Pavle.
Dragan	Zdravo, Pavle. Kako si?
Pavle	Dobro. Sreo sam jutros Zorana. On mi reče da si se vratio s puta. Kako je bilo u Engleskoj?
Dragan	Odlično, pričaću ti. Šta ima novo kod tebe?
Pavle	Ništa naročito. Znaš zašto te zovem? Večeras je na televiziji prenos košarke, Jugoslavija – Grčka. Zoran dolazi kod mene da gledamo zajedno. Dođi i ti.

Dragan	Hoću, svakako. Biće to dobra utakmica.
Pavle	Pobedićemo, to se zna.
Dragan	Kada počinje prenos?
Pavle	U sedam. Samo nemoj da zakasniš. Ja ne ustajem da otvorim vrata kad počne utakmica.
Dragan	Znam, znam . . . Neću zakasniti. Zdravo.

QUICK VOCAB

sretati, srećem; sresti, sretnem	*to meet*
On mi reče . . .	*He told me . . .*
put	*journey*
svakako	*certainly*
pobeđivati, pobeđujem; pobediti, pobedim	*to win*
to se zna	*of course*; lit. *that is known*

How it works

More about reflexive verbs

Verbs can be used with the reflexive pronoun to give an impersonal or general meaning such as *one does this* or *you do this*. It may also sometimes convey the sense of a passive construction such as *how is this said?* Look at the examples:

Tamo se samo jede i pije.	*There one just eats and drinks.*
Tamo se slušaju starogradske pesme.	*There one listens to old-time songs./You can listen to old-time songs there.*

(similarly: **Tamo možeš da slušaš starogradske pesme.**)

To se zna.	*That is known.*
Kako se kaže . . . ?	*How do you say . . . ?*
Ovde se govori engleski.	*English is spoken here.*

Other tenses: aorist and pluperfect

You have learnt the main patterns of tenses and use of aspects in Serbian. There are some other tense forms which can still be heard infrequently. The aorist, formed from perfective verbs to express an action completed in the past, survives in colloquial usage with a restricted number of verbs. For example, you may come across the verb **reći** *to say, tell* in the forms **rekoh** *I said* and **reče** *s/he said*. You may hear these words in conversation instead of the slightly longer and more conventional forms **rekao sam** and **rekao/la je**.

You are aware that you may express the pluperfect in Serbian by adding **već** *already* to a perfective verb in the past tense. There is a separate tense form for the pluperfect which is nowadays only rarely used. It is made by adding the verbal adjective from **biti** to the past tense. Both the following examples mean *Jovan had already arrived* . . . :

Jovan je već stigao . . .
Jovan je bio stigao . . .

Phrases and expressions

1 There are three verbs used in Serbian to mean *to meet* depending on the context:

naći se	*to meet, have a date* (for an informal gathering)
sastati se	*to meet, convene* (on a formal or business occasion)
sresti, sresti se	*to meet, bump into* (an accidental meeting)

Insight

Note the difference between:

Sreli smo se u gradu.	*We met in town* (by accident).
Našli smo se u gradu.	*We met in town* (as arranged).

2 The preposition **kod** *at the house of* (followed by gen. case) has an extended usage as in the examples:

Naći ćemo se kod pozorišta.	*We'll meet at the theatre.* (beside, in front of)
Šta ima novo kod tebe?	*What's new with you?* (in your life)

Nemam kod sebe njegov broj telefona.	*I don't have his telephone number with me.*

3 There are two other verbs used reflexively in this unit with the sense of *each other* or *one another*: **videti se** and **pozdraviti se**.

Videćemo se.	*We'll see each other.*
Pozdravili smo se.	*We said our goodbyes.* (to one another)

Practice

1 You have come to Belgrade on a business trip and have to arrange to meet your Serbian colleague Nebojša Vujić so you phone his office. Fill in your part of the conversation:

◀) **CD 2, TR 9, 07.11**

Sekretarica	Halo. Izvolite?
Vi	*Hello. May I speak to Mr Nebojša Vujić, please?*
Sekretarica	Izvinite, on trenutno nije u kancelariji.
Vi	*Do you know when he will be back?*
Sekretarica	Nisam sigurna. Otišao je na neki sastanak. A ko ga traži?
Vi	_____ here.
Sekretarica	Hoćete li da ostavite neku poruku?
Vi	*Please, tell him that I am in Belgrade and that I would like to see him. Can you write down my telephone number?*
Sekretarica	Naravno. Izvolite, kažite.
Vi	*My number is 483-652.*
Sekretarica	Dobro. Zapisala sam. Gospodin Vujić će vam se sigurno javiti.
Vi	*Thank you. Goodbye.*

2 Now you have to phone your Serbian friend Branka to arrange to meet her. Fill in your part of the conversation:

◀) **CD 2, TR 9, 08.55**

Vi	*Good morning. Is Branka at home, please?*
Branka	Ja sam. A ko je tamo?
Vi	*Hi, Branka.* _____ here.
Branka	Zdravo. Odakle zoveš? Jesi li u Beogradu?

Vi	*Yes, I am. I arrived yesterday.*
Branka	Sjajno. Kad ćemo da se vidimo?
Vi	*Are you free this evening?*
Branka	Jesam, slobodna sam.
Vi	*Excellent. Where shall we meet?*
Branka	Najbolje je da dođeš kod mene na piće. Onda možemo da iziđemo u neki restoran na večeru.
Vi	*At what time?*
Branka	Dođi oko pola osam.
Vi	*Fine, I'll be at your place at 7.30.*

Test yourself

Rearrange the following lines to make a telephone conversation. The distinction between the two voices is indicated by the use of italics for the second of them.

a Хало, овде Даница Предић. Дајте ми господина Зорана Бојића.

b *Добар дан, Данице. Милан овде. Одакле се јављате?*

c Могла бих да свратим сутра пре подне код вас у канцеларију.

d *И колико остајете?*

e Из Београда. Стигла сам јутрос.

f *Драго ми је што ћемо се видети. До виђења.*

g У реду, бићу код вас сутра у једанаест.

h *Одлично. Када бисмо могли да се видимо?*

i Остајем у Београду до петка.

j *Дођите око једанаест ако вам одговара.*

20

....

Accommodation

In this unit you will learn:

- About reading and making up adverts for accommodation, services and jobs

---

Finding a flat

Activity A

🔊 **CD 2, TR 10**

Vesna is talking to Barbara about her accommodation. She finds out that Barbara has to find new accommodation. Listen to the recording and answer the following questions before reading the dialogue:

Questions
i Why does Barbara have to move from her hall of residence?
ii Has she already found a job?
iii Who else is staying on in Belgrade?

Весна	Где станујеш? Знам да си раније била у студентском дому. Јеси ли још увек тамо?
Барбара	Јесам. Станујем у дому откад сам пре годину дана дошла у Београд.
Весна	И како ти је тамо?
Барбара	Није лоше. Соба уопште није скупа и имамо прилично јефтину мензу. Али се ускоро селим. Идем из дома крајем године.

Весна	Зашто?
Барбара	Зато што завршавам студије, нећу више бити студенткиња. Мораћу да нађем неки стан.
Весна	Остаћеш у Београду? Не планираш да се вратиш кући после студија?
Барбара	Не, добила сам овде посао. Предаваћу немачки на факултету.
Весна	То је сјајно. Али јесу ли ти рекли да је скупо изнајмити стан у Београду? Јефтиније би ти било да нађеш собу.
Барбара	У праву си. Ипак, волела бих да имам свој стан. Ако треба да зарадим мало више да бих платила кирију, даваћу приватне часове.
Весна	Какав стан би хтела да изнајмиш?
Барбара	Једнособан стан би ми био довољан. Важно је само да не буде далеко од центра.
Весна	Значи, остајеш овде. Баш ми је драго.
Барбара	Нисам само ја одлучила да останем. Ни Роберт још не одлази. Добио је доста понуда да преводи и да даје приватне часове енглеског.
Весна	И то је одлично, Моћи ћемо да се дружимо као и до сада.

студентски дом	*student hall of residence*
откад	*since*
уопште не	*not at all*
селити се, преселити се	*to move*
студије	*studies*
предавати, предајем	*to teach*
ипак	*however, nevertheless*
зарађивати, зарађујем, зарадити	*to earn*
кирија	*rent*
приватан	*private*
довољан	*sufficient*
понуда	*offer*
преводити, превести, преведем	*to translate*
дружити се	*to be friends*

Adverts for accommodation

Activity B

Barbara has told Vesna that she is looking for a one-roomed flat not far from the centre of town. Here are some advertisements for flats taken from the **мали огласи** *small ads* section of the newspaper. Read them and find out which one might be of interest to Barbara. What is the contact telephone number for that offer?

МАЛИ ОГЛАСИ

ИЗДАЈЕМ двособан комфоран стан, први спрат, гаража, шест месеци унапред. 011/3422-805.

ИЗДАЈЕМ једнособан стан у ужем центру, 45 квм, намештен, централно грејање, интерфон. 011/3400-662.

ИЗДАЈЕ СЕ кућа у мирном крају града (намештена или ненамештена), са гаражом и баштом. Предност имају брачни парови са децом, дипломате, и сл. Плаћање годину дана унапред. Тел. 617-334, од 12–23.

ПРИМАМ на стан студенте прве године факултета. Тел. 011/2190-154.

оглас	*advertisement*
издавати, издајем, издати, издам	*to rent (out)*
комфоран	*comfortable*
унапред	*in advance*
45 квм	*45 m²*
ужи центар	*the very centre*
узак	*narrow*
намештен	*furnished*
централно грејање	*central heating*
интерфон	*intercom*
предност	*advantage*
брачни пар	*married couple*
дипломата	*diplomat*

QUICK VOCAB

Activity C

Below are some advertisments placed by people who are looking for accommodation. Read them and give the contact telephone number for each of the following:

i A foreigner looking for a flat with a terrace.
ii Three female students looking for a two-roomed flat.
iii A family wanting to rent a flat for a long period.
iv An Englishman looking for a two-roomed flat.
v Somebody looking for a bedsit or one-roomed flat.
vi Somebody looking for a flat and business space.

> **ПОТРЕБНА** гарсоњера или једнособан стан у ширем центру. Тел. 011/4566-785.

> **ТРИ СТУДЕНТКИЊЕ** траже двособан стан, кухиња, купатило, 50 евра/особа. Тел. 032/28-256.

> **СТРАНЦУ** потребан већи, леп, празан стан са великом терасом. 3435-591

> **ЕНГЛЕЗ** тражи двособан стан у ужем центру, празан или намештен, ЦГ и телефон. Плаћање по договору и унапред. Тел. 3346-854.

> **ХИТНО** тражимо ненамештен тространи стан и пословни простор, центар.Тел. 545-384.

> **ПОРОДИЦИ** потребан стан са централним грејањем и телефоном на дужи период. Плаћање по договору. 481-252

гарсоњера	*bedsit*
шири центар	*wider centre*
широк	*wide*

празан	*empty*
тераса	*terrace*
по договору	*by agreement*
простор	*space*

How it works

More about comparatives

Comparative forms of adjectives are used in Serbian not just to mean *bigger* but also to convey a sense of *somewhat large* as in the examples:

већи стан	*a biggish flat*
мањи стан	*a smallish flat*
у ужем центру	*in the very centre* (lit. *narrower*)
у ширем центру	*in the wider centre*
на дужи период	*for a long let, for a lengthy period*

Practice

1 Using the advertisements given above as models, make up advertisements for accommodation for:

  a a married couple looking for a three-roomed, unfurnished flat, with telephone, central heating and garden.
  b a foreigner looking for a flat with telephone, central heating, garage, for a long let, paying in advance.

2 Below are some advertisements for jobs. Using these models, make up one for yourself as a private teacher of English:

> **НЕМАЧКИ** језик, приватни часови, конверзација, преводи, искуство у Немачкој. Повољно.
> 011/3666-943, 063/6490-782.

> **ДАЈЕМ** часове енглеског, граматика, превод, конверзација. Сви узрасти. 011/389-675.

ФРАНЦУСКИ за децу и одрасле. Долазим кући.
Тел. 452-093.

ЕНГЛЕСКИ за економисте, пословни језик,
интензивни курсеви. Тел. 746-261.

конверзација	*conversation*
превод	*translation*
искуство	*experience*
повољан	*reasonable* (of prices)
граматика	*grammar*
узраст	*age*
одрастао	*adult*
економиста	*economist*
интензиван	*intense*
курс	*course*

QUICK VOCAB

Test yourself

1 You are making enquiries about a flat in Belgrade. Match the questions with the answers.

I	Koliki je stan?	**a**	Stan se izdaje nenamešten.
II	Gde se nalazi?	**b**	Na žalost, nema lifta.
III	Na kojem je spratu?	**c**	Da, ima.
IV	Postoji li u kući lift?	**d**	Ne, plaćanje je mesečno.
V	Ima li stan centralno grejanje?	**e**	Trosoban.
VI	Kakav je nameštaj?	**f**	Na trećem.
VII	Da li se kirija plaća unapred?	**g**	Sutra posle podne.
VIII	Kada može da se vidi stan?	**h**	U mirnom kraju nedaleko od centra.

2 You have come to the end of our last unit. We want to say: **Čestitamo!** Can you tell what this expression means?

   a Welcome!   **b** Congratulations!   **c** Cheers!

310

Key to the exercises

Unit 1

1 Љ lj; у u; ш š; с s; ф f; ћ ć; и i; в v **2** Њ Nj; К K; Р R; Б B; Ђ Đ; Л L; Ц C; Н N **3** POŠTA; APOTEKA; BANKA; MENJAČNICA; PEKARA; ROBNA KUĆA **4** Крагујевац; Ужице; Суботица; Приштина; Нови Сад; Београд; Ниш **5 a** iv **b** x **c** vii **d** ix **e** i **f** ii **g** viii **h** vi **i** v **j** iii **6** Rome; Paris; Moscow; Thames **7** c; b; a; d; f; h; e; g **8 a** Mel Gibson; **b** Sean Connery; **c** Tom Hanks; **d** Clint Eastwood; **e** Meryl Streep; **f** Meg Ryan; **g** Melanie Griffith; **h** Gwyneth Paltrow **9** Dobro jutro/Добро јутро **10** Dobar dan/Добар дан **11** Dobro veče/Добро вече **12** Zdravo/Здраво **13** Do viđenja/До виђења **14** Laku noć/Лаку ноћ **15** Dobar dan, gospođo Petrović./Добар дан, госпођо Петровић.

Test yourself

1 b; **2** a; **3** c; **4** c; **5** b; **6** c; **7** a; **8** b; **9** a; **10** b

Unit 2

A: Dobro jutro, gospođo Petrović. **B:** Kako ste? **C:** Zdravo. **D:** Drago mi je. **E:** Da vas upoznam. Ovo je moj muž, Zoran. **F:** Ovo je moja drugarica, Vesna.

1 a Dobro veče./Zdravo./Dobro jutro. **b** Zdravo. **2 a** Dobar dan, gospodine Lukiću. Kako ste? **b** I ja sam dobro, hvala. **3** Zdravo. Kako si? **4** Drago mi je. Ja sam . . . **5** Da vas upoznam. Ovo je moja žena/moj muž. **6 a** Kako se zoveš? **b** Zovem se . . . **7** Ovo je moj drug/moja drugarica.

Test yourself

1 a; 2 b; 3 c; 4 b; 5 a; 6 a; 7 b; 8 a; 9 b; 10 c

Unit 3

A: Da li govorite engleski? **B:** Razumem srpski, ali ne govorim dobro. **C:** Učim jezik. **D: i** Ричард; **ii** Натали.

1 a Италијан; **b** српски; **c** Рус; **d** енглески; **e** Немица; **f** француски. **2 a** Ja sam Natali. Ja sam Francuskinja. Govorim francuski. **b** Ja sam Mario. Ja sam Italijan. Govorim italijanski. **c** Ja sam Ričard. Ja sam Amerikanac. Govorim engleski. **d** Ja sam Jovan. Ja sam Srbin. Govorim srpski. **4** Драго ми је. Ја сам Ричард Томпсон./ Не, ја сам Енглез./Разумем мало. Учим језик./Хвала. **5 a** govorim **b** razumete **c** ne učiš **d** ne govorim **e** razumeš **f** ste **g** si **h** sam. **6 a** Srbin; srpski i engleski; **b** Srpkinja; srpski i francuski; **c** Engleskinja; engleski, ruski i srpski. **7 a** Zdravo. **b** Kako si? **c** She understands a lot, but speaks a little.

8 a *Бојан Поповић* Бојан Поповић

b *Милена Рајић* Милена Рајић

c *Владан Гордић* Владан Гордић

d *Љиљана Жикић* Љиљана Жикић

Test yourself

1 b; 2 c; 3 b; 4 a; 5 c; 6 b; 7 a; 8 b; 9 a; 10 a

Unit 4

A: i молим вас **ii** Једно пиво, молим вас. **iii** Два пива, молим вас.
B: i Ја бих једну кафу. **ii** Дајте ми . . . **iii** Две кафе, молим вас.
C: i Шта желите? **ii** три пива.

1 a white and red; **b** чај; **c** lemonade; **d** yes; **e** raspberry juice.
2 a a Coca-Cola; **b** a coffee; **c** a beer. **3 a** Два чаја, молим вас. **b** Једну ракију и једну кафу, молим вас. **c** Две лимунаде, молим вас. **4** PIĆE; pivo; belo vino; crno vino; rakija; viski; džin; turska kafa; čaj; kisela voda; limunada; koka-kola; tonik; sok od maline. **5** Шта желите?/И ја бих кафу. Хоћете ли чашу киселе воде?/Добро вече. Две кафе и две киселе воде, молим вас. **6 a** вино, пиво; **b** ракију; **c** сока; **d** боровнице; **e** кафу, лимунаде; **f** чај; **g** пива; **h** кока-коле. **7 a** Шта желите? **b** Дајте нам четири кафе, један сок од поморанџе, једну киселу воду и два пива. **8 a** Три пива, молим вас. **b** Три чаше лимунаде, молим вас. **c** Три ракије, молим вас. **d** Три сока од јабуке, молим вас. **e** Три џуса, молим вас. **f** Три кока-коле, молим вас.

Test yourself

1 a; **2** c; **3** b; **4** a; **5** b; **6** b; **7** c; **8** a; **9** b; **10** c

---

Unit 5

A: i 40 dinars **ii** 33 dinars; **B:** One ham and one cheese sandwich. **C:** Ja bih jedan omlet i salatu od paradajza, molim vas. **D:** Drinks: three brandies, mineral water, red wine. Dishes: four soups, three steaks, one Wiener schnitzel, two Serbian salads, two tomato salads.

1 хлеб; кифле; бурек са сиром; бурек са месом; јогурт **2** She bought one loaf, four kifle and three yoghurts and has to pay 84 dinars. **3** petnaest; šesnaest; dvadeset osam; trideset sedam; četrdeset četiri; pedeset devet; šezdeset dva; sedamdeset šest; sto dvadeset tri; sto šezdeset pet; sto osamdeset devet; sto devedeset jedan; петнаест; шеснаест; двадесет осам; тридесет седам; четрдесет четири; педесет девет; шездесет два; седамдесет шест; сто двадесет три; сто шездесет пет; сто осамдесет девет; сто деведесет један **5** kifle; sendviči; jabuke; vina; pomorandže; sokovi **6** 3 kafe; 5 sendviča; 7 koka-kola; 10 jogurta; 17 pašteta; 20 sokova; 24 hleba **7** Dobro veče. Imate li jelovnik?/Da. Dajte mi, molim vas, goveđu supu./Ja bih jedan biftek i šopsku salatu, molim vas./Čašu vina, molim vas./Crno, molim vas/Račun, molim vas. **8 a** She is not hungry. **b** Grilled chicken. **c** Yes, he is. **d** A green salad. **e** A Serbian salad. **9 a** 18.00–24.00. **b** Margarita and Vladimir. **c** 340 dinars.

___

Test yourself

1 b; **2** a; **3** c; **4** b; **5** c; **6** b; **7** a; **8** b; **9** a; **10** c

___

Unit 6

A: Robert also wants to buy a map of Serbia. **B:** The map costs 120 dinars. **C: i** 3; **ii** 1 litre; **iii** 1 kilo; **iv** 1 kilo; **v** 100 g. **D: i** kilo of bread, 100 g of ham, 1 yoghurt, 1 strawberry jam; **ii** milk.

1 Молим вас, да ли продајете разгледнице?/Колико коштају?/Дајте ми пет, молим вас. И да ли имате план града?/Не, хвала. То је све. **2 a** Они; **b** Она; **c** Они; **d** Она; **e** Оне; **f** Она; **g** Оно; **h** Они; **i** Оне; **(j)** Они. **3 a** 460; **b** 630; **c** 580; **d** 550. No. The dictionary a was the cheapest. **4** двеста осамдесет шест, четиристо осамнаест, шестсто педесет девет, деветсто четрдесет седам, триста шездесет један, хиљаду шестсто, две хиљаде петсто осамдесет. **5 a** Дајте ми две флаше сока. **b** Дајте ми пет флаша пива. **c** Дајте ми литар млека. **d** Дајте ми два кила хлеба. **e** Дајте ми пола кила јабука. **f** Дајте ми кило парадајза. **g** Дајте ми двеста грама кафе. **h** Дајте ми триста грама сира. **7** Добар дан. Хоћу да купим хлеб и млеко./Дајте ми пола кила хлеба, молим вас, и литар млека./Дајте ми и флашу киселе воде./Имате ли јабуке?/У реду. Дајте ми кило./Не, хвала. Ништа више. **8 a** Они морају да уче француски. **b** Да ли она хоће да говори немачки? **c** Ја нећу да купим сендвиче. **d** Да ли ти можеш да разумеш српски? **(e)** Он неће да пије чај. **f** Ви не морате да купите кафу. **g** Ми хоћемо да имамо добар речник.

___

Test yourself

1 c; **2** c; **3** b; **4** a; **5** c; **6** b; **7** a; **8** b; **9** c; **10** b

Unit 7

B: No, it is near the square. **C:** Serbian language. **D: i** Gde stanuješ? **ii** Stanujem u ulici … broj … **iii** It is opposite Tašmajdan, near St Marko's church. **E: i** In Belgrade near the hotel *Slavija*. **ii** Between the Kosmaj cinema and the Republic Square.

1 a u parku; **b** u školi; **c** u gradu; **d** u apoteci; **e** na trgu; **f** u knjižari; **g** u pozorištu; **h** u hotelu; **i** u školi; **j** u kafani. **2 a** njena; **b** njihov; **c** njegova; **d** moj; **e** njegovo; **f** naša; **g** tvoje; **h** vaš. **3 a** 436-257; **b** 638-972. **4 a** not true; **b** true; **c** true; **d** not true; **e** true; **f** not true. **5** Possible answers: **a** Železnička stanica je blizu parka, preko puta samoposluge. **b** Banka je pored bolnice, blizu trga. **c** Crkva je u parku, blizu železničke stanice. **d** Muzej je na trgu, pored knjižare. **e** Pošta je preko puta bolnice, daleko od železničke stanice. **6** Follow Practice 5. **7** Jesam. Ali sada živim u Beogradu. Odakle ste vi?/ Da li živite tamo?/Gde radite?/Ja radim u školi./Imam lep stan blizu centra grada. **8 a** Njegova adresa je Bulevar kralja Aleksandra 237. **b** Ima. Njegov broj faksa je 422-679. **c** Njen kućni broj je 3231-677 **d** Njen broj na poslu je 1284-012. **e** Ona stanuje u ulici Kneza Miloša broj 65. **f** Njena adresa je milicapav@eunet.rs

Test yourself

1 c; **2** a; **3** c; **4** c; **5** b; **6** a; **7** c; **8** b; **9** a; **10** b

Unit 8

A: Restaurant *Vuk* is in Vuk Karadžić Street marked 17 on the map. **B:** Walking along Knez Mihailo Street they have crossed Vuk Karadžić Street and are approaching the next corner. **C:** They have not walked far enough down the small side street on which the restaurant is situated. **D: i** Аутобус стоји испред музеја. **ii** Извините, не разумем. Поновите, молим вас. **E: i** Five minutes walking distance. **ii** Пошта је петнаест минута пешке. **iii** Где је поштанско сандуче?

1 a The museum. **b** Left. **c** On the right. **d** First street on the right, on the right side. **2 a** ii; **b** iii; **c** i; **d** iii. **3** Possible answers: **a** Скрените у прву улицу лево, а онда у прву улицу десно. Пошта је са леве стране, на ћошку. **b** Идите право на трг. Позориште је на тргу, са леве стране. **c** Идите право и скрените у другу улицу лево. Самопослуга је са десне стране, на ћошку. **d** Скрените у прву улицу лево, идите право и скрените у другу улицу десно. **4** Follow the examples in Practice 2 and 3. **5 a** на тргу; **b** у кафану; **c** у граду; **d** у биоскоп; **e** у ресторан на вечеру; **f** у апотеку; **g** у град; **h** на трг; **i** на пиво; **j** у апотеци. **6 a** Хлеб можете да купите у пекари./Идите право. Пекара је на ћошку са десне стране. **b** Шампон можете да купите у самопослузи./Идите право. Самопослуга је на ћошку десно, преко пута музеја. **c** Марке можете да купите на пошти./Идите право и скрените у трећу улицу десно. **d** Аспирин можете да купите у апотеци./Апотека је одмах овде десно. **7** Извините, како могу да дођем до музеја?/Који аутобус иде тамо?/Молим вас, где је аутобуска станица? Да ли је близу?/Извините, не разумем. Поновите, молим вас./ Сада разумем. Хвала. **8 a** парка; **b** трамвај; **c** аутобусом; **d** Веру и Зорана; **e** пошту; марке; **f** тргу; кафане; **g** центру; града; музеја.

Test yourself

1 c; **2** b; **3** c; **4** a; **5** b; **6** a; **7** b; **8** c; **9** c; **10** b

Unit 9

A: Immediately after he got his suitcase. **B:** No, he didn't. **C:** 273. **D: i** Njegoševa 4. **ii** It has 130 rooms and apartments. **E:** He changes £50 for 4950 dinars.

1 a Putovao je avionom. **b** Dobio je vizu u ambasadi u Londonu. **c** Da, bio je udoban. **d** Stevan Marić je čekao Marka na izlazu. **e** Pili su kafu na aerodromu. **f** Da, već je bio u Beogradu. **g** Ne, nisu čekali. **h** Uzeli su taksi. **2 a** Vera je pila kafu. **b** Barbara i Vesna su išle u školu peške. **c** Marko je putovao avionom. **d** Mi smo živeli blizu parka. **e** Ja sam kupila kartu. **f** Dragan i Jelena su čekali taksi. **g** Vi ste bili u centru grada? **h** Robert je stigao na aerodrom. **3 a** Nisam znala dobro Beograd. **b** Vesna nije išla u Narodnu biblioteku Srbije. **c** Nismo dobili vaše pismo. **d** Nisi gledao taj film. **e** Milan i Dragan nisu bili na poslu. **f** Nisam imao stan u Beogradu. **g** Nije dobro govorio srpski. **h** Niste videli njegovu ženu. **4** Hotel Splendid. **5 a** 9.00 Mr. Lazarević, in town; **b** 10.15 Mr Dragojević; **c** 11.30 Mrs Danilović; **d** 1.15–2.40, lunch with Mr Lalić; **e** 2.50 British Embassy; **f** 4.00 Mr Lazarević, in the hotel. **6 a** Sada je devet sati. **b** Sada je deset i petnaest. **c** Sada je dva i dvadeset pet. **d** Sada je dvadeset do pet; **e** Sada je pet do osam. **f** Sada je pola devet. **7 a** evro; **b** Kakav je kurs za funtu? **c** Želim da promenim pedeset funti. **d** Želim da promenim sto evra. **e** Želim da promenim dvesta dolara.

Test yourself

1 a; **2** b; **3** b; **4** a; **5** b; **6** c; **7** c; **8** b; **9** c; **10** a

Unit 10

A: i She is a teacher. **ii** English language. **B: i** Koliko imaš godina? **ii** Imam dvadeset dve godine. **C: i** It has three rooms. **ii** In Sheffield. **D: i** In a village near Belgrade. **ii** A bottle of plum brandy. **E: i** A book and a CD. **ii** That they were very kind.

1 a Milica Babić; **b** Beograd; **c** prevodilac; **d** tridest četiri; **e** udata; **f** Aleksandar; **g** novinar; **h** tridesetšest; **i** jednaćerka; **j** Ivana, pet. **2** Da, jesam./Studiram istoriju i srpski jezik./ Žive u Londonu./Moja mama ne radi, a tata je lekar./Imam sestru i brata./Moja sestra ima dvadeset sedam godina./Ne, ne živi. Ona je već udata. Radi kao nastavnica u Birmingemu./Moj brat ima sedamnaest godina./On još ide u školu. **3** Possible answers: Zovem se Gordana. Ja sam studentkinja. Imam dvadeset jednu godinu. Moja mama se zove Milica. Ona radi kao učiteljica. Ima pedeset godina. Moj tata se zove Branko. On je advokat. Ima pedeset četiri godine. Imam brata. Zove se Bojan. On ima dvadeset osam godina. Radi kao novinar. **4 a** Zoranova; **b** Jelenina; **c** Robertovi; **d** Majin; **e** Jovanovo i Mirino; **f** Milanova. **5 a** Stevan je njen brat.

b Љубица је њихова бака. **c** Дејан је њен брат. **d** Биљана је његова тетка. **e** Маја је његова сестра од тетке. **f** Марко је његов син. **g** Ана и Јелена су његове ћерке. **6** Possible answers: Имам ___ година. Живим у ____ Радим као ____ Ожењен сам./Удата сам. Мој муж/моја жена се зове . . . Имам сина/ћерку. Има. . . . година. Зове се . . . **7 a** сестри и брату; **b** родитељима.; **c** пријатељицама; **d** хотелима; **e** оцу; **f** ћеркама.

Test yourself

1 a; **2** c; **3** b; **4** a; **5** b; **6** b; **7** c; **8** a; **9** b; **10** c

Unit 11

A: i They are going by bus. **ii** They are going to rent a holiday flat. **B: i** No, she doesn't. **ii** Yes, there are different sport activities organized there. **C: i** By train. **ii** Private accommodation. They booked a cheap room in the centre of the old town. **D: i** They are going to visit Zoran's brother. **ii** They are going to stay at Vera's cousin's. She has a villa there. **E: i** No, there is also a road through Prokuplje. **ii** Žiča is the nearest, Sopoćani the furthest.

1 a Ana i Vesna će iznajmiti udoban apartman. **b** Čitaću knjigu. **c** Uroš neće igrati fudbal. **d** Da li ćete gledati taj film? **e** Kako će ići u grad? **f** Nećemo imati kuhinju. **g** Neću ga videti. **h** Moći ćete da putujete autobusom. **2 a** ih; **b** nju; **c** ga; **d** vas; **e** te; **f** nje; **g** me; **h** nas. **3 a** Hotel *Grand*. **b** Hotel *Olga Dedijer*. **c** Hotel *Grand*. **d** 5600 dinars per person. **e** Children up to 2 years old are accepted free of charge; from 2 to 12 years get 30% discount. **f** Rooms with two, three and four beds. **g** In the apartment complex *Konaci*. **h** Yes, they have one at *Konaci*. **4** Possible answers: Idem na Kopaonik. Putovaću autobusom/vozom/kolima. Iznajmiću sobu/apartman. Ostaću tamo dve nedelje. Šetaću po šumi./Sunčaću se i čitaću knjige./Ići ću na izlete./Igraću fudbal/tenis. **5 a** true; **b** false; **c** true; **d** false; **e** false, **f** true. **6** Od Beograda do Vrnjačke Banje postoje dva puta. Možete da putujete preko Kraljeva ili preko Jagodine i Kruševca. **7 a** Ići će na more, u Budvu. **b** Ne, ići će sa drugaricom. **c** Putovaće vozom. **d** Ostaće dve nedelje. **e** Neće. On ne voli mnogo more, voli planine. Ići će na Kopaonik. **f** Neće. Putovaće kolima. **g** Još nije. **8 a** hleba; **b** vode; **c** vremena; **d** dobrih restorana; **e** jeftinih soba; **f** ljudi; **g** lepih šuma; **h** benzina.

Test yourself

1 c; **2** c; **3** a; **4** c; **5** b; **6** a; **7** c; **8** b; **9** a; **10** b

Unit 12

A: i At 7.15. **ii** 810 dinars. **B: i** Two. **ii** The first leaves at 7.00; the second at 7.17. **iii** At 14.45. **C: i** Next day at 1.00. **ii** A first-class return ticket. **D:** departure 2 July; return 28 July.

1 a Шест сати. **b** У два сата ноћу. **c** У осам сати ујутро. **d** Десет минута. **2** Молим вас, колико кошта карта за Будву?/Повратна./ Дајте ми две повратне карте за суботу, петнаести јул./Увече./ Да ли тај аутобус иде преко Краљева?/У колико сати стиже у Будву?/У реду./Тридесетог јула./Изволите. Хвала. **3 a** 20 July–3 August; **b** 1–15 August; **c** 5–19 August. They'll all be back after 19 August. **4 a** великим; **b** лепом; **c** старим; **d** новом; **e** мојим **f** нашем; **g** густој; **h** њеним. **5 a** вам; **b** њима **c** ми; **d** нам; **e** мном; **f** му; **g** тобом; **h** јој. **6 a** У седам и петнаест. **b** Суботом су летови у седам и петнаест, у четрнаест и четрдесет пет и у двадесет и педесет. Недељом нема лета у седам и петнаест. **c** Понедељком, уторком, средом и четвртком нема летова увече. Петком, суботом и недељом има један лет у двадесет и десет. **7** Молим вас, желим да купим једну карту за Подгорицу./ Четрнаестог марта./Ујутро./У реду. То ми одговара./Повратну./ Фиксиран. Има ли неки лет за Београд четрнаестог увече?/Дајте ми, молим вас, карту за први лет. Колико кошта повратна карта?/У реду. Узећу карту.

Test yourself

1 c; **2** a; **3** c; **4** b; **5** b; **6** c; **7** a; **8** a; **9** c; **10** a

Unit 13

A: i At 6.00. **ii** By car. **iii** From 7.00 to 3.00. **B: i** By bus. **ii** At 10.00. **iii** She is studying English literature and is preparing an essay on Shakespeare. **C: i** No, he lives near them. **ii** To a park near their home. **D: i** Sometimes it is pleasant and warm, and sometimes rainy and cool. **ii** They leave town and go to the mountains or the seaside.

1 a Zoran: u 7.00. Jelena: u 6.00. **b** Zoran: kolima; Jelena: autobusom. **c** Zoran: u 9.00. Jelena: u 8.00. **d** Zoran: kod kuće; Jelena: na poslu. **e** Zoran: u 4.00; Jelena: u 3.00. **2** Possible answers: Ustajem u . . . sati. Idem na posao/u školu/na fakultet u . . . Idem kolima/peške/autobusom. Put traje deset/dvadeset minuta. Počinjem da radim/ imam prvi čas u . . . Ručam na poslu/u menzi/na fakultetu. Završavam posao/poslednji čas se završava u . . . Dolazim kući u . . . Uveče gledam televiziju/čitam/izlazim u grad/ idem u bioskop. **3 a** Sutra ću ga videti. **b** Ispričali su joj gde su bili. **c** Vesna ga je zaboravila kod kuće. **d** Obično ih zovemo u goste subotom. **e** Mnogo ga je voleo. **f** Kupiće mu je. **g** Bili su juče u biblioteci i videli su je tamo. **h** Nisam im ga dala. **4 a** da kupi; **b** da budem; **c** da dođeš; **d** da pozovu; **e** da bude; **f** da sedimo; **g** da budete; **h** da putujem. **5 a** bude; **b** bude duvao; **c** budemo završili; **d** budem; **e** bude znao; **f** bude čitala; **g** bude imala; **h** budete. **6 a** Sunčano i toplo. **b** Ne, biće oblačno sa pljuskovima. **c** Ne, duvaće slab vetar. **d** Oko dvadeset devet stepeni. **e** Oblačno i svežije. **7 a** Sveže je i pada kiša. **b** Oblačno i sveže. **c** Sunčano i toplo. **8** Use Activity D as a model.

Test yourself

1 a; **2** a; **3** c; **4** b; **5** c; **6** a; **7** b; **8** c; **9** a; **10** b

Unit 14

A: i Tennis and football. **ii** To a sport centre near his home. **B: i** He goes skiing. **ii** Football. **C:** It is about the history of the town Višegrad from the sixteenth to the twentieth century.

D: i She has to look after Uroš. **ii** To go to watch the first performance and take Uroš with them. **E: i** Because they don't want to see either a ballet or an opera. **ii** Yes, they have. **iii** Because Dragan's parents are coming for dinner. **iv** *Putujuće pozorište Šopalović*. **F: i** Row 5 on the left, seats 5 and 6. **ii** About 10.30.

1 a In winter he likes to go skiing. In summer he plays tennis. **b** No, he never plays football. **c** She likes swimming. **d** No, she doesn't. She prefers to go out with friends or to listen to music. **2 a** хладније; **b** већем; **c** мањи; **d** старијом; **e** виши; **f** дужи; **g** лепшу; **h** бољег. **3 a** нешто; **b** нико; **c** ништа; **d** ико; **e** негде; **f** никада. **4 a** коме; **b** никога; **c** чиме; **d** ким; **e** никоме; **f** нечему. **5 a** Вери се допадају тенис и пливање. Милану се допадају фудбал, хокеј, кошарка и ватерполо. **b** Вера воли да иде у биоскоп, у позориште и на концерт. Милан воли да иде у биоскоп, у позориште и на фудбалске утакмице. **c** Мени се допада/допадају . . . Волим да идем у/на . . . **6** Кад имам времена, волим да идем у биоскоп и у позориште. Свиђа ми се и музика./Да, идем./То би било добро. Волео бих и да идем у *Народно позориште* да гледам оперу./Много волим фудбал. Да ли бисмо могли да идемо на фудбалску утакмицу у суботу?/Да, иде ми се у шетњу. **7 a** волели; **b** Желео/ла; **c** могао; **d** Морали; **e** дошао/ла; **f** падала; остала; **g** слушали; **h** имао/ла; ишао/ла. **8 a** *Citizen Kane, Some Like It Hot, Apocalypse Now, High Noon, Psycho, Cabaret.* **b** Orson Welles. **c** A comedy. **d** Marilyn Monroe. **e** Дајте ми, молим вас, две карте у партеру за филм *Тачно у подне*.

Test yourself

1 c; **2** b; **3** c; **4** b; **5** b; **6** a; **7** c; **8** b; **9** c; **10** b

Unit 15

A: i Four. **ii** To go to fetch bread. **B: i** With his girlfriend. **ii** Maja. **C: i** It has four rooms. **ii** In the bathroom. **D: i** Three years. **ii** Five months ago. **E: i** No, she hasn't. **ii** To be in the country and talk to people.

1 a Rekla je da je Marko juče došao u Beograd. **b** Rekla je da su ga pozvali na ručak. **c** Rekla je da će doći sutra oko jedan sat.

d Rekla je da će i Maja biti na ručku. **e** Rekla je da sutra nema predavanja na fakultetu. **f** Rekla je da će Marko imati u Beogradu mnogo posla. **g** Rekla je da misli da ostaje do kraja nedelje. **h** Rekla je da bi on voleo da nas vidi. **2 a** Pitao sam da li Marko ima mnogo posla u Beogradu. **b** Pitao sam da li boravi kod njih ili u hotelu. **c** Pitao sam koliko dugo će ostati ovde. **d** Pitao sam u koliko sati će doći na ručak. **e** Pitao sam da li im je potrebna neka pomoć. **f** Pitao sam treba li nešto da im kupimo. **g** Pitao sam da li možemo da svratimo posle ručka. **h** Pitao sam da li bi ona htela da nam čuva decu sutra uveče. **3 a** Krevet stavite u spavaću sobu. **b** Kredenac stavite u trpezariju. **c** Frižider stavite u kuhinju. **d** Radni sto stavite u radnu sobu. **e** Sto i stolice stavite u trpezariju. **f** Orman stavite u spavaću sobu. **g** Policu za knjige stavite u radnu sobu. **h** Trosed stavite u dnevnu sobu. **4** Possible answer: Milan ima četvorosoban stan. Ima jednu spavaću sobu, kuhinju, kupatilo, dnevnu sobu, radnu sobu i trpezariju. U spavaćoj sobi ima . . . U dnevnoj sobi drži . . . etc. **5 a** koji; **b** kojom; **c** koji; **d** koju; **e** kojem; **f** koja; **g** kojoj; **h** kome. **6** Kakav stan imaš?/Da li živiš sama?/Imaš li svoju sobu?/A gde stanuju tvoji roditelji?/Šta znači reč **komšiluk**? Ne znam tu reč./A kako se kaže na srpskom *a neighbour*?/Ja imam dobre komšije. Uvek su ljubazni i pitaju me da li mi treba neka pomoć.

Test yourself

1 c;   2 a;   3 b;   4 a;   5 a;   6 c;   7 c;   8 b;   9 c;   10 c

---

Unit 16

A: i No, but there is one who lives nearby. **ii** In a few minutes. **B: i** Two or three days. **ii** No, but she has to be careful not to walk too much. **C: i** He has a toothache. **ii** Antibiotics. **D: a** коса; **b** око; **c** рука; **d** прст; **e** нога. **i** Боли ме глава. **ii** Боли га стомак. **iii** Повредио/ла сам колено.

1 Нисам јуче ишла у школу. Нисам се осећала добро./Болела ме је страшно глава./Не осећам се добро. Све ме боли. Мислим да сам прехлађена./Не знам. Али узела сам аспирин./У реду. Слажем се. Да ли можеш да кажеш господину Лукићу да сам болесна и да нећу доћи на час?/Хвала ти. Јавићу ти се после подне. **2 a** He has a sore throat. **b** No. **c** Yes, he had 39 yesterday. **d** Antibiotics. **e** He has to take aspirin and to drink a lot of tea. **f** Four or five days. **g** In a week.

Test yourself

1 b; **2** a; **3** b; **4** b; **5** a; **6** I e; II d; III a; IV c; V b

Unit 17

A: i 42; **ii** One red and one yellow. **B:** She is replacing summer clothes in her wardrobe with those she will need during winter. **C: i** The next day. **ii** That same day in the evening.

1 a crvena; **b** crne; **c** svetloplava; **d** žuta; **e** braon; **f** plava; **g** beli. **2** Htela bih da kupim košulju. Kakve košulje imate?/Sviđa mi se. Koje boje imate?/Mogu li, molim vas, da vidim belu?/Ja nosim broj trideset osam./Mogu li da probam?/Dobra je. Uzeću je. Gde mogu da platim? **3 a** Yes. **b** Yes. **c** No. **d** Yes. **e** Yes. **4 a** Hteo/Htela bih da promenim novac. Gde je menjačnica? **b** Da li u hotelu mogu da kupim novine? **c** Imate li frizerski salon? **d** Gde mogu da parkiram kola? **e** Imate li lekara u hotelu?

Test yourself

1 b; **2** c; **3** a; **4** b; **5** a; **6** I d; II e; III a; IV b; V c

Unit 18

A: i His secretary. **ii** On 24 September at nine o'clock at the reception of the hotel *Park*. **B:** Dušan is going to send a car to pick him up. **C:** At 3.30 at the latest.   **D:** To be in front of the hotel *Park* at two o'clock.

1 a iii; **b** i; **c** iii.   **2** Possible answer: Поштована господо, хтео/хтела бих да у вашем хотелу резервишем једну двокреветну собу са купатилом од 10. до 17. маја. Са поштовањем . . .   **3** Possible answer: Драги Милане, ја сам у Београду, у хотелу *Парк*, соба број 203. Бићу у хотелу данас после подне. Јавите ми се или ми оставите поруку на рецепцији. Срдачан поздрав . . .

Test yourself

1 i c; **ii** a; **2 i** a; **ii** c;

Unit 19

A: i Biljana. **ii** Yes, she did, but she couldn't find him.   **B: i** In England. **ii** At the end of October or the beginning of November.   **C: i** Dajte mi, molim vas, gospođu . . ./Mogu li da govorim sa gospođom . . . **ii** Imate li neku poruku?   **D:** At half past four in the square, at the theatre.   **E:** At 8 o'clock.   **F:** Basketball match Yugoslavia–Greece.

1 Halo. Mogu li, molim vas, da govorim sa gospodinom Nebojšom Vujićem?/Da li znate kada će se vratiti?/__ ovde./Recite mu, molim vas, da sam u Beogradu i da bih voleo/la da ga vidim. Možete li da zapišete moj telefonski broj?/Moj broj je 483–652/Hvala. Do viđenja.   **2** Dobro jutro. Da li je Branka kod kuće, molim vas?/Zdravo, Branka, ovde __/Da, jesam. Došao/la sam juče./Jesi li slobodna večeras?/Odlično. Gde ćemo da se nađemo?/U koliko sati?/Dobro, biću kod tebe u pola osam.

Test yourself

a; b;   e; d;   i; h;   c; j;   g; f

Unit 20

A: i She is finishing her studies and is not going to be a student any more. **ii** She has got a job at the university teaching German. **iii** Robert. **B:** 011/3400–662 **C: i** 3435–591; **ii** 032/28–256; **iii** 481–252; **iv** 3346–854; **v** 011/4566–785; **vi** 545–384.

1 a Брачни пар тражи тросован ненамештен стан са телефоном, централним грејањем и баштом. Тел . . . **b** Странцу потребан стан са телефоном, централним грејањем и гаражом на дужи период. Плаћање унапред. Тел . . . **2** Possible answer: Енглез/Енглескиња даје приватне часове енглеског језика. Сви узрасти. Повољно. Тел . . .

Test yourself

1 I e; **II** h; **III** f; **IV** b; **V** c; **VI** a; **VII** d; **VIII** g; **2** b

Transcripts

Unit 1

Practice 4
Крагујевац; Ужице; Суботица; Приштина; Нови Сад; Београд; Ниш.

Practice 7
Урош Максимовић; Драган Јовановић; Милан Лукић; Зоран Марковић; Весна Костић; Јелена Мићић; Вера Петровић; Бранка Шантић.

Unit 2

Practice 1
Dobro veče.
Dobro veče, gospođo Zorić. Kako ste?
Dobro sam, hvala. A kako ste vi?
I ja sam dobro, hvala.

Zdravo, Vera.
Zdravo, Vesna. Kako si?
Dobro, hvala. A ti?
I ja sam dobro.

Dobro jutro. Kako ste, gospodine Iliću?
Ja sam dobro, hvala. A vi?
Dobro sam, hvala.

Unit 3

Practice 6
Ja sam Milan. Ja sam Srbin. Govorim srpski i engleski.
Ja sam Ana. Ja sam Srpkinja. Govorim srpski i francuski.
Ja sam Laura. Ja sam Engleskinja. Govorim engleski, ruski i srpski.

Unit 4

Practice 2

Конобар	Добар дан. Изволите?
Весна	Дајте ми, молим вас, једну кока-колу.
Конобар	А за вас, госпођице?
Барбара	Ја бих кафу, молим вас.
Конобар	А ви, господине?
Роберт	Дајте ми једно пиво.

Unit 5

Practice 2

Prodavačica	Dobro jutro. Šta želite?
Barbara	Dajte mi, molim vas, jedan hleb i četiri kifle.
Prodavačica	Izvolite.
Barbara	Imate li jogurt?
Prodavačica	Imamo.
Barbara	Dajte mi i tri jogurta.
Prodavačica	Izvolite. To je osamdeset četiri dinara.

Practice 8

Dragan	Hoćemo li predjelo, Jelena?
Jelena	Ja ne bih. Nisam gladna.
Dragan	U redu. Šta hoćeš za jelo?
Jelena	Ja bih piletinu na žaru. A ti?
Dragan	Ja bih jednu bečku šniclu. Hoćeš li salatu?
Jelena	Hoću zelenu salatu.
Dragan	A ja hoću srpsku salatu. Konobaru, molim vas, jednu piletinu na žaru, jednu bečku šniclu, jednu zelenu i jednu srpsku salatu.
Konobar	Odmah, gospodine.

Unit 6

Practice 3

a Молим вас, колико кошта овај енглеско-српски речник?

Тај речник кошта четиристо шездесет динара.

b Молим вас, колико кошта овај речник?

Он кошта шестсто тридесет динара.

c Молим вас, колико кошта овај енглеско-српски речник?

Кошта петсто осамдесет динара.

d А овај речник, колико он кошта?

Тај речник кошта петсто педесет динара.

Unit 7

Practice 3

a Dobar dan. Dajte mi, molim vas, broj telefona Milana Jankovića.

Njegova adresa je Molerova 46.

Milan Janković. Samo trenutak. To je 436–257.

Hvala lepo.

b Dobro veče. Molim vas, broj telefona restorana Kolarac.

Restoran Kolarac je 638–972.

Hvala.

Molim.

Unit 8

Practice 1

Извините, молим вас, да ли знате где се налази музеј?

Идите право, а онда скрените лево. Музеј је на крају улице.

А где је, молим вас, пошта?

Пошта је десно, иза ћошка.

А где је хотел *Лондон*?

Скрените у прву улицу десно. Хотел је са десне стране.

Unit 9

Practice 5

U devet sati sastanak sa gospodinom Lazarevićem u gradu; u deset i petnaest sastanak sa gospodinom Dragojevićem; u pola dvanaest sastanak sa gospođom Danilović; od jedan i petnaest do dvadeset do tri ručak sa gospodinom Lalićem; u deset do tri sastanak u Britanskoj ambasadi; u četiri sata opet sastanak sa gospodinom Lazarevićem u hotelu.

Unit 10

Practice 1

Зовем се Милица Бабић. Живим у Београду. Ја сам преводилац. Имам тридесет четири године. Удата сам. Мој муж се зове Александар. Он је новинар. Има тридесет шест година. Имамо једну ћерку. Наша ћерка се зове Ивана и има пет година.

Unit 11

Practice 7

Milan	Kuda ideš na letovanje, Branka?
Branka	Idem na more, u Budvu.
Milan	Hoćeš li ići sama?
Branka	Ne, ići ću sa drugaricom.
Milan	Kako ćete putovati?
Branka	Ići ćemo vozom.
Milan	I koliko ćete ostati?
Branka	Dve nedelje. A ti? Kakvi su tvoji planovi?
Milan	Ja ne volim mnogo more. Volim planine. Ići ću na Kopaonik.
Branka	Hoćeš li ići autobusom?
Milan	Ne, ići ću kolima, ali još ne znam kada. Još nisam rezervisao hotelsku sobu.

Unit 12

Practice 3

Милан	Ја идем на море двадесетог јула. Вратићу се у Београд трећег августа. Хоћеш ли ти, Миро, бити овде у августу?
Мира	Не, бићу на одмору од првог до петнаестог. После петнаестог августа сам у Београду.
Милан	А ти, Јанко?
Јанко	Ја путујем на Копаоник петог и враћам се деветнаестог августа. После сам овде.

Unit 13

Practice 1

Robert	U koliko sati ustajete, gospodine Petroviću?
Zoran	Ustajem obično u sedam sati.
Robert	A vi, gospođo Jelena?
Jelena	Kad idem na posao, ustajem u šest.
Robert	I kako idete na posao?
Zoran	Ja uvek idem na posao kolima.
Jelena	Ja nemam kola. Idem autobusom.
Robert	Kada počinjete da radite?
Zoran	U devet sati.
Jelena	A ja počinjem u osam.
Robert	I gde ručate?
Zoran	Ručam sa ženom kod kuće posle posla.
Jelena	Ja obično kupim sendvič i pojedem ga na poslu.
Robert	Kada završavate posao?
Zoran	U četiri sata.
Jelena	A ja radim do tri.

Unit 14

Practice 1

Барбара	Кажи ми, шта радиш када си слободан? Да ли се бавиш неким спортом?
Ричард	Зими волим да идем на скијање. А лети често играм тенис.
Барбара	А фудбал?
Ричард	Никад не играм фудбал. Нисам добар фудбалер. А ти?
Барбара	Мени се допада пливање. Идем на базен кад год могу.
Ричард	Да ли гледаш спортске преносе на телевизији?
Барбара	Не, не волим да гледам телевизију. Више волим да идем у град са друштвом или да слушам музику.

Unit 16

Practice 2

Лекар	Добар дан. Изволите, седите. Кажите ми, шта није у реду?
Болесник	Добар дан, докторе. Не осећам се добро. Боли ме грло.
Лекар	Да ли кашљете?
Болесник	Не, не кашљем.
Лекар	Имате ли температуру?
Болесник	Јуче сам имао високу температуру, тридесет девет.
Лекар	Да видим . . . Имате инфекцију. Даћу вам рецепт за антибиотик.
Болесник	Треба ли да узимам још нешто?
Лекар	Узимајте и аспирин, и пијте много чаја.
Болесник	Да ли морам да лежим?
Лекар	Да, останите у кревету четири-пет дана. Дођите опет код мене за недељу дана.

Unit 17

Practice 1

Majka	Koju haljinu hoćeš da nosiš, crvenu ili belu?
Ana	Crvenu. Već sam je stavila u kofer.
Majka	A pantalone?
Ana	Poneću crne pantalone.
Majka	Hoćeš da ti spakujem neke košulje?
Ana	Spakuj mi, molim te, svetloplavu svilenu bluzu i žutu košulju.
Majka	I šta još?
Ana	Tamo će biti toplo. Poneću i braon šorc.
Majka	A šta ćeš ako bude hladno?
Ana	Mislila sam o tome. Odlučila sam da ponesem jaknu.
Majka	Koju, plavu?
Ana	Da, plavu. Ali, čekaj, nešto sam zaboravila . . . kupaći kostim. Nisam ga stavila na spisak. Poneću onaj beli.

Unit 18

Practice 1

Марко	Добар дан, Стеване. Овде Марко.
Стеван	Добар дан, Марко. Како сте?
Марко	Добро, хвала. Хтео сам да вас питам можемо ли да се нађемо данас око подне.
Стеван	Наравно. Где сте? Јесте ли у граду?
Марко	Не, још сам у хотелу. Сада полазим у град.
Стеван	Хоћете ли да дођете код мене у канцеларију?
Марко	Не, то ми не одговара. Шта мислите, да се нађемо негде у центру за један сат?
Стеван	У реду. Чекаћу вас на Тргу Републике, испред биоскопа Јадран у пола дванаест.
Марко	Одлично. Видећемо се тамо. До виђења.

Grammar glossary

adjective   An adjective is a word used to qualify or describe a noun or pronoun, e.g. *Dragan is tall*. **Dragan je visok**. *She is young*. **Ona je mlada**.

adverb   Adverbs are used to qualify or modify an adjective or a verb, e.g. *She is very young*. **Ona je veoma mlada**. *Vesna sings well*. **Vesna dobro peva**.

agreement   Agreement is when words which are used together have the same grammatical number, gender or case.

case   Cases in Serbian are indicated by changes made to nouns, adjectives and pronouns. Serbian has seven cases: nominative, vocative, accusative, genitive, dative, instrumental, locative. Cases tell you the function of a noun in a sentence.

comparative   When making comparisons we need the comparative form of the adjective. In English this is usually done by adding *-er* to the adjective or by putting *more* in front. *I am taller than you*. **Ja sam viši od tebe**.

conditional   This is a form of the verb to show that an event might have happened or might yet take place.

enclitics   Serbian has two forms of the verb *to be* **biti** and *to want* **hteti** in the present tense and two forms for personal pronouns in cases other than the nominative (see **Pronouns** and **Case**). The shorter form of these alternatives is called the enclitic with rules for when and how they are to be used.

gender   In English the term gender refers to whether human beings or animals are male or female. In Serbian, as in many European languages, all nouns have a gender which is masculine, feminine or neuter. Sometimes the grammatical gender of a noun may tell you if the word refers to a male or female being but it is not primarily a biological reference. In Serbian the word *hotel* **hotel** is masculine, while *chair* **stolica** is feminine and *sea* **more** is neuter. Adjectives which are used to describe these words must agree with the gender of the noun and change accordingly. There are rules which help you to determine the gender of nouns and adjectives.

imperative The imperative is the form of the verb used to give directions, instructions, orders or commands.

infinitive The infinitive is the basic form of the verb used for dictionary entries. It is often the form used when two verbs are used together, e.g. *She likes to live in London.* **Ona voli živeti u Londonu.** Serbian also has an alternative infinitive construction, e.g. *She likes to live in London.* **Ona voli da živi u Londonu.**

noun Nouns are words which name things and people, e.g. *room* **soba**, *person* **čovek**.

number Number is the term used to indicate whether words are singular or plural.

object The object of a verb indicates what or who is on the receiving end of an action, unlike the subject which tells you who is performing the action (see **Subject**). There are two types of object. The direct object indicates on what or whom the action is performed, e.g. *Vesna likes coffee.* **Vesna voli kafu.** *Coffee* is the direct object in this sentence as it is the object being liked and here is expressed in the accusative case. The indirect object in a sentence indicates what or who is the beneficiary of an action, e.g. *He bought a book for his brother.* **Kupio je bratu knjigu.** *Brother* is the indirect object in this sentence as he is the beneficiary of the action, the one for whom the book has been bought, and here is expressed in the dative dase. Indirect objects in English are often preceded by *to* or *for*.

person Person is the term which refers to the separate parts of a verb. Verbs have six persons, three in singular (I, you, he/she/it) and three in plural (we, you, they) and endings of verbs change to indicate which person is the subject.

plural See **singular**.

possessive adjectives and pronouns Possessive adjectives such as *my* and pronouns such as *mine* indicate who possesses what in a sentence. *This is my coffee. That coffee is yours.* **Ovo je moja kafa. Ta kafa je vaša.**

334

preposition   Prepositions are words which generally show relationships between people or things, e.g. *Zoran is in the room.* **Zoran je u sobi.**

pronouns   Pronouns are often used to substitute for nouns which have usually been mentioned once already. *This is my husband. He is standing in the square.* **Ovo je moj muž. On stoji na trgu.** Such pronouns as *I* **ja**, *he* **on** are called personal pronouns and are often omitted in Serbian because the ending of the verb indicates the person (see **person**), e.g. *This is my husband. He is standing in the square.* **Ovo je moj muž. Stoji na trgu.**

reflexive verb   These are constructions in which the word **se**, meaning *oneself*, accompanies the verb.

singular   The terms singular and plural are used to contrast between one and more than one, e.g. *book/books* **knjiga/knjige.**

subject   The subject names the person or thing who is performing the action of the verb of a sentence, e.g. *Vesna likes coffee.* **Vesna voli kafu.** *Vesna* is the subject as she is the one who likes coffee and is expressed here in the nominative case.

superlative   The superlative part of the adjective is formed in English by adding *-est* to the adjective or by using *most*. *This shirt is the cheapest of all.* **Ova košulja je najjeftinija od svih.** *This coat is the most expensive.* **Ovaj kaput je najskuplji.**

tense   Tense indicates the time when the action of the verb in a sentences takes place.

verb   Verbs usually indicate the action of a sentence, e.g. *He is playing football.* **On igra fudbal.** They may indicate sensations, e.g. *I feel fine.* **Osećam se dobro.** They may also be used to show a state, e.g. *Today is a fine day.* **Danas je lep dan.**

verbal aspect   The aspect of a verb tells you more about the quality of the action in a sentence. It tells you if the action was or will be completed, if the action took place or will take place on more than one occasion, if the action was or will be in process but not completed for some reason. Serbian has an imperfective aspect (for unfinished or regular actions, e.g. *to write* **pisati**) and a perfective aspect (for completed actions e.g. *to write* **napisati**) e.g. *He wrote to his brother every day.* **Pisao je bratu svaki dan.** *Yesterday he wrote a letter to his brother.* **Juče je napisao pismo bratu.**

Grammar summary

In this section you can find model endings for regular nouns, adjectives and for the present tense of verbs in table form, including changes to the personal pronouns.

Nouns

Masculine

	hard ending		soft ending	
	Singular	Plural	Singular	Plural
nom.	hotel	hoteli	muž	muževi
voc.	hotele	hoteli	mužu	muževi
acc.	hotel	hotele	muža	muževe
gen.	hotela	hotela	muža	muževa
dat.	hotelu	hotelima	mužu	muževima
ins.	hotelom	hotelima	mužem	muževima
loc.	hotelu	hotelima	mužu	muževima

Feminine

	-a ending		consonant ending	
	Singular	Plural	Singular	Plural
nom.	žena	žene	stvar	stvari
voc.	ženo	žene	stvar	stvari
acc.	ženu	žene	stvar	stvari
gen.	žene	žena	stvari	stvari
dat.	ženi	ženama	stvari	stvarima
ins.	ženom	ženama	stvari*	stvarima
loc.	ženi	ženama	stvari	stvarima

(*alternative ins. stvarju)

Neuter

	-o ending		-e ending	
	Singular	Plural	Singular	Plural
nom.	mesto	mesta	polje	polja
voc.	mesto	mesta	polje	polja

acc.	mesto	mesta	polje	polja
gen.	mesta	mesta	polja	polja
dat.	mestu	mestima	polju	poljima
ins.	mestom	mestima	poljem	poljima
loc.	mestu	mestima	polju	poljima

Adjectives

Masculine

	Singular	Singular (ending in soft consonant)
nom.	nov/novi	svež/sveži
voc.	novi	sveži
acc.	as nom. or gen.	as nom. or gen.
gen.	novog(a)	svežeg(a)
dat.	novom(e)	svežem(u)
ins.	novim	svežim
loc.	novom(e)	svežem(u)

Feminine

	Singular	Singular (ending in soft consonant)
nom.	nova	sveža
voc.	nova	sveža
acc.	novu	svežu
gen.	nove	sveže
dat.	novoj	svežoj
ins.	novom	svežom
loc.	novoj	svežoj

Neuter

	Singular	Singular (ending in soft consonant)
nom.	novo	sveže
voc.	novo	sveže
acc.	novo	sveže
gen.	novog(a)	svežeg(a)
dat.	novom(e)	svežem(u)
ins.	novim	svežim
loc.	novom(e)	svežem(u)

Plural (adjectives ending in a soft consonant follow same pattern)		
	masc.	fem.	neut.
nom.	novi	nove	nova
voc.	novi	nove	nova
acc.	nove	nove	nova
gen.	novih	novih	novih
dat.	novim(a)	novim(a)	novim(a)
ins.	novim(a)	novim(a)	novim(a)
loc.	novim(a)	novim(a)	novim(a)

Present tense of verbs

a type

ja	gledam	mi	gledamo
ti	gledaš	vi	gledate
on	gleda	oni	gledaju

e type

ja	pijem	mi	pijemo
ti	piješ	vi	pijete
on	pije	oni	piju

i type

ja	govorim	mi	govorimo
ti	govoriš	vi	govorite
on	govori	oni	govore

Personal pronouns

Singular

nom.	ja	ti	on	ona	ono
acc.	mene	tebe	njega	nju	njega
	me	te	ga	je, ju	ga
gen.	mene	tebe	njega	nje	njega
	me	te	ga	je	ga
dat.	meni	tebi	njemu	njoj	njemu
	mi	ti	mu	joj	mu
ins.	mnom(e)	tobom	njim(e)	njom(e)	njim(e)
loc.	meni	tebi	njemu	njoj	njemu

Plural

nom.	mi	vi	oni	one	ona
acc.	nas	vas	njih	njih	njih
	nas	vas	ih	ih	ih
gen.	nas	vas	njih	njih	njih
	nas	vas	ih	ih	ih
dat.	nama	vama	njima	njima	njima
	nam	vam	im	im	im
ins.	nama	vama	njima	njima	njima
loc.	nama	vama	njima	njima	njima

Vocabulary section

This section contains the words used in this book listed alphabetically, first from Serbian to English and then from English to Serbian. The following abbreviations are used: m. masculine; f. feminine; n. neuter; sing. singular; pl. plural; acc. accusative; gen. genitive; dat. dative; ins. instrumental; loc. locative; adj. adjective. Nouns in Serbian are given in the nominative singular form, and adjectives are given in the masculine nominative singular form. Verbs in Serbian are listed with the imperfective form before the perfective. Names of countries in the Serbian–English vocabulary are followed by the adjective, the noun denoting a male inhabitant and the noun denoting a female inhabitant. Serbian prepositions are followed by the case which they govern.

Serbian–English vocabulary

a   *and, but*
adresa f.   *address*
advokat m.   *lawyer*
aerodrom m.   *airport*
agencija f.   *agency*
ako   *if*
aktivnost f.   *activity*
ali   *but*
alkohol m.   *alcohol*
ambasada f.   *embassy*
Amerika f.   *America*
   američki adj.
   Amerikanac m.
   Amerikanka f.
antibiotik m.   *antibiotic*
apartman m.   *apartment,*
   holiday flat
apoteka f.   *pharmacy*
apotekar m. apotekarka f.
   pharmacist
april m.   *April*
atletika f.   *athletics*
Australija f.   *Australia*
autobus m.   *bus*
autobuska stanica f.   *bus*
   station
automobil, auto m.   *car*
autoput m.   *motorway*
avgust m.   *August*
avion m.   *aeroplane*
Azija f.   *Asia*

baba, baka f.   *grandmother*
bakalnica f.   *grocery shop*

baklava f.   *baklava*
balet m.   *ballet*
balkon m.   *circle (theatre),*
   balcony
banja f.   *spa*
banka f.   *bank*
bar m.   *bar*
baš   *really, quite*
bašta f.   *garden*
baviti se   *to be engaged in*
bazen m.   *swimming pool*
benzin m.   *petrol*
benzinska pumpa f.   *petrol*
   station
beo adj.   *white*
besplatan adj.   *free (of cost)*
bez (+ gen.)   *without*
biblioteka f.   *library*
biftek m.   *beef steak*
bioskop m.   *cinema*
biti   *to be*
biznis m.   *business*
blagajna f.   *ticket office*
blagajnik m. blagajnica f.
   ticket seller
blizina f.   *vicinity*
blizu (+ gen.)   *near*
blok m.   *block*
bluza f.   *blouse*
boja f.   *colour*
bojati se   *to fear, be afraid*
bol m.   *pain*
bolesnik m. bolesnica f.   *patient*
bolestan adj.   *ill*

boleti   *to hurt, ache*
bolnica f.   *hospital*
boravak m.   *stay*
boravište n.   *residence*
boraviti   *to stay*
borovnica f.   *blueberry*
Bosna f.   *Bosnia*
Božić m.   *Christmas*
bračni par m.   *married couple*
braća f.   *brothers*
brak m.   *marriage*
brat m.   *brother*
brdo n.   *hill*
briga f.   *worry*
brinuti   *to worry*
broj m.   *number*
brz adj.   *quick*
budilnik m.   *alarm clock*
buditi; probuditi   *to wake*
bulevar m.   *boulevard*
burek m.   *pie made with leaves of filo pastry*
buter m.   *butter*
butik m.   *boutique*

carina f.   *customs*
cena f.   *price*
centar m.   *centre*
centrala f.   *telephone switchboard*
centralno grejanje n.   *central heating*
ceo adj.   *whole*
cigareta f.   *cigarette*
cipela f.   *shoe*
crkva f.   *church*
crn adj.   *black (red of wine)*
Crna Gora f.   *Montenegro*
crven adj.   *red*

cvekla f.   *beetroot*
čaj m.   *tea*
čas m.   *class, hour*
čaša f.   *glass*
čekati   *to wait*
često   *often*
četvrtak m.   *Thursday*
čiji adj.   *whose*
činiti se   *to seem*
čist adj.   *clean*
čitati; pročitati   *to read*
čorba f.   *broth*
čovek m.   *person, man*
čudan adj.   *strange*
čuti   *to hear*
čuvati   *to look after*
ćao   *hi*
ćerka f.   *daughter*
ćevapčići m. pl.   *small kebabs*
ćošak m.   *corner*

da   *yes*
dalek adj.   *far*
daleko od (+ gen.)   *far from*
dan m.   *day*
danas   *today*
davati; dati   *to give*
davati se   *to be showing (of a film or a play)*
deca f.   *children*
decembar m.   *December*
dečko m.   *boy, boyfriend*
deda m.   *grandfather*
deliti; podeliti   *to share*
delovati   *to take effect*
desno   *right*
dešavati se; desiti se   *to happen*
dete n.   *child*
detinjstvo n.   *childhood*

devize f. pl.   *foreign currency*
devojka f.   *girl, young lady,*
  girlfriend
dezinfikovati   *to disinfect*
dinar m.   *dinar*
diplomata m.   *diplomat*
divan adj.   *wonderful*
dnevna soba f.   *sitting room*
dnevni adj.   *daily*
do (+ gen.)   *to, up to*
dobar adj.   *good*
dobijati; dobiti   *to receive, get*
dobro došli   *welcome*
dogovoriti se   *to agree*
dogovor m.   *agreement*
dok   *while*
dolar m.   *dollar*
dolaziti; doći   *to come*
dole   *down, down there*
dolina f.   *valley*
domaći adj.   *home, home-made*
domaćica f.   *housewife*
donje rublje n.   *underwear*
donositi; doneti   *to bring*
dopadati se   *to like*
doplata f.   *additional payment*
doručak m.   *breakfast*
doručkovati   *to breakfast*
dosadan adj.   *boring*
dosta (+ gen.)   *enough, a lot*
dostavljati; dostaviti   *to*
  deliver
do viđenja   *goodbye*
dovoljan adj.   *sufficient*
doživljaj m.   *experience*
drag adj.   *dear*
dragocenosti f. pl.   *valuables*
drama f.   *drama*

drug m. drugarica f.   *friend*
drugi adj.   *second, other,*
  another
drukčiji adj.   *different*
društvo n.   *company, group of*
  friends
družiti se   *to be friends*
drven adj.   *wooden*
drvo n.   *tree*
držati   *to keep*
dug adj.   *long*
duhovit adj.   *witty*
duvati   *to blow*
dva/dve   *two*
džem m.   *jam*
džemper m.   *jumper*
džin m.   *gin*
džus m.   *orange juice*

ekonomista m.   *economist*
elektronska pošta f.   *e-mail*
Engleska f.   *England*
  engleski adj.
  Englez m.
  Engleskinja f.
esej m.   *essay*
evo (+ gen.)   *here is/are*
evro m.   *euro*
Evropa f.   *Europe*
evropski adj.   *European*

faktura f.   *invoice*
fakultet m.   *faculty*
farmerke f. pl.   *jeans*
februar m.   *February*
fijoka f.   *drawer*
fiksiran adj.   *fixed*
film m.   *film*
firma f.   *firm, company*

flaša f. *bottle*
fotelja f. *armchair*
fotografija f. *photograph*
Francuska f. *France*
  francuski adj.
  Francuz m.
  Francuskinja f.
freska f. *fresco*
frizerski salon m. *hairdress-ing salon*
frižider m. *fridge*
fudbal m. *football*
fudbaler m. *football player*
funta f. *pound*

galeb m. *seagull*
galerija f. *gallery*
garaža f. *garage*
garsonjera f. *bedsit*
gde *where*
gladan adj. *hungry*
glava f. *head*
glavni adj. *main*
gledati; pogledati *to watch, look at*
glumac m. *actor*
glumica f. *actress*
godina f. *year*
godišnje doba n. *season of the year*
gorak adj. *bitter*
gore *up, up there*
gornji adj. *upper*
gospoda f. *gentlemen*
gospodin m. *Mr, gentleman*
gospođa f. *Mrs, lady*
gospođica f. *Miss, young lady*
gost m. *guest*
goveđi adj. *beef*

govoriti *to speak*
grad m. *town*
građanin m. *citizen*
gram m. *gram*
gramatika f. *grammar*
granica f. *border, frontier*
Grčka f. *Greece*
  grčki adj.
  Grk m.
  Grkinja f.
grlo n. *throat*
grmljavina f. *thunder*
grudi f. pl. *chest*
gust adj. *thick*
gužva f. *traffic jam, crowd*

hajde *come on*
haljina f. *dress*
hemijsko čišćenje n. *dry cleaning*
hiljada f. *thousand*
hitan adj. *urgent*
hladan adj. *cold*
hleb m. *loaf, bread*
hobi m. *hobby*
hodati *to walk*
hodnik m *corridor*
hokej m. *hockey*
hotel m. *hotel*
hrana f. *food*
Hrvatska f. *Croatia*
  hrvatski adj.
  Hrvat m.
  Hrvatica f.
hteti *to want*
hvala *thank you*

i *and, too, also*
ići *to go*
idući adj. *next*

igrati   *to play*
ili   *or*
imati   *to have*
ime n.   *name*
infekcija f.   *infection*
informacija f.   *information*
inostranstvo n.   *abroad*
intenzivan adj.   *intense*
interfon m.   *intercom*
internet-kafe m.   *internet café*
inženjer m.   *engineer*
ipak   *however, nevertheless*
iskustvo n.   *experience*
ispod (+ gen.)   *below*
ispred (+ gen.)   *in front of*
isti adj.   *same*
istok m.   *east*
istorija f.   *history*
Italija f.   *Italy*
   italijanski adj.
   Italijan m.
   Italijanka f.
iz (+ gen)   *from, out of*
iza (+ gen.)   *behind*
izdavati, izdati   *to rent (out)*
izgledati   *to appear*
izgovor m.   *pronounciation*
izlaz m.   *exit, way out*
izlaziti; izići   *to go out*
izlet m.   *excursion*
između (+ gen.)   *between*
iznad (+ gen.)   *above*
iznajmljivati; iznajmiti   *to rent, hire*
izraz m.   *expression*
izvinite   *excuse me*
izvinjavati se; izviniti se   *to apologize*
izvoziti   *to export*

ja   *I*
jabuka f.   *apple*
jagoda f.   *strawberry*
jak adj.   *strong*
jakna f.   *jacket*
januar m.   *January*
javljati se; javiti se   *to get in touch*
jedan adj.   *one*
jeftin adj.   *cheap*
jelo n.   *dish, meal, food*
jelovnik m.   *menu*
jer   *for, because*
jesen f.   *autumn*
jesti; pojesti   *to eat*
jezero n.   *lake*
jezik m.   *language*
jogurt m.   *yoghurt*
još   *more, also, still*
juče   *yesterday*
jug   *south*
Jugoslavija   *Yugoslavia*
jugoslovenski adj.   *Yugoslav*
jul   *July*
jun   *June*
jutro n.   *morning*
jutros   *this morning*

kada f.   *bath*
kada   *when*
kafa f.   *coffee*
kafana f.   *café*
kafić m.   *café-bar*
kakav adj.   *what kind of*
kako   *how*
kancelarija f.   *office*
kao   *as, like*
kaput m.   *coat*
karta f.   *ticket*

kasa f.   *checkout, till*
kasniti; zakasniti   *to be late*
kasno   *late*
kašika f.   *spoon*
kašljati   *to cough*
katedra f.   *university
   department*
kazati   *to say, tell*
kifla f.   *kifla*
kijavica f.   *cold*
kilo n.   *kilo*
kilometar m.   *kilometre*
kiosk m.   *kiosk*
kirija f.   *rent*
kisela voda f.   *mineral water*
kiša f.   *rain*
kišni mantil m.   *raincoat*
kišovit adj.   *rainy*
ključ m.   *key*
knjiga f.   *book*
knjižara f.   *bookshop*
književnost f.   *literature*
ko   *who*
kod (+ gen)   *at, to the
   home/office of*
kofer m.   *suitcase*
koji adj.   *which, what*
koka-kola f.   *Coca-Cola*
kola n. pl.   *car*
kolač m.   *cake*
kolega m. koleginica f.
   colleague
koleno n.   *knee*
koliko   *how much, how many*
komedija f.   *comedy*
komforan adj.   *comfortable*
komoda f.   *chest of drawers*
kompjuter m.   *computer*

komšija m. komšinica f.
   neighbour
komšiluk m.   *neighbourhood*
konj m.   *horse*
konobar m.   *waiter*
konobarica f.   *waitress*
konverzacija f.   *conversation*
koristiti; iskoristiti   *to use*
kosa f.   *hair*
kostim m.   *suit (female)*
košarka f.   *basketball*
koštati   *to cost*
košulja f.   *shirt*
kraj m.   *area, end*
krastavac m.   *cucumber*
kravata f.   *tie*
kredenac m.   *sideboard*
kredit m.   *credit*
kreditna kartica f.   *credit card*
kretati; krenuti   *to set off*
krevet m.   *bed*
kroz (+ acc.)   *through*
kruna f.   *crown*
kuća f.   *house*
kuda   *where to*
kuhinja f.   *kitchen*
kultura f.   *culture*
kulturan adj.   *cultural*
kupaće gaćice f. pl.   *swimming
   trunks*
kupaći kostim m.   *swimming
   costume*
kupatilo n.   *bathroom*
kupovati; kupiti   *to buy*
kupovina f.   *shopping*
kupus m.   *cabbage*
kurs m.   *exchange rate, course*
kusur m.   *change*

kutija f. *box*
kuvati; skuvati *to cook*

labud m. *swan*
lak adj. *easy*
lavabo n. *sink*
leđa n. pl. *back*
lek m. *medicine*
lekar m. lekarka f. *doctor*
lep adj. *nice, beautiful*
lepinja f. *lepinja* (bread bun)
lepota f. *beauty*
let m. *flight*
leteti *to fly*
letnji adj. *summer*
leto n. *summer*
letovanje n. *summer holidays*
levo *left*
ležati *to lie*
limenka f. *tin can*
limun m. *lemon*
limunada f. *lemonade*
litar m. *litre*
livada f. *meadow*
lokacija f. *location*
lokal m. *telephone extension*
lomiti; slomiti *to break*
loš adj. *bad*
ljubav f. *love*
ljubazan adj. *kind*
ljubić m. *love story*
ljudi m. pl. *people, men*
ljutiti se *to be angry*

maj m. *May*
majica f. *T-shirt*
majka f. *mother*
Makedonija f. *Macedonia*
  makedonski adj.

Makedonac m.
Makedonka f.
mali adj. *small, little*
malina f. *raspberry*
malo *a little*
mama f. *mum*
manastir m. *monastery*
mapa f. *map*
marka f. *stamp*
mart m. *March*
maslina f. *olive*
mast f. *ointment*
mašina za veš f. *washing machine*
međunarodni adj. *international*
mek adj. *soft*
menjačnica f. *exchange office*
menjati; promeniti *to change*
menza f. *canteen*
mesec m. *month, Moon*
meso n. *meat*
mesto n. *place, space*
metar m. *metre*
mi *we*
milion m. *million*
minut m. *minute*
miran adj. *peaceful, quiet*
misliti *to think*
mišljenje n. *opinion*
mlad adj. *young*
mladić m. *young man, youth, boyfriend*
mleko n. *milk*
mnogi adj. *numerous, many*
mnogo (+ gen.) *many, much, a lot of*
moći *be able to, can*

moderan adj. *modern*
moj adj. *my*
moliti; zamoliti *to ask, to beg*
morati *to have to, want*
more n. *sea*
most m. *bridge*
možda *perhaps*
muški adj. *male*
muzej m. *museum*
muzika f. *music*
muž m. *husband*

na (+ acc.) *to, onto*
na (+ loc.) *on*
na žalost *unfortunately*
nabavljati; nabaviti *to acquire*
nacionalnost f. *nationality*
nadati se *to hope*
nalaziti; naći *to find*
nalaziti se *to be situated*
nameravati *to intend*
nameštaj m. *furniture*
namešten adj. *furnished*
napolju *outside*
napred *in front*
napuštati; napustiti *to leave*
naravno *of course*
naročit *special, particular*
narodni adj. *national*
naručivati; naručiti *to order*
naselje n. *settlement*
nastavljati; nastaviti *to continue*
nastavnik m. nastavnica f. *teacher*
naš adj. *our*
natrag *back*
ne *no, not*
nedelja f. *week, Sunday*

nedeljno *weekly*
negde *somewhere*
nego *than*
nekada *once*
neki adj. *some, certain*
neko *somebody*
nekoliko (+ gen.) *a few*
nema *there is not, there are not*
Nemačka f. *Germany*
  nemački adj.
  Nemac m.
  Nemica f.
nešto *something*
ni *nor*
nigde *nowhere*
nikada *never*
niko *nobody*
ništa *nothing*
noć f. *night*
noćas *tonight*
noćenje n. *overnight stay*
noga f. *leg, foot*
nos m. *nose*
nositi *to carry, to wear*
nov adj. *new*
novac m. *money*
novembar m. *November*
novinar m. novinarka f. *journalist*
novine f. pl. *newspaper*
nož m. *knife*
nula f. *zero*
njegov adj. *his*
njen adj. *her*
njihov adj. *their*

o (+ loc.) *about*
obaveštavati; obavestiti *to inform*

obavezan adj.   *obligatory*
obdanište n.   *nursery school*
obećavati; obećati   *to promise*
obično   *usually*
obilazak m.   *visit*
oblačno   *cloudy*
od (+ gen.)   *from*
odakle   *where from*
odbojka f.   *volleyball*
odeća f.   *clothes*
odelo n.   *suit*
odgovarati   *to suit*
odlagati; odložiti   *to delay,*
  postpone
odlazak m.   *departure*
odlaziti; otići   *to leave, go*
  away
odličan adj.   *excellent*
odlučivati; odlučiti   *to decide*
odmah   *immediately, at once*
odmarati se; odmoriti se   *to*
  rest
odmor m.   *holiday, rest*
odobravati; odobriti   *to permit*
odrastao adj.   *adult*
odvajati; odvojiti   *to set aside*
oglas m.   *advertisement*
oko n.   *eye*
okretati; okrenuti   *to turn*
oktobar m.   *October*
omiljen adj.   *favourite*
omlet m.   *omelette*
on   *he*
ona   *she*
onaj adj.   *that*
onda   *then, next*
oni (-e, -a)   *they*
ono   *it*

opasan adj.   *dangerous*
opera f.   *opera*
opet   *again*
oprema f.   *equipment*
organizovati   *to organize*
orman m.   *wardrobe*
osećati se; osetiti se   *to feel*
osim (+ gen.)   *except*
osoba f.   *person*
ostajati; ostati   *to stay,*
  remain
ostavljati; ostaviti   *to leave*
  (behind)
otac m.   *father*
otkad   *since*
otprilike   *approximately*
otvarati; otvoriti   *to open*
otvoren adj.   *open*
ovaj adj.   *this*
ovde   *here*
ozbiljan adj.   *serious*
oženjen adj.   *married*
  (of a man)

padati; pasti   *to fall*
pakovati; spakovati   *to pack*
pantalone f. pl.   *trousers*
papuče f. pl.   *slippers*
paradajz m.   *tomato*
park m.   *park*
parking m.   *car park*
parkirati   *to park*
parter m.   *stalls (theatre)*
pasoš m.   *passport*
pašteta f.   *pasty*
patike f. pl.   *training shoes*
pauza f.   *pause, break*
paziti   *to be careful*
pečurka f.   *mushroom*

peći; ispeći *to roast*
peglati *to iron*
pekara f. *bakery*
period m. *period*
peške *on foot*
petak m. *Friday*
pevač m. pevačica f. *singer*
picerija f. *pizzeria*
piće n. *drink*
pidžama f. *pyjamas*
pileći adj. *chicken*
piletina f. *chicken*
pisac m. *writer*
pisati; napisati *to write*
pismo n. *letter*
pitati *to ask*
piti; popiti *to drink*
pivo n. *beer*
plaćati; platiti *to pay*
plan m. *plan*
planina f. *mountain*
planirati *to plan*
plata f. *pay, salary*
plav adj. *blue, blonde*
plaža f. *beach*
plivati *to swim*
pljeskavica f. *hamburger*
pljusak m. *shower*
po (+ dat.) *around*
pobeđivati; pobediti *to win*
početak m. *beginning*
počinjati; početi *to begin*
pod m. *floor*
podne n. *midday*
poezija f. *poetry*
pogačica f. *pie (small)*
pogled m. *view*
pogodan adj. *convenient*
pokazivati; pokazati *to show*

poklon m. *present*
pola *half*
polako *slowly*
polazak m. *departure*
polaziti; poći *to set off*
polica f. *shelf*
polje n. *field*
pomagati; pomoći *to help*
pomoć f. *help*
pomorandža f. *orange*
ponavljati; ponoviti *to repeat*
ponedeljak m. *Monday*
ponekad *sometimes*
ponoć f. *midnight*
ponuda f. *offer*
popularan adj. *popular*
popust m. *discount*
pored (+ gen) *next to, by,*
  beside
porodica f. *family*
porudžbina f. *order*
poruka f. *message*
posao m. *work, job*
posećivati; posetiti *to visit*
posedovati *to possess*
poseta f. *visit*
poslastičarnica f. *cake shop*
posle (+ gen.) *after*
poslednji adj. *last (final)*
poslovni adj. *business*
postavljati; postaviti *to set*
poster m. *poster*
postojati *to be, exist*
posuđe n. *dishes*
pošta f. *post office*
poštansko sanduče n. *postbox,*
  mailbox
pošto *since, because*
poštovan adj. *respected*

potok m. *stream*
potpisivati; potpisati *to sign*
potreban adj. *necessary*
povoljan adj. *reasonable (of prices)*
povratak m. *return*
povređivati; povrediti *to injure*
pozdravljati se; pozdraviti se *to greet, take one's leave*
poziv m. *invitation*
pozivati; pozvati *to invite*
pozorište n. *theatre*
prati; oprati *to wash*
prav adj. *right, correct, straight*
pravac m. *direction*
praviti; napraviti *to make*
pravo *straight on, directly*
prazan adj. *empty*
praznik m. *holiday (public)*
pre (+ gen.) *before, ago*
prebacivati; prebaciti *to transfer*
predavanje n. *lecture*
predavati *to teach*
predgrađe n. *suburb*
predjelo n. *first course*
predlagati; predložiti *to suggest*
predlog m. *proposal*
prednost f. *advantage*
predstava f. *performance*
predstavnik m. *representative*
pregledati *to examine*
pregovori m. *negotiations*
prehlađen adj. *having a cold*
prekidati; prekinuti *to interrupt*
preko (+ gen.) *via, across*
preko puta (+ gen.) *opposite*

prelaziti; preći *to cross*
prema (+ dat.) *towards*
prenos m. *broadcast*
pretežno *mostly*
prevod m. *translation*
prevodilac m. *translator*
prevoditi; prevesti *to translate*
prevoz m. *transport*
prezime n. *surname*
priča f. *story*
pričati; ispričati *to talk, tell*
prijatan adj. *pleasant*
prijatelj m. prijateljica f. *friend*
prijateljski adj. *friendly*
prilika f. *opportunity*
prilično *quite, rather*
primati; primiti *to receive*
primećivati; primetiti *to notice*
pripovetka f. *short story*
priroda f. *nature*
prisustvovati *to be present*
privatan adj. *private*
prizemlje n. *ground floor*
priznavati; priznati *to confess, recognize*
probati *to try*
problem m. *problem*
prodavac m. *salesman*
prodavačica f. *saleswoman*
prodavati; prodati *to sell*
prodavnica f. *shop*
program m. *programme*
proizvod m. *product*
proizvoditi *to produce*
prolaziti; proći *to pass*
proleće n. *spring*
promenljiv adj. *changeable*
prostor m. *space*

prošli adj.   *last (previous)*
protiv (+ gen)   *against*
proveravati; proveriti   *to check*
provoditi; provesti   *to spend*
   (time)
prozor m.   *window*
prst m.   *finger, toe*
pršut m.   *smoked ham*
prtljag m.   *luggage*
prvi adj.   *first*
pun adj.   *full*
put m.   *road, way, journey,*
   time
putnički adj.   *travel, travelling*
putovanje n.   *journey, trip*
putovati   *to travel*

račun m.   *bill*
radio m.   *radio*
raditi; uraditi   *to work, do*
radna soba f.   *study*
radni sto m.   *desk*
radnja f.   *shop*
radovati se   *to look*
   forward to
rakija f.   *brandy*
rame n.   *shoulder*
rana f.   *wound*
rano   *early*
raspakovati se   *to unpack*
raspust m.   *vacation, school*
   holidays
rat m.   *war*
razglednica f.   *postcard*
razgovarati   *to talk, chat*
razgovor m.   *talk,*
   conversation
razni adj.   *various, different*
razumeti   *to understand*

razvoj m.   *development*
ražnjići m. pl.   *small skewers*
   of meat
recepcija f.   *reception*
recepcioner m.   *receptionist*
recept m.   *prescription*
reč f.   *word*
rečnik m.   *dictionary*
reći   *to say, tell*
red m.   *row, order*
reka f.   *river*
rerna f.   *oven*
restoran m.   *restaurant*
retko   *rarely*
rezervacija f.   *reservation*
rezervisati   *to book*
riba f.   *fish*
ringla f.   *hotplate*
robna kuća f.   *department*
   store
roditelj m.   *parent*
rođak m. rođaka f.   *relative*
rođendan m.   *birthday*
roman m.   *novel*
roštilj m.   *barbecue*
ručak m.   *lunch*
ručati   *to have lunch*
ruka f.   *arm, hand*
rukomet m.   *handball*
Rusija f.   *Russia*
   ruski adj.
   Rus m.
   Ruskinja f.

sa (+ gen.)   *from, off*
sa (+ ins.)   *with*
sada   *now*
sakupljati; sakupiti   *to gather*
sala f.   *hall*

salata f.   *salad*
salon m.   *salon*
salveta f.   *serviette*
sam adj.   *alone*
samo   *only*
samoposluga f.   *supermarket*
sandale f. pl.   *sandals*
saobraćaj m.   *traffic*
sapun m.   *soap*
saradnja f.   *co-operation*
sastajati se; sastati se   *to meet*
sastanak m.   *meeting*
sasvim   *completely*
sat m.   *hour*
sav adj.   *all*
sauna f.   *sauna*
scena f.   *stage*
sebe   *oneself*
sećati se; setiti se   *to remember*
sedeti   *to be sitting*
sedište n.   *seat*
sef m.   *safe*
sekretar m. sekretarica f.
   secretary
sekretarica f.   *answer machine*
seliti se; preseliti se   *to move*
   (house)
selo n.   *village*
semafor m.   *traffic lights*
sendvič m.   *sandwich*
septembar m.   *September*
sesti   *to sit down*
sestra f.   *sister*
sever m.   *north*
siguran adj.   *sure, certain*
sijati   *to shine*
silaziti; sići   *to get off, get down*
sin m.   *son*

sinoć   *last night*
sir m.   *cheese*
sjajan adj.   *marvellous*
skijanje n.   *skiing*
skijati se   *to ski*
skoro   *almost*
skretanje n.   *turn*
skretati; skrenuti   *to turn*
skup adj.   *expensive*
slab adj.   *weak*
sladak adj.   *sweet*
sladoled m.   *ice cream*
slati; poslati   *to send*
slatkiši m. pl.   *sweets*
slaviti; proslaviti   *to celebrate*
sledeći adj.   *next*
sličan adj.   *similar*
slika f.   *picture*
slobodan adj.   *free, vacant*
slušati   *to listen*
službenik m. službenica f.
   clerk
služiti   *to serve*
smeđ adj.   *brown*
smeštaj m.   *accommodation*
smetati   *to bother*
sneg m.   *snow*
soba f.   *room*
sobarica f.   *maid*
sok m.   *juice*
sparno   *muggy*
spavaća kola n. pl.   *sleeping car*
spavaća soba f.   *bedroom*
spavati   *to sleep*
spisak m.   *list*
spomenik m.   *monument*
spor adj.   *slow*
sport m.   *sport*

sportist m.   *sportsman*
sportski centar m.   *sports centre*
spremati; spremiti   *to prepare*
spremati se; spremiti se   *to get ready*
sprat m.   *floor*
Srbija f.   *Serbia*
  srpski adj.
  Srbin m.
  Srpkinja f.
srce n.   *heart*
srećan adj.   *happy*
sreda f.   *Wednesday*
sredina f.   *middle*
srednji adj.   *medium*
sretati; sresti   *to meet*
stadion m.   *stadium*
stajati   *to be standing*
stan m.   *flat*
stanica f.   *station, stop*
stanovati   *to live, reside*
stanje n.   *situation, condition*
star adj.   *old*
stati   *to stop*
stavljati; staviti   *to place, put*
staza f.   *path*
stepen m.   *degree*
stizati; stići   *to arrive*
sto   *hundred*
sto m.   *table*
stolica f.   *chair*
stolnjak m.   *tablecloth*
stomak m.   *stomach*
stran adj.   *foreign*
strana f.   *side*
stranac m. strankinja f.   *foreigner*

stranka f.   *party*
strašno   *terribly*
stric m.   *uncle (father's brother)*
strina f.   *aunt (wife of stric)*
student m. studentkinja f.   *student*
studentski dom m.   *student hall of residence*
studije f. pl.   *studies*
studirati   *to study*
stvar f.   *thing*
stvarno   *really*
subota f.   *Saturday*
sudopera f.   *sink*
sudovi m. pl.   *dishes*
suknja f.   *skirt*
sumnjati   *to doubt*
sunčati se   *to sunbathe*
sunce n.   *sun*
sunčan adj.   *sunny*
supa f.   *soup*
suprug m.   *husband*
supruga f.   *wife*
sutra   *tomorrow*
suv adj.   *dry*
suvenir m.   *souvenir*
suviše   *too, too much*
svadba f.   *wedding*
svakako   *certainly*
svaki adj.   *every*
svež adj.   *fresh*
sviđati se   *to like*
svila f.   *silk*
svilen adj.   *silk*
svoj adj.   *one's own*
svraćati; svratiti   *to drop in, call at*

svugde   *everywhere*
šalter m.   *window (in a bank etc.)*
šampon m.   *shampoo*
šef m.   *boss*
šerpa f.   *pan*
šetati; prošetati   *to walk, go for a walk*
šetnja f.   *walk*
širok adj.   *wide*
škola f.   *school*
šljivovica f.   *plum brandy*
šofer m.   *driver*
šorc m.   *shorts*
šporet m.   *cooker*
šta   *what*
štampa f.   *press*
šuma f.   *forest*
šunka f.   *ham*

tableta f.   *tablet*
tačan adj.   *exact*
tada   *at that time*
taj adj.   *that*
tako   *so*
taksi m.   *taxi*
tamo   *there*
tanak adj.   *thin*
tanjir m.   *plate*
tata m.   *dad*
teča m.   *uncle (husband of tetka)*
telefon m.   *telephone*
telefonirati   *to telephone*
televizija f.   *television*
televizor m.   *television set*
temperatura f.   *temperature*
tenis m.   *tennis*
tepih m.   *carpet*

terasa f.   *terrace*
teren m.   *pitch, court*
teretana f.   *gym*
tetka f.   *aunt (sister of mother or father)*
težak adj.   *difficult*
ti   *you (sing.)*
ticati se   *to concern*
tih adj.   *quiet*
tokom (+ gen.)   *during*
toliko (+ gen.)   *so many, so much*
tonik m.   *tonic*
topao adj.   *warm*
torba f.   *bag*
trajati   *to last*
tramvaj m.   *tram*
trava f.   *grass*
tražiti   *to look for, ask for*
trebati   *should, ought to, need*
treći adj.   *third*
trenutak m.   *moment*
trg m.   *square*
tri   *three*
triler m.   *thriller*
trolejbus m.   *trolleybus*
trosed m.   *sofa (three seats)*
trpezarija f.   *dining room*
tržni centar m.   *shopping centre*
turist m.   *tourist*
tuš m.   *shower*
tuširati se; istuširati se   *to shower*
tužan adj.   *sad*
tvoj adj.   *your (sing.)*
tvrđava f.   *fortress*

u (+ acc.)   *to*
u (+ loc.)   *in*

ubeđivati; ubediti *to persuade*
učenik m. učenica f. *pupil*
učitelj m. učiteljica f. *teacher*
učiti; naučiti *to learn*
udata *married (of a woman)*
udavati se; udati se *to get married (of a woman)*
udoban adj. *comfortable*
udžbenik m. *textbook*
ujak m. *uncle (mother's brother)*
ujna f. *aunt (wife of ujak)*
ujutro *in the morning*
uključivati; uključiti *to include*
ulaz m. *entry, way in*
ulaziti; ući *to enter*
ulica f. *street*
uloga f. *role*
umeren adj. *moderate*
unapred *in advance*
univerzitet m. *university*
unuk m. *grandson*
unuka f. *granddaughter*
unutra *inside*
uopšte *in general*
upoznavati; upoznati *to introduce, get to know*
uskoro *soon*
usluga f. *service*
usput *on the way*
usta n. pl. *mouth*
ustajati; ustati *to get up*
utakmica f. *match (sports)*
utorak m. *Tuesday*
uveče *in the evening*
uvek *always*
uvo n. *ear*
uvoziti *to import*

uzak *narrow*
uzimati; uzeti *to take*
uzrast m. *age*

vaditi; izvaditi *to take out*
valuta f. *currency*
valjda *probably*
vaš adj. *your (pl.)*
vaterpolo m. *water polo*
važan adj. *important*
veče n. *evening*
večera f. *dinner*
večeras *this evening*
večerati *to have dinner*
već *already*
vek m. *century*
velik adj. *big*
venčavati se; venčati se *to get married*
veoma *very*
veseo adj. *jolly, merry*
vetar m. *wind*
veza f. *connection*
vi *you (pl.)*
videti *to see*
vila f. *villa*
viljuška f. *fork*
vino n. *wine*
viski m. *whisky*
visok adj. *tall, high*
više *more*
viza f. *visa*
voće n. *fruit*
voda f. *water*
voditi; povesti *to take, lead*
voleti *to like, love*
voz m. *train*
vozilo n. *vehicle*
voziti *to drive*

vraćati se; vratiti se   *to return*
vrata n. pl.   *door*
vreme n.   *time, weather*
vrh m.   *peak*
vrlo   *very*
vruć adj.   *hot*
vrućina f.   *heat*
vunen adj.   *woollen*

za (+ acc.)   *for, in (time)*
za (+ ins.)   *behind*
zabavan adj.   *amusing, entertaining*
zaboravljati; zaboraviti   *to forget*
zadovoljan adj.   *pleased, satisfied*
zadovoljstvo n.   *satisfaction*
zahvalan adj.   *grateful*
zahvaljivati; zahvaliti   *to thank*
zainteresovan adj.   *interested*
zaista   *really*
zajedno   *together*
zakazan adj.   *arranged*
zaključak m.   *conclusion*
zaljubljen adj.   *in love*
zamenjivati; zameniti   *to exchange*
zamrzivač m.   *freezer*
zanimanje n.   *profession*
zanimati   *to interest*
zapad   *west*
zapisivati; zapisati   *to write down*
zarađivati; zaraditi   *to earn*
zašto   *why*

zato   *therefore*
zato što   *because*
zatvarati; zatvoriti   *to close*
zatvoren adj.   *closed*
zauzet adj.   *busy*
zavisiti   *to depend*
zavoj m.   *bandage*
završavati; završiti   *to finish*
zbog (+ gen.)   *because of*
zdravo   *hi, cheerio*
zelen adj.   *green*
zemlja f.   *country*
zgrada f.   *building*
zid m.   *wall*
zima f.   *winter*
zimovanje n.   *winter holiday*
značiti   *to mean*
znamenitost f.   *landmark, sight*
znati   *to know*
zub m.   *tooth*
zubar m. zubarka f.   *dentist*
zubna pasta f.   *toothpaste*
zvati; pozvati   *to call*
zvoniti; zazvoniti   *to ring*
žedan adj.   *thirsty*
želeti   *to wish, want*
železnička stanica f.   *railway station*
žena f.   *wife, woman*
ženski   *female*
ženiti se; oženiti se   *to get married (of a man)*
živeti   *to live*
žurka f.   *party*
žut adj.   *yellow*

English–Serbian vocabulary

able, to be   moći
about   o (+ loc.)
above   iznad (+ gen.)
abroad   inostranstvo n.
accommodation   smeštaj m.
ache, to   boleti
acquire, to   nabavljati; nabaviti
across   preko (+ gen.)
activity   aktivnost f.
actor   glumac m.
actress   glumica f.
additional payment   doplata f.
address   adresa f.
adult   odrastao adj.
advantage   prednost f.
advertisement   oglas m.
aeroplane   avion m.
afraid, to be   bojati se
after   posle (+ gen.)
again   opet
against   protiv (+ gen.)
age   uzrast m.
agency   agencija f.
ago   pre
agree, to   dogovoriti se
agreement   dogovor m.
airport   aerodrom m.
alarm clock   budilnik m.
alcohol   alkohol m.
all   sav adj.
almost   skoro
alone   sam adj.
already   već
always   uvek

America   Amerika f.
amusing   zabavan adj.
and   a, i
angry, to be   ljutiti se
another   drugi adj.
antibiotic   antibiotik m.
apartment   apartman m.
apologize, to   izvinjavati se;
   izviniti se
appear, to   izgledati
apple   jabuka f.
approximately   otprilike
April   april m.
area   kraj m.
arm   ruka f.
armchair   fotelja f.
around   po (+ dat.)
arranged   zakazan adj.
arrive, to   stizati; stići
as   kao
Asia   Azija f.
ask, to   moliti; zamoliti, pitati
ask for, to   tražiti
at   kod (+ gen.)
athletics   atletika f.
August   avgust m.
aunt   strina f. tetka f. ujna f.
Australia   Australija f.
autumn   jesen f.

back   natrag
back   leđa n. pl.
bad   loš adj.
bag   torba f.
bakery   pekara f.

358

baklava baklava f.
balcony balkon m.
ballet balet m.
bandage zavoj m.
bank banka f.
bar bar m.
barbecue roštilj m.
basketball košarka f.
bath kada f.
bathroom kupatilo n.
be, to biti
beach plaža f.
beautiful lep adj.
beauty lepota f.
because zato što
because of zbog (+ gen.)
bed krevet m.
bedroom spavaća soba f.
bedsit garsonjera f.
beer pivo n.
beetroot cvekla f.
before pre (+ gen.)
beg, to moliti; zamoliti
begin, to počinjati; početi
beginning početak m.
behind iza (+ gen.), za (+ ins.)
below ispod (+ gen.)
beside pored (+ gen.)
between između (+ gen.)
big velik adj.
bill račun m.
birthday rođendan m.
bitter gorak adj. kiseo adj.
black crn adj.
block blok m.
blonde plav adj.
blouse bluza f.
blow, to duvati

blue plav adj.
blueberry borovnica f.
book knjiga f.
bookshop knjižara f.
border granica f.
boring dosadan adj.
Bosnia Bosna f.
boss šef m.
bother, to smetati
bottle flaša f.
boulevard bulevar m.
boutique butik m.
box kutija f.
boy dečko m.
boyfriend dečko m.
   mladić m.
brandy rakija f.
bread hleb m.
break pauza f.
break, to lomiti; slomiti
breakfast doručak m.
breakfast, to
   have doručkovati
bridge most m.
bring, to donositi; doneti
broadcast prenos m.
broth čorba f.
brother brat m.
brown smeđ adj.
building zgrada f.
bus autobus m.
bus station autobuska
   stanica f.
business biznis m.
busy zauzet adj.
but a, ali
butter buter m.
buy, to kupovati; kupiti

cabbage kupus m.
café kafana f.
café-bar kafić m.
cake kolač m.
cake shop poslatičarnica f.
call, to zvati; pozvati
call at, to svraćati; svratiti
can moći
canteen menza f.
car auto m. automobil m.
  kola n. pl.
careful, to be paziti
car park parking m.
carpet tepih m.
carry, to nositi
celebrate, to slaviti; proslaviti
centre centar m.
century vek m.
certain siguran adj.
certainly svakako
chair stolica f.
change kusur m.
change, to menjati; promeniti
changeable promenljiv adj.
chat, to razgovarati
cheap jeftin adj.
check, to proveravati; proveriti
checkout kasa f.
cheerio zdravo
cheese sir m.
chest grudi f. pl.
chest of drawers komoda f.
chicken pileći adj.
chicken piletina f.
child dete n.
childhood detinjstvo n.
Christmas Božić m.
church crkva f.

cigarette cigareta f.
cinema bioskop m.
circle (theatre) balkon m.
citizen građanin m.
class čas m.
clean čist adj.
clerk službenik m službenica f.
close, to zatvarati; zatvoriti
closed zatvoren adj.
clothes odeća f.
cloudy oblačno
coat kaput m.
Coca-Cola koka-kola f.
coffee kafa f.
cold hladan adj.
cold kijavica f.
colleague kolega m.
  koleginica f.
colour boja f.
come, to dolaziti; doći
comedy komedija f.
comfortable komforan adj.
  udoban adj.
company društvo n. firma f.
completely sasvim
computer kompjuter m.
concern, to ticati se
conclusion zaključak m.
condition stanje n.
confess, to priznavati; priznati
connection veza f.
continue, to nastavljati;
  nastaviti
convenient pogodan adj.
conversation razgovor m.
cook, to kuvati; skuvati
cooker šporet m.
co-operation saradnja f.

corner ćošak m.
correct prav adj.
corridor hodnik m.
course kurs m.
cost, to koštati
cough, to kašljati
country zemlja f.
court (games) teren m.
credit kredit m.
credit card kreditna kartica f.
Croatia Hrvatska f.
cross, to prelaziti; preći
crowd gužva f.
crown kruna f.
cucumber krastavac m.
cultural kulturan adj.
culture kultura f.
currency valuta f.
customs carina f.

dad tata m.
daily dnevni adj.
dangerous opasan adj.
daughter ćerka f.
day dan m.
dear drag adj.
December decembar m.
decide, to odlučivati; odlučiti
degree stepen m.
delay, to odlagati; odložiti
deliver, to dostavljati;
   dostaviti
dentist zubar m. zubarka f.
department store robna kuća f.
departure odlazak m.,
   polazak m.
depend, to zavisiti
desk radni sto m.
development razvoj m.

dictionary rečnik m.
different drukčiji adj. razni
   adj.
difficult težak adj.
dinar dinar m.
dining room trpezarija f.
dinner večera f.
dinner, to have večerati
diplomat diplomata m.
direction pravac m.
directly pravo
discuss, to razgovarati
dish jelo n.
dishes posuđe n. sudovi m. pl.
disinfect, to dezinfikovati
do, to raditi; uraditi
doctor lekar m. lekarka f.
door vrata n. pl.
doubt, to sumnjati
down dole
drama drama f.
drawer fijoka f.
dress haljina f.
drink piće n.
drink, to piti; popiti
drive, to voziti
driver šofer m.
drop in, to svraćati; svratiti
dry suv adj.
dry cleaning hemijsko
   čišćenje n.
during tokom (+ gen.)

ear uvo n.
early rano
earn, to zarađivati; zaraditi
east istok m.
easy lak adj.
eat, to jesti; pojesti

economist ekonomista m.
else još
e-mail elektronska pošta f.
  mejl m.
embassy ambasada f.
empty prazan adj.
end kraj m.
engaged in, to be baviti se
engineer inženjer m.
England Engleska f.
enough dosta (+ gen.)
enter, to ulaziti; ući
entertaining zabavan adj.
entry ulaz m.
equipment oprema f.
essay esej m.
euro evro m.
Europe Evropa f.
evening veče n.
every svaki adj.
everywhere svugde
exact tačan adj.
examine, to pregledati
excellent odličan adj.
except osim (+ gen.)
exchange, to zamenjivati;
  zameniti
exchange office menjačnica f.
exchange rate kurs m.
excursion izlet m.
exist, to postojati
exit izlaz m.
expensive skup adj.
experience doživljaj m.
  iskustvo n.
export, to izvoziti
expression izraz m.
eye oko n.

faculty fakultet m.
fall, to padati; pasti
family porodica f.
far dalek adj.
far from daleko od (+ gen.)
father otac m.
favourite omiljen adj.
fear, to bojati se
February februar m.
feel, to osećati se; osetiti se
female ženski adj.
few nekoliko (+ gen.)
field polje n.
film film m.
find, to nalaziti; naći
finger prst m.
finish, to završavati; završiti
firm firma f.
first prvi adj.
fish riba f.
fixed fiksiran adj.
flat stan m.
flight let m.
floor pod m. sprat m.
fly, to leteti
food hrana f. jelo n.
foot noga f.
football fudbal m.
football player fudbaler m.
for za (+ acc.), na (+ acc.)
foreign stran adj.
foreign currency devize f. pl.
foreigner stranac m.
  strankinja f.
forest šuma f.
forget, to zaboravljati;
  zaboraviti
fork viljuška f.

fortress tvrđava f.
France Francuska f.
free besplatan adj. slobodan adj.
freezer zamrzivač m.
fresco freska f.
fresh svež adj.
Friday petak m.
fridge frižider m.
friend drug m. drugarica f. prijatelj m. prijateljica f.
friendly prijateljski adj.
friends, to be družiti se
from iz (+ gen.), od (+ gen.), sa (+ gen.)
from here odavde
from there odatle
frontier granica f.
fruit voće n.
full pun adj.
furnished namešten adj.
furniture nameštaj m.

gallery galerija f.
garage garaža f.
garden bašta f.
gentleman gospodin m.
Germany Nemačka f.
get, to dobijati; dobiti
get in touch, to javljati se; javiti se
get off, to silaziti; sići
get to know, to upoznavati; upoznati
get up, to ustajati; ustati
gin džin m.
girl devojka f.
girlfriend devojka f.
give, to davati; dati

glass čaša f.
go, to ići
go away, to odlaziti; otići
go down, to silaziti; sići
go for a walk, to šetati; prošetati
go out, to izlaziti; izići
good dobar adj.
goodbye do viđenja
gram gram m.
grammar gramatika f.
granddaughter unuka f.
grandfather deda m.
grandmother baka f. baba f.
grandson unuk m.
grass trava f.
grateful zahvalan adj.
gather, to sakupljati; sakupiti
Greece Grčka f.
green zelen adj.
greet, to pozdravljati; pozdraviti
grilled na žaru
grocery shop bakalnica f.
ground floor prizemlje n.
guest gost m.
gym teretana f.

hair kosa f.
hairdressing salon frizerski salon m.
half pola
hall sala f.
ham šunka f.
hand ruka f.
handball rukomet m.
happen, to dešavati se; desiti se
happy srećan adj.
have, to imati

have to, to morati
he on
head glava f.
hear, to čuti
heart srce n.
heat vrućina f.
help pomoć f.
help, to pomagati; pomoći
her njen adj.
here ovde
hi zdravo, ćao
high visok adj.
hill brdo n.
hire, to iznajmljivati; iznajmiti
his njegov adj.
historical istorijski adj.
history istorija f.
hobby hobi m.
hockey hokej m.
holiday odmor m. praznik m.
home-made domaći adj.
hope, to nadati se
horse konj m.
hospital bolnica f.
hot vruć adj.
hotel hotel m.
hotplate ringla f.
hour čas m. sat m.
house kuća f.
housewife domaćica f.
how kako
how many koliko (+ gen.)
how much koliko (+ gen.)
however ipak
hundred sto
hungry gladan adj.
hurt, to boleti
husband muž m. suprug m.

I ja
ice cream sladoled m.
if ako
ill bolestan adj.
immediately odmah
import, to uvoziti
important važan adj.
in u (+ loc.)
include, to uključivati; uključiti
infection infekcija f.
in front napred
in front of ispred (+ gen.)
inform, to obaveštavati;
  obavestiti
information informacija f.
injure, to povređivati; povrediti
in love zaljubljen adj.
inside unutra
intend, to nameravati
intense intenzivan adj.
intercom interfon m.
interest, to zanimati
interested zainteresovan adj.
international međunarodni adj.
internet café internet-kafe m.
interrupt, to prekidati;
  prekinuti
introduce, to upoznavati;
  upoznati
invitation poziv m.
invite, to pozivati; pozvati
invoice faktura f.
iron pegla f.
it ono
Italy Italija f.

jacket jakna f.
jam džem m.
January januar m.

jeans farmerke f. pl.
job posao m.
jolly veseo adj.
journalist novinar m.
  novinarka f.
journey put m. putovanje n.
juice sok m.
July jul m.
jumper džemper m.
June jun m.

keep, to držati
key ključ m.
kilo kilo n.
kilometre kilometar m.
kind ljubazan adj.
kiosk kiosk m.
kitchen kuhinja f.
knee koleno n.
knife nož m.
know, to znati

lady gospođa f.
lake jezero n.
landmark znamenitost f.
language jezik m.
large velik adj.
last poslednji adj. prošli adj.
last, to trajati
late kasno
late, to be kasniti; zakasniti
lawyer advokat m.
lead, to voditi; povesti
learn, to učiti; naučiti
leave, to napuštati; napustiti,
  odlaziti; otići
leave behind, to ostavljati;
  ostaviti
lecture predavanje n.

left levo
leg noga f.
lemon limun m.
lemonade limunada f.
less manje (+ gen.)
letter pismo n.
library biblioteka f.
lie, to ležati
life život m.
like kao
like, to dopadati se, sviđati
  se, voleti
list spisak m.
listen, to slušati
literature književnost f.
litre litar m.
little mali adj.
live, to stanovati, živeti
loaf hleb m.
location lokacija f.
long dug adj.
look after, to čuvati
look at, to gledati; pogledati
look for, to tražiti
look forward, to radovati se
love ljubav f.
love, to voleti
luggage prtljag m.
lunch ručak m.
lunch, to have ručati

Macedonia Makedonija f.
maid sobarica f.
mailbox poštansko sanduče n.
main glavni adj.
make, to praviti; napraviti
male muški adj.
man čovek m.
many mnogo (+ gen.)

map mapa f.

March mart m.

marriage brak m.

married udata (*of a woman*), oženjen (*of a man*)

married, to get venčavati se; venčati se, udavati se; udati se (*of a woman*), ženiti se; oženiti se (*of a man*)

married couple bračni par m.

marvelous sjajan adj.

match (sports) utakmica f.

May maj m.

meadow livada f.

meal jelo n.

mean, to značiti

meat meso n.

medicine lek m.

medium srednji adj.

meet, to sastajati se; sastati se; sretati; sresti

meeting sastanak m.

menu jelovnik m.

merry veseo adj.

message poruka f.

metre metar m.

midday podne n.

middle sredina f.

midnight ponoć f.

milk mleko n.

million milion m.

minute minut m.

moderate umeren adj.

modern moderan adj.

moment trenutak m.

monastery manastir m.

Monday ponedeljak m.

money novac m.

Montenegro Crna Gora f.

month mesec m.

monument spomenik m.

moon mesec

more još, više (+ gen.)

morning jutro n.

mostly pretežno

mother majka f.

motorway autoput m.

mountain planina f.

mouth usta n. pl.

move house, to seliti se; preseliti se

much mnogo (+ gen.)

muggy sparno

mum mama f.

museum muzej m.

mushroom pečurka f.

music muzika f.

must morati

my moj adj.

name ime n.

narrow uzak adj.

national narodni adj.

nationality nacionalnost f.

nature priroda f.

near blizu (+ gen.)

necessary potreban adj.

negotiations pregovori m. pl.

neighbour komšija m. komšinica f.

neighbourhood komšiluk m.

neither ni

never nikada

nevertheless ipak

new nov adj.

newspaper novine f. pl.

next onda

next sledeći adj. idući adj.
next to pored (+ gen.)
nice lep adj.
night noć f.
no ne
nobody niko
north sever m.
nose nos m.
not ne
notice, to primećivati; primetiti
nothing ništa
novel roman m.
November novembar m.
now sada
nowhere nigde
number broj m.
numerous mnogi adj.
nursery school obdanište n.

obligatory obavezan adj.
October oktobar m.
of course naravno
offer ponuda f.
office kancelarija f.
often često
ointment mast f.
old star adj.
olive maslina f.
omelette omlet m.
on na (+ loc.)
once nekada
one jedan adj.
oneself sebe
one's own svoj adj.
on foot peške
only samo
open otvoren adj.
open, to otvarati; otvoriti
opera opera f.

opinion mišljenje n.
opportunity prilika f.
opposite preko puta (+ gen.)
or ili
orange pomorandža f.
orange juice džus m.
order porudžbina f. red m.
order, to naručivati; naručiti
organize, to organizovati
other drugi adj.
ought trebati
our naš adj.
outside napolju
oven rerna f.
overnight stay noćenje n.

pack, to pakovati; spakovati
pain bol m.
pan šerpa f.
parent roditelj m.
park park m.
park, to parkirati
particular naročit adj.
party stranka f. žurka f.
pass, to prolaziti; proći
passport pasoš m.
pasty pašteta f.
path staza f.
patient bolesnik m. bolesnica f.
pause pauza f.
pay plata f.
pay, to plaćati; platiti
peaceful miran adj.
peak vrh m.
performance predstava f.
perhaps možda
period period m.
permit, to odobravati; odobriti
person čovek m. osoba f.

persuade, to ubeđivati; ubediti
petrol benzin m.
petrol station benzinska
  pumpa f.
pharmacist apotekar m.
  apotekarka f.
pharmacy apoteka f.
photograph fotografija f.
picture slika f.
pitch (sports) teren m.
pizzeria picerija f.
place mesto n.
place, to stavljati; staviti
plan plan m.
plan, to planirati; isplanirati
plate tanjir m.
play, to igrati
pleasant prijatan adj.
pleased zadovoljan adj.
plum brandy šljivovica f.
poetry poezija f.
popular popularan adj.
possess, to posedovati
postbox poštansko sanduče n.
postcard razglednica f.
poster poster m.
post office pošta f.
postpone, to odlagati; odložiti
pound funta f.
prepare, to spremati; spremiti
prescription recept m.
present poklon m.
present, to be prisustvovati
price cena f.
private privatan adj.
probably valjda
problem problem m.
produce, to proizvoditi

product proizvod m.
profession zanimanje n.
programme program m.
promise, to obećavati; obećati
pronunciation izgovor m.
proposal predlog m.
pupil učenik m. učenica f.
put, to stavljati; staviti
pyjamas pidžama f.

quick brz adj.
quiet miran adj. tih adj.
quite baš, prilično

radio radio m.
railway station železnička
  stanica f.
rain kiša f.
raincoat kišni mantil m.
rainy kišovit adj.
rarely retko
raspberry malina f.
rather prilično
read, to čitati; pročitati
ready, to get spremati se;
  spremiti se
real pravi adj.
really baš, stvarno, zaista
reasonable (of prices)
  povoljan adj.
receive, to dobijati; dobiti,
  primati; primiti
reception recepcija f.
receptionist recepcioner m.
recognize, to priznavati;
  priznati
red crven adj.
relative rođak m. rođaka f.
remain, to ostajati; ostati

remember, to sećati se; setiti se
rent kirija f.
rent, to iznajmljivati; iznajmiti
rent out, to izdavati; izdati
repeat, to ponavljati; ponoviti
representative predstavnik m.
reservation rezervacija f.
reserve, to rezervisati
residence boravište n.
respected poštovan adj.
rest odmor m.
rest, to odmarati se;
  odmoriti se
restaurant restoran m.
return povratak m.
return, to vraćati se; vratiti se
right desno
right prav adj.
ring, to zvoniti; zazvoniti
river reka f.
road put m.
roast, to peći; ispeći
role uloga f.
room soba f.
row red m.
Russia Rusija f.

sad tužan adj.
safe sef m.
salad salata f.
salary plata f.
salesman prodavac m.
saleswoman prodavačica f.
salon salon m.
same isti adj.
sandals sandale f. pl.
sandwich sendvič m.
satisfaction zadovoljstvo n.
satisfied zadovoljan adj.

Saturday subota f.
sauna sauna f.
say, to kazati, reći
school škola f.
school holidays raspust m.
sea more n.
seagull galeb m.
season (of the year) godišnje
  doba n.
seat sedište n.
second drugi adj.
secretary sekretar m. sekretarica f.
see, to videti
seem, to činiti se
sell, to prodavati; prodati
send, to slati; poslati
September septembar m.
Serbia Srbija f.
serious ozbiljan adj.
serve, to služiti; poslužiti
service usluga f.
serviette salveta f.
set, to postavljati; postaviti
set aside, to odvajati; odvojiti
set off, to kretati; krenuti,
  polaziti; poći
settlement naselje n.
shampoo šampon m.
share, to deliti; podeliti
she ona
shelf polica f.
shine, to sijati
shirt košulja f.
shoes cipele f. pl.
shop prodavnica f. radnja f.
shopping kupovina f.
shopping centre tržni centar m.

short story   pripovetka f.
shorts   šorc m.
should   trebati
shoulder   rame n.
show, to   pokazivati; pokazati
shower   pljusak m. tuš m.
shower, to have a   tuširati se;
   istuširati se
side   strana f.
sideboard   kredenac m.
sight   znamenitost f.
sign, to   potpisivati; potpisati
silk   svila f.
silk   svilen adj.
similar   sličan adj.
since   jer, otkad, pošto
singer   pevač m. pevačica f.
sink   lavabo m. sudopera f.
sit down, to   sesti
sitting, to be   sedeti
sitting room   dnevna soba f.
situated, to be   nalaziti se
situation   stanje n.
ski, to   skijati se
skiing   skijanje n.
skirt   suknja f.
sleep, to   spavati
sleeping car   spavaća kola n. pl.
slippers   papuče f. pl.
slow   spor adj.
slowly   polako
small   mali adj.
smoked ham   pršut m.
snow   sneg m.
so   tako
soap   sapun m.
soft   mek adj.
so many   toliko (+ gen.)
some   neki adj.

somebody   neko
something   nešto
sometimes   ponekad
somewhere   negde
so much   toliko (+ gen.)
son   sin m.
soon   uskoro
soup   supa f.
sour   kiseo adj.
south   jug m.
souvenir   suvenir m.
spa   banja f.
space   mesto n. prostor m.
speak, to   govoriti
special   naročit adj.
spend (time), to   provoditi;
   provesti
spoon   kašika f.
sport   sport m.
sports centre   sportski
   centar m.
sportsman   sportist m.
spring   proleće n.
square   trg m.
stadium   stadion m.
stage   scena f.
stalls (theatre)   parter m.
stamp   marka f.
standing, to be   stajati
starter   predjelo n.
station   stanica f.
stay   boravak m.
stay, to   boraviti, ostajati; ostati
steak   biftek m.
still   još uvek
stomach   stomak m.
stop   stanica f.
stop, to   stati
storey   sprat m.

story priča f.
straight on pravo
strange čudan adj.
strawberry jagoda f.
stream potok m.
street ulica f.
strong jak adj.
student student m.
   studentkinja f.
student hall of residence
   studentski dom m.
studies studije f. pl.
study radna soba f.
study, to studirati
suburb predgrađe n.
sufficient dovoljan adj.
suggest, to predlagati;
   predložiti
suit kostim m. (*female*),
   odelo n.
suit, to odgovarati
suitcase kofer m.
summer leto n.
summer holidays letovanje n.
sun sunce n.
sunbathe, to sunčati se
Sunday nedelja f.
sunny sunčan adj.
supermarket samoposluga f.
sure siguran adj.
surname prezime n.
swan labud m.
sweet sladak adj.
sweets slatkiši m. pl.
swim, to plivati
swimming costume kupaći
   kostim m.
swimming pool bazen m.

swimming trunks kupaće
   gaćice f. pl.

table sto m.
tablet tableta f.
take, to uzimati; uzeti, voditi;
   povesti
take effect, to delovati
take one's leave, to pozdravljati se; pozdraviti se
take out, to vaditi; izvaditi
talk razgovor m.
talk, to pričati, razgovarati
tall visok adj.
taxi taksi m.
tea čaj m.
teach, to predavati
teacher nastavnik m. nastavnica f. učitelj m. učiteljica
telephone telefon m.
telephone, to telefonirati
telephone extension lokal m.
telephone switchboard
   centrala f.
television televizija f.
television set televizor m.
tell, to kazati, reći
temperature temperatura f.
tennis tenis m.
terrace terasa f.
terribly strašno
textbook udžbenik m.
than nego
thank, to zahvaljivati; zahvaliti
thank you hvala
that onaj adj. taj adj.
theatre pozorište n.
their njihov adj.
then onda, tada

there tamo
therefore zato
they oni (-e, -a)
thick gust adj.
thin tanak adj.
thing stvar f.
think, to misliti
third treći adj.
thirsty žedan adj.
this ovaj adj.
thousand hiljada f.
three tri
thriller triler m.
throat grlo n.
through kroz (+ acc.)
thunder grmljavina f.
Thursday četvrtak m.
ticket karta f.
ticket office blagajna f.
ticket seller blagajnik m.
  blagajnica f.
tie kravata f.
till kasa f.
time vreme n.
tin can limenka f.
to u (+ acc.), na (+ acc.), do
  (+ gen.)
today danas
toe prst m.
together zajedno
tomorrow sutra
tonic tonik m.
tonight noćas
too much suviše
tooth zub m.
toothpaste zubna pasta f.
tourist turist m.
towards prema (+ dat.)

town grad m.
traffic saobraćaj m.
traffic jam gužva f.
traffic lights semafor m.
train voz m.
training shoes patike f. pl.
tram tramvaj m.
transfer, to prebacivati;
  prebaciti
translate, to prevoditi;
  prevesti
translation prevod m.
translator prevodilac m.
transport prevoz m.
travel, to putovati
travelling putnički adj.
tree drvo n.
trip putovanje n.
trolleybus trolejbus m.
trousers pantalone f. pl.
try, to probati
T-shirt majica f.
Tuesday utorak m.
turn skretanje n.
turn, to skretati; skrenuti,
  okretati; okrenuti
two dva, dve

uncle stric m. teča m. ujak m.
understand, to razumeti
underwear donje rublje n.
unfortunately na žalost
university univerzitet m.
university department
  katedra f.
unpack, to raspakovati se
up gore
upper gornji adj.
urgent hitan adj.

use, to   koristiti; iskoristiti
usually   obično

vacant   slobodan adj.
vacation (university)
   raspust m.
valuables   dragocenosti f. pl.
various   razni adj.
vehicle   vozilo n.
very   veoma, vrlo
via   preko (+ gen.)
vicinity   blizina f.
view   pogled m.
villa   vila f.
village   selo n.
visa   viza f.
visit   obilazak m. poseta f.
visit, to   posećivati; posetiti
volleyball   odbojka f.

wait, to   čekati
waiter   konobar m.
waitress   konobarica f.
wake, to   buditi; probuditi
walk   šetnja f.
walk, to   hodati, šetati;
   prošetati
wall   zid m.
want, to   hteti, želeti
war   rat m.
war   ratni adj.
wardrobe   orman m.
warm   topao adj.
wash, to   prati; oprati
washing machine   mašina za
   veš f.
watch, to   gledati; pogledati
water   voda f.
waterpolo   vaterpolo m.

way   put m.
we   mi
weak   slab adj.
wear, to   nositi
weather   vreme n.
wedding   svadba f.
Wednesday   sreda f.
week   nedelja f.
weekly   nedeljno
welcome   dobro došli
west   zapad m.
what   šta
what kind of   kakav adj.
when   kada
where   gde
where from   odakle
where to   kuda
which   koji adj.
while   dok
whisky   viski m.
white   beo adj.
who   ko, koji adj.
whose   čiji adj.
why   zašto
wide   širok adj.
wife   supruga f. žena f.
win, to   pobeđivati; pobediti
wind   vetar m.
window   prozor m.
window (in bank)   šalter m.
wine   vino n.
winter   zima f.
winter holiday   zimovanje n.
wish, to   želeti
with   sa (+ ins.)
without   bez (+ gen.)
witty   duhovit adj.
woman   žena f.

wonderful divan adj.
wooden drven adj.
woollen vunen adj.
word reč f.
work posao m.
work, to raditi; uraditi
worry briga f.
worry, to brinuti
wound rana f.
write, to pisati; napisati
write down, to zapisivati; zapisati
writer pisac m.

year godina f.
yellow žut adj.
yes da
yesterday juče
yoghurt jogurt m.
you ti (sing.), vi (pl.)
young mlad adj.
your tvoj (sing.) adj., vaš (pl.) adj.
youth mladić m.
Yugoslav jugoslovenski adj.
Yugoslavia Jugoslavija f.

zero nula f.

Grammar index

Taking it further

History, culture and politics

Leslie Benson, *Yugoslavia: A Concise History*, Palgrave, London, 2001

Misha Glenny, *The Balkans 1804–1999: Nationalism, War and the Great Powers*, Granta Books, London, 1999

Eric D. Gordy, *The Culture of Power in Serbia: Nationalism and the Destruction of Alternatives*, Pennsylvania State University Press, 1999

Dina Iordanova, *Cinema of Flames: Balkan Film, Culture and the Media*, British Film Institute, London, 2001

Tim Judah, *The Serbs: History, Myth and the Destruction of Yugoslavia*, Yale University Press, 1997

David A. Norris, *In the Wake of the Balkan Myth: Questions of Identity and Modernity*, Macmillan, London, 1999

Stevan K. Pavlowitch, *Serbia: The History of an Idea*, New York University Press, 2002

Robert Thomas, *Serbia under Milošević: Politics in the 1990s*, Hurst, London, 1999

Dictionaries

Morton Benson, *Standard English–Serbo-Croatian, Serbo-Croatian–English Dictionary*, Cambridge University Press, 1998

Zdravko Ignjatović (et al), *ESSE English–Serbian Serbian–English Dictionary*, The Institute for Foreign Languages, Belgrade, 2002

Internet sources

- beograd.com   links to general sites
- www.mfa.gov.rs   Ministry of Foreign Affairs
- www.serbiancafe.co.uk   general information and chat site
- www.serbia-tourism.org   tourist information for Serbia
- www.visit-montenegro.com   tourist information for Montenegro

"Global scale" of the Common European Framework of Reference for Languages: learning, teaching, assessment (CEFR)

Advanced	**CEFR LEVEL C2**	Can understand with ease virtually everything heard or read. Can summarise information from different spoken and written sources, reconstructing arguments and accounts in a coherent presentation. Can express him/herself spontaneously, very fluently and precisely, differentiating finer shades of meaning even in more complex situations.
Advanced	**CEFR LEVEL C1**	Can understand a wide range of demanding, longer texts, and recognise implicit meaning. Can express him/herself fluently and spontaneously without much obvious searching for expressions. Can use language flexibly and effectively for social, academic and professional purposes. Can produce clear, well-structured, detailed text on complex subjects, showing controlled use of organisational patterns, connectors and cohesive devices.
Intermediate	**CEFR LEVEL B2 (A Level)**	Can understand the main ideas of complex text on both concrete and abstract topics, including technical discussions in his/her field of specialisation. Can interact with a degree of fluency and spontaneity that makes regular interaction with native speakers quite possible without strain for either party. Can produce clear, detailed text on a wide range of subjects and explain a viewpoint on a topical issue giving the advantages and disadvantages of various options.
Intermediate	**CEFR LEVEL B1 (Higher GCSE)**	Can understand the main points of clear standard input on familiar matters regularly encountered in work, school, leisure, etc. Can deal with most situations likely to arise whilst travelling in an area where the language is spoken. Can produce simple connected text on topics which are familiar or of personal interest. Can describe experiences and events, dreams, hopes and ambitions and briefly give reasons and explanations for opinions and plans.
Beginner	**CEFR LEVEL A2: (Foundation GCSE)**	Can understand sentences and frequently used expressions related to areas of most immediate relevance (e.g. very basic personal and family information, shopping, local geography, employment). Can communicate in simple and routine tasks requiring a simple and direct exchange of information on familiar and routine matters. Can describe in simple terms aspects of his/her background, immediate environment and matters in areas of immediate need.
Beginner	**CEFR LEVEL A1**	Can understand and use familiar everyday expressions and very basic phrases aimed at the satisfaction of needs of a concrete type. Can introduce him/herself and others and can ask and answer questions about personal details such as where he/she lives, people he/she knows and things he/she has. Can interact in a simple way provided the other person talks slowly and clearly and is prepared to help.